Lady Tigers
IN THE CONCRETE JUNGLE

Lady Tigers

IN THE CONCRETE JUNGLE

HOW SOFTBALL AND SISTERHOOD
SAVED LIVES IN THE SOUTH BRONX

DIBS BAER

PEGASUS BOOKS
NEW YORK LONDON

LADY TIGERS IN THE CONCRETE JUNGLE

Pegasus Books Ltd.
148 W 37th Street, 13th Floor
New York, NY 10018

First Pegasus Books cloth edition October 2019

Interior design by Maria Fernandez

The people and events in this book are true to life. Some names,
events, and locations have been altered to protect privacy.

Library of Congress Cataloging-in-Publication Data is available.

ISBN: 978-1-64313-065-1

10 9 8 7 6 5 4 3 2 1

Printed in the United States of America
Distributed by W. W. Norton & Company
www.pegasusbooks.us

For my mom,
who came to every single one of my games,
sun, rain, sleet, or snow.

CONTENTS

Prologue: Tryouts & Shootouts   ix

⚾ PART I: PRE-GAME   1

1: Building Character   3

2: Caught in the Cycle   19

3: A Bronx Tale or Two   27

4: As Sick As Your Secrets   41

5: Love & Loss   45

6: The Angel Kid   55

7: Gut Punch   63

8: A Teacher Gets Schooled   75

⚾ PART II: PRACTICE   95

9: Where's the Beef?   97

10: An Ultimatum   123

11: A New Beginning   147

12: Innocence Lost   167

⚾ PART III: PLAY BALL   179

13: Win One For the Mister   181

14: Blowout in the Bronx   189

15: Sliding into Worst   199

16: The Show   217

17: Go Forth & Set the World on Fire   231

Epilogue: Winning Cures All   241

Acknowledgments   251

Prologue

TRYOUTS & SHOOTOUTS

Chris Astacio sat down on a bucket of Wiffle balls in the middle of the basketball court and waited for the girls to arrive. It was the only place to sit, really, in the empty, run-down gym. The wooden benches were missing nuts and bolts and looked like they could collapse under a gentle breeze. Broken windows had yet to be replaced, and caved in ceiling panels dangled over the court, which had giant cracks and dangerous, uneven surfaces. The boys' basketball team may have won their division last year, but you'd never know it. There was no scoreboard, no pennants hanging from the rafters, no school pride evident on the bare walls at all. Not a single colorful banner or poster proclaiming the fierceness of the Tigers, the school mascot. All six basketball hoops were net-less so they wouldn't be stolen; the rims bent from kids climbing, hanging, and sitting on them.

"They think it's funny when they sit up there," Chris thought, shaking his head. "It's not funny."

A half hour passed and nobody came into the gym. Chris was genuinely puzzled. He must have passed out five hundred flyers, printed in big, vibrant orange and black block letters to get maximum attention:

COME JOIN THE 1ST EVER GIRLS' SOFTBALL TEAM!

Every morning for a week, he'd stood in the doorway of Jordan L. Mott Middle School handing out flyers to any and all females who passed by. He taped them to walls and blanketed every dark corner of the school, especially all the secret places the girls hung out when they cut class—alcoves, back staircases, and bathrooms. He lobbied boys on the baseball team to send their sisters and girlfriends, hoping they'd be good players, too. In Chris's poetry and PE classes (an odd combo, but that was Mott), he recruited the best female athletes, like Angie, star of the girls' basketball team, and Yoshie, who'd thrown a volleyball at him like a bullet in the gym. She was always playing sports in the yard with the boys.

"Do you play softball?" he asked Yoshie.

"Is that like baseball?" she said.

"Yeah."

"Then I play."

She said she'd be there. They all said they'd be there. On his way to the gym that day, he was actually a little nervous, thinking, "There will be so many girls, what ever *will* I do?" But there were no girls in the gym. Just the bucket of Wiffle balls, a plastic bat, and a couple of used, beat-up gloves. Oh, and stifling heat. It was a beautiful September day, an Indian summer kind of afternoon, maybe the girls thought tryouts were outside?

Chris walked out to the schoolyard to investigate. It was vacant and eerily quiet. At most schools, when the bell rings at 2:30 P.M., you might hear the sounds of screaming, happy kids outside. But Mott wasn't most schools. It was located in the South Bronx, at the corner of 167th Street and College Avenue, in one of the most gang-infested, poverty-stricken neighborhoods in New York City. So yeah, there was a schoolyard, about half the size of a football field, but it wasn't the kind of place anyone wanted to hang out long. The playground was on cracked concrete, and the baseball "field," with faded foul lines painted years ago, was littered with broken glass and syringes. A forbidding black chain-link fence surrounded the school, which was right across the street from a ten-story housing project—close enough that kids could throw frozen eggs and potatoes off the roof into the schoolyard. And they did.

Dodging projectile eggs were the least of the students' worries. The schoolyard was barren of human beings because the surrounding city blocks were a battlefield for the small but vicious rival gangs who'd taken over 167th to 169th Streets. Lord have mercy on a student who accidentally wandered down the wrong street. These gang members, known to spray bullets haphazardly and indiscriminately around the school, were heartless killers. A couple years prior, a South Bronx gang mistook a beloved Little League coach for a rival and shot him in the head in front of his apartment building. Police vans patrolled the blocks around the school constantly but that didn't stop the shootings. Chris, a 34-year-old, muscular Puerto Rican-Colombian covered in colorful tattoos, could easily be mistaken for a gang member. The tattoos had nothing to do with gang life, of course. They were homages to the most significant moments in his life so far. A large cross on his bicep honored his late sister, a blue puzzle piece on his forearm was a nod to his daughter's autism, and a skull connected to a tree of life symbolized his battle with cancer. But nobody could see that from far away. He was like a lamb for the slaughter standing out in the schoolyard by himself, so he hurried back into the gym.

To be honest, he wasn't that safe inside either. Mott JHS, aka MS 22, was notoriously violent and named one of the twelve most dangerous schools in the five boroughs. Gang culture had seeped into the school like toxic mold. A decade before, after getting an F rating, some genius administrator had decided to break the 800 students up into three separate "academies"—called UConn, John Jay, and Columbia—so they'd get more individual attention from teachers. But it was a horrible mistake. The academies just further segregated the student body, which was 72 percent Latino and 25 percent black, and separated the smarter kids from the most badly behaved. In effect, the school had added three more rival gangs to the neighborhood.

The school was almost as much of a war zone as the streets. The one time school staff had all three academies in the yard, an all out rumble broke out. Chris's life had been threatened more than once by out-of-control, preteen gangbangers, and he'd broken up more than a few ferocious fights between female students, who, if looked at sideways, gouged each other's eyes out with nails filed into deadly points. It was those bloody brawls that inspired Chris to start the softball team. Whatever scarce resources existed at the school always went to the seemingly futile attempt to turn the boys' lives around. Nobody seemed to care about the girls. Chris did.

But screw it. An hour had passed and Chris was ready to throw in the towel. He sat back down on the bucket, put his head in his hands, and stared down at the ground. Chris had so desperately wanted to make an impact at the school and he'd already failed miserably. Such a stupid idea, he thought. What a waste . . .

"Is this the baseball tryouts?"

Chris lifted his head and saw two girls he recognized slightly, Hamniky, aka Nicky, and Gheynee, walking into the gym.

"Softball," he corrected.

"Whatever," Nicky shot back rudely.

"Are *you* the coach?" Gheynee asked.

It was the first time in his life he'd ever been called "Coach." He liked it. It made his heart swell with pride a little.

"Yes, I'm Coach Astacio."

"Is this baseball tryouts?" Nicky asked again impatiently.

"Softball."

As Gheynee eyeballed Chris up and down suspiciously, he suddenly remembered who she was. She'd been in his PE class and he'd never pronounced her name right. He always said "Gay-nee," and it was actually "Shay-nee." She obviously remembered him, too, and hadn't forgiven him.

"I don't like you," Gheynee sniped.

"Well, that's okay, I like you," Chris said.

"If my mom calls, you tell her I'm here," Nicky ordered.

The light bulb went on. Chris remembered the girls' story—they're sisters. Their mother recently got out of prison, and they were living with her for the first time in their lives. It was major upheaval, being torn away from the aunt they grew up with and actually called "Mami." They weren't adjusting well to their new life with their real mother. They didn't know her, and they were scared of her.

Suddenly, another set of sisters, Kimberly and Claudia, strolled in. Chris recognized Kimberly, because she was so tall for an eighth-grader. She was a good student who loved math and science. Claudia, a sixth-grader, was her half-sister and new to the school. She was Kimberly's little shadow, but not necessarily because they liked each other. They had different dads but their mother forced them to go everywhere together.

"Is it okay if she joins, too?" Kimberly asked.

"Of course," Chris said.

"Do we have to do anything today?" Nicky asked. "I don't feel like it. I've had a hard day."

"We can't really do anything with this amount of girls anyway," Chris said.

"Do we have to leave?" Nicky asked.

"It's fine, you can hang out."

They sprawled out on the dirty floor, which hadn't been mopped or waxed in weeks. Three of the girls, Kimberly, Claudia, and Nicky, were all in the same academy, UConn, which had the smartest, most well-behaved kids, so they knew each other and had no beefs. Chris sat quietly and listened to them gossip about boys they liked and girls they hated. At first, the banality of the conversation made his eyes glaze over. But as he watched them, he realized something profound. They didn't want to go home. Whether they were scared to walk down the street or scared of what would greet them at home, it was clear they were in no hurry to leave. They might not give a shit about softball, but they seemed very content chilling with Chris in the gym.

Chris thought about all of the girls he'd met over the last year, his first teaching at the school. How many horror stories he'd heard about shootings and abuse and drugs and abandonment and fucked-up families. That's why he'd created this softball team. To be clear, it's not like Chris *loved* softball. He didn't know anything about softball and had never even played. He knew how to play baseball and figured softball wasn't much different. Chris also picked the sport because it seemed to require the least amount of money—the school refused to give him one penny for his passion project. It was never about "softball." He started the team to be a safe space for the most troubled girls in the school. The ones who needed to be handled with care, and more important, the ones who were hardest to handle.

He wasn't giving up. Not yet.

"Hey, guys," he said, breaking into their conversation. "We need a lot more girls for this to work. I'll make you a deal—come back tomorrow with ten more people and you can hang out in the gym for as long as you want. I don't care who comes. Literally anybody."

To his shock, the next day, at exactly 2:30 on the dot, girls started flowing into the gym. Fifteen in total. Chris wanted more, but he wasn't about to get greedy. Fifteen was more than enough to field a team. "Damn," he thought, trying to suppress a smile. He knew these girls respected and responded to tough guys. He couldn't show happiness yet, which equaled weakness in their eyes. Show vulnerability and get ripped to shreds.

"I'm here, *bitches!*"

Chris's heart sank. Rashell, arguably the meanest, scariest girl in the entire school, walked in with Nicky, Gheynee, and their posse and made her presence known immediately. To say that Rashell was intimidating was an understatement. She was the ringleader, the head honcho, the boss, but not in a positive way. She was only thirteen years old but had a woman's body and carried herself like a woman. She was mature in body but not in her head. Rashell was in UConn because she was very smart, but she didn't apply herself. She was best known for throwing chairs at and spitting on teachers. They were terrified of her. Chris had faced her wrath in PE after also mispronouncing her name: "Ray-shell" instead of "Rachel."

"That's not my *fuckin'* name," she'd shouted at him. "It's 'Rachel'! What the *fuck* is wrong with you."

She hadn't forgiven or forgotten either. She walked up to Chris and got close to his face. "I still don't like you."

"Okay, I hope that changes," he said calmly. Then he turned to Gheynee. "Welcome back."

"Fuck you."

"I love you, too," he also said calmly.

Alcielis, a dead ringer for Janet Jackson and the most girly and provocatively dressed of the bunch, picked up one of the old gloves and put it on. "Ew!" she shrieked and threw it on the ground.

"You're going to get dirty in softball," Chris explained.

None of the girls in the gym were very athletic. Heaven, whose behavior had earned her the nickname "Hell" because she cursed constantly and had zero respect for authority, was skin and bones and looked like she couldn't even lift a ball.

It was a motley crew, and obvious that most, if not all, were not there to play softball. Some of the girls Chris knew, some he didn't. Some liked him, some didn't, like boy-crazy Precious, who Chris was certain was not "precious" at all, or her cousin Shiadiamond, who looked innocent but had a rep for running with gangbangers and fighting everyone—male, female, even teachers. A lot of these girls had assaulted a teacher like it was putting on pants in the morning. Robin had spent time in juvie for attacking a security guard. Robin had always been nice to Chris in gym class and she was sporty enough that he'd recruited her for the team.

"But you gotta change your attitude," he warned her.

"I'm gonna do this for you!" she promised.

If not violent themselves, many had been on the receiving end of violence or abuse. All had some kind of heartbreaking issue. One girl, who Chris suspected was homeless, smelled horrible. Genesis, who showed up alone, was pathologically shy and had cutting marks on her arms. Nayeli complained that she'd had nothing to eat all day. Mayoli was only eleven but bragged about drinking and smoking weed.

There were a few he thought would rub off on the others in a positive way, like rifle-armed Yoshie, but she hadn't shown up. Fraternal twins Kyara and Tyara were both intelligent, got good grades, and genuinely wanted to learn about softball. Johanna was very sweet but spoke zero English. Grateshka, whose brother was on the baseball team, came from a very solid home and was one of the only ones there who had a mother *and* a father. But she was also a class clown and had turned everyone's attention to Gianella's humongous forehead. The roasting was fierce.

"Fivehead!"

"It's like your entire face is on your chin!"

"Hey, Tyra Banks!"

Gianella was used to it, and laughed along, too, but to change the subject, she yelled, "I need to get some ass!"

If Chris didn't act fast, this could turn chaotic. He gathered the girls around him to get started. "I'm Coach Astacio, welcome to the softball tryouts," he said to a smattering of weak claps and blank stares. Undeterred, he launched into a short speech about the game of softball, explaining the simple things first, like the mechanics of how to throw the ball and hold the bat. Every few sentences, Grateshka interrupted him with lewd comments and corny jokes. Chris was annoyed. Grateshka came from a good family with a mother and father, she was the only girl who had great parents, so why was she acting like a clown?

Chris knew attention spans were short, so it was time to get moving. He told the girls to throw Wiffle balls around and swing the bat to gauge where they were at. There were a few girls that stuck out and a few that struck out: Aleiri was a disaster, with zero eye-hand coordination. Grateshka, however, had a big swing to match her big mouth. Precious looked so frail but surprisingly had a very powerful arm. Nicky, who seemed the most promising, and Rashell were good at all of it: throwing, catching, and swinging. He made sure to give them all lots of praise, something they rarely got in school or at home.

Next, Chris set up a clinic of three stations—playing catch, hitting the ball, and learning the rules of the game. He did something smart at first.

He gave the "best" players, Nicky and Rashell, important jobs, overseeing the catching and hitting stations, while he would explain the rules of the game at another station. Rashell might not have liked Chris, but he knew she liked being in charge.

"Now you teach them, like I taught you," he explained.

That was a genius move, but then he screwed up with a rookie mistake. He let the girls break themselves up into groups and they naturally gravitated into their academy cliques.

UConn: Nicky, Rashell, Gianella, Kimberly, Alcielis

Columbia: Precious, Shiadiamond, Gheynee, Heaven, Grateshka, Aleiri

John Jay: Nayeli, Jeelin, Genesis, Mayoli, Claudia

Before he knew it, the competing stations were jawing at each other.

"Why is she next to me?"

"Are you talking to me?"

"What is she looking at?"

He made a mental note to mix the girls up more in the future.

Despite all the side-eye, the first practice was going better than Chris had dreamed. And they seemed genuinely interested in learning about the game. Even though Yankee Stadium was less than a mile away, they were clueless and starting from scratch. His station was like *Softball for Dummies*, explaining basics like the positions, three strikes, and three outs. They asked productive questions like:

"If I hit the ball in the outfield, where do I run?"

"If the ball is hit to me, where do I throw it?"

"What's a bunt?"

They were having meaningful conversations, and Chris had to contain his excitement again. "Yes, this is going to happen," he thought.

Just as practice was starting to flow, the gym doors burst open and Angie, star of the girls' basketball tem, flew in like a tornado, trailed by her friend Achelin.

"What the fuck is *this*?" Angie sneered.

The girls stopped what they were doing and turned to stare. They all knew who she was. A tomboy. The baddest of the bad from John Jay.

Everyone was scared of John Jay girls. Except maybe for the biggest badass from UConn.

"Who the FUCK is she talking to?" Rashell yelled.

Uh-oh. Chris knew this was a disaster in the making. Achelin was a fighter, triggered by the smallest slight. He tried to shut up Angie and get her to leave quickly. But she wasn't going anywhere. Angie stalked the gym, shit-talking all the girls and pointing out everyone and everything wrong.

"Wiffle balls? Is this a fucking joke? You don't even have your own gloves! *She's* on the team? Oh, hell naw. Do you even have uniforms? I ain't playin on no team that don't have a uniform!" Her dissing was working. He could see it register in the other girls' eyes. Angie was cutting off Chris's manhood right in front of his team. It was all unraveling. He was gonna lose them.

After five minutes of pure torture, Angie finally stormed out with Achelin in tow. But the damage was done. Chris decided the only way to save it was to be honest. "Angie's right," he admitted. "We're not a team, we don't have uniforms, and, to be real, we don't have any promise. I'm not gonna sugarcoat this. The truth is, there's no money and no equipment. But it's gonna come, please just trust me and be patient. I'll be damned if I let you girls fail."

It was silent for a second, then Nicky spoke up.

"Fuck them!"

Chris smiled from ear to ear and, this time, he didn't care who saw it.

Part One

PRE-GAME

Chapter One

BUILDING CHARACTER

Failure was not an option for Chris. It never had been. In his house growing up in the '80s, there was a firm "no excuses" policy, largely due to the fact that Chris's dad, Andre "June" Astacio, was a Vietnam vet, drafted into the war when he was just eighteen years old. June was cryptic about his military deployment, and his battle scars, physical and emotional, were buried deep. Occasionally, a harrowing story would slip out. On one mission in the jungle, shrapnel missed tearing through June's face by inches. Several of his friends weren't so fortunate, blown to bits by grenades, right in front of his eyes. "If I could survive Vietnam," he always said, "then everything else was easy in life."

Of course, that was a fallacy and totally unrealistic. Everything else was not easy for the Astacios. Everyone in his family was expected to be as strong as June, though it was obvious he struggled with post-traumatic stress disorder after he came home, gulping down White Russians until he got drunk enough to drown the pain. He landed a job working the floor at Syms clothing store to provide for his wife, Cecilia, and growing family, but they were still dirt-poor. The family depended on food stamps for a short time before June and Chris's mom, Cecilia, decided the Astacios would not fall into the trap of relying on public assistance. Cecilia started collecting loose change, saving it in a jar. As she and June became more self-sufficient financially, the change jar was used for special occasions. Chris went to the circus for the first time after his mom emptied the jar of coins and bought them tickets. He didn't really like the circus, especially the stench of the elephants, but it was a special treat, nonetheless.

They may have had nothing, but they had each other. Cecilia and her children attended Christian church religiously, at least three times per week. She taught them to be God-fearing. Unfortunately June was not yet on board with religion. He resented God for the horrors he'd witnessed abroad, plus the everyday struggles he had to deal with once he returned home. What kind of God would allow the atrocities that transpired in Vietnam? What kind of God would allow his first daughter, Michelle, to be taken away by a cheating ex-wife?

Michelle was the oldest Astacio but she lived with her biological mom and addict stepdad a few blocks away. Chris was the second oldest, then Nick, Cindy, and Danny, and they all lived with June and Cecilia in their first floor, one-bedroom apartment on Sedgwick Avenue in the North Bronx. Chris and Nick shared the one bedroom, while his parents and the other children slept in the living room on a sofa bed and a cot. Chris never invited friends over because he was embarrassed by their tight quarters. He wore the same clothes to school almost every single day, though his mom taught him how to mix and match to the fullest. If he had only two pairs of jeans and a few shirts to his name, then he had an infinite number of outfits. *Dios no lo quiera*, he got a hole in his jeans. Today, you could probably wear pants that are ripped to shreds and get away with it. Back then, distressed jeans weren't cool or stylish, it was a sign of poverty, so his mom sewed on patches, also humiliating. In second grade, his high-water pants had patches on both knees and the other kids used to make fun of him. But he didn't tell his mom because he understood their circumstances. She would always tell Chris, "Jesus was poor but he was still King."

Chris's neighborhood, a melting pot of Puerto Rican and Dominican immigrants, was also a mix of working class and those on public assistance. His block wasn't rich by any standard, but it was safe, safer and less poor than even a couple blocks over. That's where the gangs were. Chris didn't know the names of them; he just knew which streets not to walk down. When he was a kid, he played stickball in the ones he knew were not war zones.

Still, they sometimes had trouble with the block below them, and kids from his block got jumped, too. One day while Chris was playing stickball, out of nowhere, some kids rolled up and one put a knife to Chris's friend's neck.

"What now, muthafucka?" he threatened.

Chris's friend's little brother ran up to the knife-wielding gangbanger and pleaded with him not to kill his sibling.

"Relax, no one is killing anyone today," the kid said. "Just stay away from our block."

So they stayed away from that block.

Chris loved playing baseball. He was a natural athlete, and, like every other red-blooded boy in the Bronx, was obsessed with the Yankees. He and his dad often took the subway down to Yankee Stadium, scored a couple of tickets in the cheap seats (back when that was actually an option), then snuck down to the good seats together. He used to be scared that they'd get caught but his dad was fearless.

"Who cares?" June would shrug.

Chris dreamed of stepping onto that legendary field one day, of playing alongside his idols Wade Boggs and Daryl Strawberry. He even imitated Strawberry's signature batting stance—bat held high, a little shimmy and the high kick. Stickball was a religion to Chris. He played nonstop, only taking a break when a car went by or he got hungry. He'd run over to his apartment, knock on the first-floor kitchen window, and his mom would hand him a hot dog or a sandwich. Then back to playing ball.

Truth is, Chris never went hungry. Even when times were super tight, Chris and his siblings were able to scrounge for pennies to buy food. June, who came to the United States from Puerto Rico when he was thirteen, was the most adamant that the Astacios never rely on public assistance, lest they be stigmatized as being lazy. He stood on the floor at Syms selling clothing for thirty-five years, despite enduring stomach ulcers, diabetes, a stroke, and eventually a heart attack. He instilled a sense of pride in hard work in his children, and, in the boys, machismo. His focus wasn't money or material things, it was all about strength of body, mind, character.

As far back as he can remember, Chris, as the oldest boy, was expected to be a leader and he felt immense pressure to be perfect. He was extremely bright; his buddies always gave him shit about it and nicknamed him "the smart kid." He had to be the best at everything, like when he learned to write, he made sure his penmanship was the neatest in his class. From day one, Chris was supposed to be the success story of his family, and he took that responsibility seriously.

There was only one hitch and it was major—even as a young kid, Chris was riddled with severe anxiety. He was super tiny for his age and bullied about his size mercilessly. It was easy to push him around because he couldn't defend himself, though his father offered the unhelpful and useless advice, "Just punch them in the stomach!" Chris was so small, when he got his junior high school diploma, someone shouted, "Hey, there's a kindergartner graduating!" By the time he got to high school, he was still barely five feet tall. Chris was ashamed of his appearance and never felt "normal." Petrified of talking or getting called on in class, he was quiet as a mouse and so self-conscious he couldn't eat in front of anyone. His stomach would ache, his throat would close up, and he couldn't swallow.

This small, skinny, fragile boy was in tremendous emotional and physical pain but he couldn't tell anyone for a couple of reasons. One, because he was a child, he didn't know what "anxiety" was and didn't know what to call it; and two, in his family, being mentally ill was taboo. Until very recently, his dad refused to get help for PTSD, though he had night terrors and woke Cecilia up screaming in his sleep.

Instead of therapy, June self-medicated, a habit he picked up in 'Nam. He did what he had to do to survive, even if it meant "medicating" himself to stay awake for thirty-six hours. Before Chris was born, June drank and smoked like a chimney. After Chris was born, he chain-smoked so incessantly, his wife would warn, "Don't go into the living room, your father is smoking," because the whole room was a thick cloud of smoke. When Chris was four, his mother gave birth to a little girl, Christina. Sixteen hours later, her lungs collapsed and she died in Cecilia's arms. June went to the cemetery with his last pack of cigarettes in his pocket, crushed it, threw it over the hill, and never smoked again.

June cursed God but ultimately felt responsible. Following the death of Christina, he began to see the light, and began praying and attending church. June was finally on the path to enlightenment and healing, but the opposite happened to Chris, who was severely traumatized by the passing of his baby sister. The night his mom went into labor, she told him, "I'll be back in a few days." But she returned the next day carrying an empty basket. Chris peered into it, puzzled, and asked, "Where's the baby?"

"God took the baby," his mother replied sadly.

"Why did God take the baby? Tell Him to give her back!"

"God can't give back the baby."

"I hate God!" Chris screamed.

According to Cecilia, that was the last thing he said for the next year.

Between his secret anxiety and his baby sister's death, Chris was a wreck, barely able to function. After Christina's death, Chris's brain, being "the smart kid," helped him keep his head above water for awhile. He was a math whiz and excelled at writing and vocabulary, probably because one summer, he read the entire dictionary. In seventh grade, out of the blue, Chris and one other female student were plucked from his neighborhood school and chosen to attend JHS 141 (David A. Stein Riverdale), a tony public middle school in the Bronx on 237th Street. Cecilia was so thrilled, she wrote in his grade school yearbook, "So proud you got into 141!"

Chris was excited, too. He felt special and like he was on his way to fulfilling his destiny as the family superstar. But he was also terrified. At the age of twelve, he'd have to take public transportation by himself for the first time and attend a school that was mostly white and Jewish, with barely any Hispanic kids. The first time he walked into class, it was a culture shock. There were blue eyes everywhere.

"Where am I?" he thought. "Damn, I'm in the wrong place."

His instincts were right on. Chris was miserable at his new school. He was teased by his new classmates about his size—they called him "Bighead" because his head was disproportionately large for his body—and got jumped at the bus stop by a gang member who had once attended Riverdale but got kicked out. "If you don't leave this bus stop, I'm gonna smack you in the face," the boy taunted.

"Why does this kid want to smack me?" Chris wondered. Before he could figure out the answer, the gangbanger slapped his face as hard as he could and emptied his pockets. When Chris's uncle, a former gangbanger from Spanish Harlem, heard about this incident, he rushed to the school and made a scene.

"Where is this motherfucka?" he yelled and cursed. "YOU better not be covering for him!" It scared the shit out of Chris because he knew if his uncle found the boy, he might have seriously hurt him or maybe even killed him. Cecilia had told Chris stories about his uncle; he knew what he was capable of. Fortunately, the kid was nowhere to be found that day.

The kids weren't the worst of Chris's problems. He got zero support from the teachers at his new school, and one in particular made it his job to torture Chris. From the first moment he stepped foot in Vincent Cuomo's homeroom class, it was over. He took one look at Chris's brown face and said coldly, "Are you in the right place?"

"I don't know," Chris said innocently, "am I?"

"For some strange reason, you *are* in the right place," he sneered.

For an entire year, Chris was subjected to Cuomo's racist wrath. When Chris did well on his first quiz, Cuomo said, "I don't know how you were accepted into this school, let alone this program." The next time Chris aced his test, Cuomo said, "You think you're smart? I'm gonna find out how you cheated on my test."

"I took my book home and studied," Chris explained.

"Oh you study? Really?" Cuomo mocked. "You'll end up to be nothing. A street kid. Always in the street. All you people are the same."

A lot of kids called this teacher "Cuomo the homo" behind his back but Chris never did. He was overly nice to his tormentor and tried to be a "perfect" student so Cuomo would like him. It was futile. Once, trying to score Brownie points, Chris volunteered to clean the blackboards. He grabbed the sponge but realized he was too short to reach the top. He didn't want the students to laugh at him jumping up and down like a monkey so he snuck back to his desk and slunk down in his seat. Suddenly, Cuomo shouted, "EVERYONE, STOP. Chris, put that piece of chalk back. I saw you take the chalk, put it back."

"I didn't take nothing," Chris insisted. "I never took no chalk."

Cuomo kept the entire class after school for an hour, threatening to keep them even longer until Chris gave back the chalk he didn't take. He felt his classmates shooting daggers at him. He knew what they were thinking: "He's Hispanic, of course he took the chalk." When Chris wouldn't confess to a crime he didn't commit, Cuomo slowly let the other students go home one by one. Finally, Chris was the last student left, and he started to get up to leave.

"You're not going anywhere," Cuomo said darkly, then pushed Chris back down in his chair hard. He picked up Chris's desk, turned it over, and dumped it on the floor. "I don't know where you put this chalk!" he spit. "I know who you are! I bet your mom has twelve kids on welfare, she breeds like a rabbit and spits babies out!"

Tears streamed down Chris's face.

"That's not true, my mom has a job . . ."

"Oh, your mom has a job? You probably don't even know who your father is!"

"No, my dad has a job, too . . ."

"Oh really, wow! You gonna use the chalk for graffiti?"

"You don't use chalk for graffiti . . ."

"Oh, now you're a smart ass? You probably steal all the time. You need the money for food."

This confused Chris. He didn't understand how stealing chalk would put money in his pocket or food on his table.

Cuomo finally let him go, but spewed more hateful words that would be forever burned in Chris's memory: "Don't even think about telling anyone what happened here. No one will ever believe you and I will always win." Chris wasn't sure whether he meant that being a teacher would discredit him or that being white gave him more leverage. As a young child in an unfamiliar educational environment, he took it to mean both. That was the first time Chris realized that being Hispanic came with a price.

Cuomo didn't want Chris at Riverdale; he didn't think he belonged there, but he had to tolerate him being there. For two years, Chris barely tolerated being at Riverdale. He was stressed out, sick to his stomach every day, and missed nearly twenty days of school. Every day he forced himself to show up, the crowded MTA bus rides to school triggered panic attacks. He hung onto the overhead straps for dear life, soothing himself with the mantra, "Almost there, almost there, almost there."

Bottom line was he just didn't fit in there. He didn't have money or trendy clothes or go on vacations, like the other kids. He was the odd man out, the outsider. He only had two friends, a Jewish kid and another Hispanic kid. They were far from being popular. Chris gravitated to Adam, the Jewish kid, because he, too, was bullied, but for a different reason. He had a minor deformity on his nose (one nostril was smaller than the other), his mom was a drunk, and he didn't know his father. Teachers didn't like Adam, either; they laughed at his chicken-scratch handwriting. Chris did not pity Adam, he understood him, and thus they were best friends. Michael, the Hispanic kid, lived just a few blocks away from Chris in a dilapidated, dark, smelly old house.

Chris, Adam, and Michael called themselves the "Three Amigos" and soon enough Chris found himself riding shotgun in their mischievous adventures, like running across the busy Henry Hudson Parkway. Chris and Michael didn't really didn't want to but felt peer pressured into it. After Adam took off, they darted through the speeding traffic like deer in headlights.

"Did you see the look on Chris's face?" Adam howled after. "You guys are such pussies!"

Adam was clearly the ringleader and goaded the other boys into his increasingly reckless schemes by calling them his favorite word: "pussies." One day Adam claimed that he had to pick something up from his rabbi at his synagogue. Chris had never been in a temple and he was amazed. The place was empty and Adam had disappeared. Ten minutes later, Adam sprinted toward them, shouting, "RUN!"

Being Hispanic, Chris and Michael didn't need to be told to run. They started running as soon as they saw Adam running. They ran out of the synagogue for a few blocks with no clue as to why they were running. Finally, they stopped to catch their breath and Adam explained that he'd robbed the collection. Chris felt awful. He didn't want to steal from God.

But peer pressure is mighty powerful and their newfound burglary capers, led by Adam, had just begun. Adam and Michael began stealing small things like candy from the candy store. Of course, Chris didn't know at first they'd been stealing until Adam mocked him. "Wait, you paid for that Milky Way? What a pussy!" So Chris started stealing with them to prove he wasn't a pussy and to get Adam's approval. He lifted jewelry for Adam's ear piercing, Marvel cards, but also books and school supplies. Chris didn't want to be a pussy but he was clearly still a nerd. Marvel cards were the craze that year. One package was a little less than $5 and it came with a substantial number of cards. Chris sold single cards to kids who wanted to complete their collections, anywhere from $1 to $5 each.

When shoplifting got boring, they turned to vandalism. They stabbed car tires and threw rocks from the MTA bus windows, shattering car windows and windshields. They collected acorns and chucked them at people. They kept score of who they hit, old ladies got bonus points. They did this for a few months until Adam decided to throw some acorns at a parked car while the bus was standing at a red light. The guy in the parked car forced his way through the backdoor of the bus and lifted Adam from his seat. The guy threatened to kill Adam but all Adam did was smile. Luckily, the guy realized how warped Adam was and decided to leave the bus. That was the last day they decided to play the acorn game. Of course that meant they had to invent something else to do.

So they hung out at Adam's apartment. Adam didn't like people to meet his mom because she was a sloppy drunk, so they hung out on the playground on the property. One day, the building's white security guard asked them to leave.

"I live here and these are my guests," Adam explained.

"You can be here but *they* can't," the guard said, nodding his head toward the brown boys.

This angered Adam. He ran back up to his kitchen and when he came back down, led the Three Amigos to the building's garbage room. He directed Chris and Michael to scoop up all of the newspaper they could find. Once they had big pile, Adam walked them back to the playground.

"Quick, help me spread newspaper everywhere," he yelled.

"Great," Chris thought, "we are going to litter the playground as revenge!" But once the park was covered, Adam reached into his backpack and pulled out a bottle of lighter fluid and drenched the newspapers. Then he took out a lighter from his pocket and lit the whole playground on fire.

"Isn't this so beautiful?" Adam beamed, all wild-eyed in a trance.

Chris's initial instinct was to get the fuck outta there, but Adam urged him and Michael to stay to take in the beauty. Soon they heard sirens in the distance, but Adam still wanted to stay. The hell with that! Chris climbed over the fence and ran home. He flipped through the channels on TV to see if they had burned down the park but there was no mention.

The next day at school, Adam ran into Chris and Michael walking down the hallway and burst into laughter. Chris was furious. Adam called them "a bunch of pussies" again. Chris started not to like their adventures anymore.

During their last year at JHS 141, the Three Amigos were still intact but just barely. Chris and Michael didn't hang out with Adam that often because every time they did, something bad happened. Walking home one day, they were approached by another group of kids traveling together, but they had more "color" in their group. They decided to rob the Three Amigos. "If you weren't hanging with that white kid, we might have just kept walking by," one of the attackers said, laughing as they ran away with their stuff.

As a form of retaliation, Adam decided that he wanted to jump a random freshman. Chris was the voice of reason and protested against this stupidity. Adam approached a kid and started pushing him around, but Chris stepped in and stopped the onslaught.

"What, are you a pussy?" Adam smirked.

"No, but at least I like pussy," Chris retorted. Of course, he was still a virgin at the time but he was trying to call him gay for attempting to jump a defenseless kid.

The last day of school was the last hurrah for the Three Amigos. After they all picked up their diplomas, they walked home together. Suddenly, Adam stopped in a small clearing. Adam dumped the contents of his backpack onto a concrete slab and lit in on fire. "No one cares that I graduated, why should I?" he said coldly, and then dramatically threw his diploma into the bonfire. Michael dumped his bag into the fire too.

Chris clutched his backpack. "Fuck no," he said. He worked hard for that diploma.

Adam continued to throw stuff onto the fire—dead tree limbs, leaves, garbage. The fire grew as tall as the top of the trees.

"This fire is out of control, man!" Chris screamed.

"You want to see out of control?" Adam took several lighters from his backpack and threw them into the flames, causing small explosions. Adam had finally gone too far. Chris bolted without looking back, as Adam's favorite word "Pussy!" echoed among the charred trees. Chris was officially done with the Three Amigos.

Two years later, he crossed paths with Adam one more time. Adam was excited to see Chris and suggested they make plans. Chris never reached out. A few months after that, Chris heard that Adam killed himself. The funeral was empty.

Riverdale could have changed the trajectory of Chris's life in a positive way. Instead, it shook him to his core and pushed him farther away from his goals and dreams. When it came time to apply for high school, Chris could have gone anywhere. New York City has the most extensive system of "School Choice" in the country and requires all students to apply to twelve schools, ranked in order of preference. Chris was accepted to Stuyvesant High School, one of the best schools in all five boroughs. But he didn't want to be "the smart kid" anymore. He didn't want to take the bus by himself; he knew he couldn't survive a subway train ride all the way down to lower Manhattan with his increasingly crippling anxiety. He just wanted to feel normal. So he chose the "zone school" closest to his house, John F. Kennedy High School, one of the worst in New York City. By 1995, it had more than 5,000 students and a dismal claim to fame—less than 25 percent of its seniors graduated. JFK was dangerous and chaotic. But Chris didn't care. He'd be with his people, his kind, the Hispanic and black kids. He'd be home.

Not surprisingly, Chris did not thrive at JFK either. In fact, he barely managed to graduate himself. Chris's high-school years became about survival, not learning or nurturing his gifts.

The school was a war zone. Chris was scared every day and that sense of fear angered him. The violence was brazen and unchecked. Students threatened to kill teachers in the classroom, they polished their guns openly in the hallway, they threw chairs out the windows. Chris tried eating lunch in the cafeteria but it was a battlefield in there, too, between the brawls and kids stealing each other's lunch money.

Nowhere was safe at JFK, especially the bathrooms. First, there were no doors on the stalls in case you had to really "go." Second, most fights and drug transactions happened in the bathroom. Chris tried his best to hold it until he went home. He'd rather use the piss-infested, bum-riddled public restrooms of the great ol' New York City park system near the Marble Hill projects. He starved himself daily so he wouldn't have to use the bathroom at school. Obviously, that decision was detrimental to his health. He couldn't concentrate because he was either exhausted or starving, not to mention distracted by the music blaring from the cars of people hanging out in the parking lot, not all of whom were even students.

Once again, his new classmates bullied him about his size, and inevitably, the bullying led to a physical altercation. In tenth grade, Chris was violently assaulted. One afternoon, his friends decided to cut class to go to the park. Chris had a test and told them he'd meet them there after. Traveling solo was a big no-no at JFK, but Chris took a chance. After his test, he walked quickly from the school to the street, through a long passage dubbed "The Strip" by the students because that's where everything bad happened. Six boys walked ahead of him talking loudly and Chris nervously decided to pass them. As he snuck by, the boisterous chatter turned to frightening whispers. Chris walked anxiously for a few minutes hoping he would make it to the end of The Strip, back to civilization. Just when Chris could see that the end of the walkway was near, he felt a blow on the back of his head. One of the boys grabbed his neck, slammed him into a fence, threw him to the ground, and smashed his face into the concrete pavement. Chris's parents had scrounged together enough money to pay for braces; now the metal ripped the inside of his mouth and the wires pierced through his gums. Blood poured from his mouth and he passed out. Chris woke in a pool of his own blood and saw a large crowd assembled around him.

Chris didn't feel pain just rage.

It was at that moment he truly hated himself.

That night, Chris begged his mother to let him take a few days off school, but of course, the Astacio house had a strict "no whining" policy. "Don't use this as an excuse to not go to school," said Cecilia, who grew up in Spanish Harlem and was no stranger to violence. "You're going tomorrow."

So Chris showed up the next day, his chin three times the size of Jay Leno's, his lip puffed three times the size of a Kardashian. His face got beat so badly one of his teeth died and eventually turned black. He was embarrassed and scared at the same time. He'd be seen as weak and an easy target. What if it happened again . . . and again . . . and again? To his surprise, when he got to school, nobody laughed at Chris or harassed him. They thought he had a lot of guts. "He got jumped and he still came to school?" they whispered. "The cojones on this kid!"

From that day on, Chris shut down and hardened up. He didn't want to be the guy who got picked on ever again. His whole demeanor changed. He started wearing baggy pants like the hoodlums. He made friends with kids in gangs or who had gang influence, so people would see him hanging out with them and not mess with him. He dropped out of honors classes and cut classes like everyone else because he didn't want to stand out and make himself a target. People didn't like "the smart kid," so he got answers wrong on tests on purpose, and instead of turning his papers in first, waited for other students to finish before him.

Chris abandoned everything that once made him happy, that kept him stable and structured. He quit the baseball team. He stopped going to church, furious with God for turning His back on him. "Where is God now if I'm being such a good kid?" he wondered. "I'm still getting harassed and tortured. Hell with this shit, I'm gonna be just like everyone else."

His anxiety, at an all time high, turned into anger. He put on a big show like he'd fight anyone. He punched holes in walls. He started carrying weapons, mostly knives. His favorite was a small blade that fit between his fingers. It made him feel safe to walk with his hand stuffed in his pocket, ready to slash any *mamabicho* who dared confront him.

Chris manufactured a reputation for being a hothead on purpose, and it worked because nobody ever jumped him again. His vibe became, "Don't mess with that short kid who always looks hungry and angry 'cause there's something off about him." Chris used his brain to outsmart his would-be attackers and get out of tricky situations. Like, he'd never liked drinking and smoking weed and now he was surrounded by kids who did. When they passed a joint around, Chris put on his new tough guy act and huffed, "Get that shit away from me!" They didn't dare peer pressure him. Chris had always been school smart, now he was street smart, too. Staying sober allowed him to make better decisions when things got scary or hairy, which happened a lot.

Still, his anxiety ruled his life and his confidence was at an all-time low. He once dreamed of playing baseball at Yankee Stadium like his heroes; now that aspiration was in the toilet. He only had one simple goal now—get out of high school alive.

He had no plan beyond that.

Chapter Two

CAUGHT IN THE CYCLE

A mother is her daughter's first friend. But the earliest memory Nicky has of her mom was not her tickling her tummy or brushing her hair or playing with toys. It was the time she and her sister Gheynee went to prison to visit Gheynee's father. They put their coloring books through the metal detector, got frisked by a couple guards, then shuttled over to the visiting room. When they walked in, they spotted their mother waving them over to the table she was sitting at with Gheynee's father, who'd been incarcerated on a drug charge. He wanted to meet his daughter for the first time, so a relative brought the girls to the prison.

As the girls sat down shyly at the table, Nicky snuck a peek at her mom out of the corner of her eye. They didn't see her much, so she always forgot what she looked like. She looked like Nicky. Actually, they were carbon copies—same thin body, same intense brown eyes, and same dark ringlets cascading down their backs. Her mom caught Nicky's eye, then looked up at her forehead.

"Why you got them ugly bangs?" she said, smile vanishing, mood darkening instantly. "They're too short." She picked up a hairbrush that'd been sitting on the table and hit Nicky over the head with it. Hard.

"What the hell?" Nicky thought. "Dis lady has issues." Maybe her mom meant to be playful but it didn't feel right. It felt awful. "When you're young and you get hit with anything," Nicky would recall later, "it hurts you."

That was the first time she remembers being hit by her mother. It wouldn't be the last. When Nicky was born, her mom was only nineteen years old and was in no position to raise a baby. She had no job, no place of her own, and Nicky's birth father lived in the Dominican Republic. (Gheynee's father came up with her unusual real first name, listed on her birth certificate as "Hamniky"—call her that at your own risk.)

Plus, her mom had mental health issues. Before Nicky was born, she'd been hospitalized for an attempted suicide. After the birth, she couldn't handle the stress and had zero patience. So, two weeks after she was born, Nicky's mom moved into her sister Gladys's apartment in Harlem, and Nicky was handed off to her aunt, who was twenty-two years older than Nicky's mom and had already grown children. A year and a half later, as soon as Gheynee was born, she, too, was given up to Mami Gladys, as the girls called her affectionately. "Gheynee was born in Mami Gladys's hands," Nicky would always say.

Nicky and Gheynee remember an idyllic childhood living with Mami Gladys, first in New York City, then in Virginia and North Carolina. Once out of New York City, they lived in nice apartments or houses with plenty of bedrooms, big backyards, and swimming pools in their complexes or just down the street. They had structure and rules. And they were tight. Nicky was into cheerleading and Gheynee was all about gymnastics, and the two would practice cartwheels, flips, and splits together outside in nearby fields. Gheynee even had a little dachshund puppy named Lexi she doted on. "I was happy all the time," she remembers.

Though their birth parents' absence understandably left a deep hole in their hearts, Mami Gladys and her super tight-knit extended family gave the girls as much love and attention as they could, and that definitely helped mitigate the emotional wound of abandonment. When they were very young, Nicky and Gheynee saw their birth mom infrequently, and usually only when Gladys brought them back to New York City to visit more family. In the meantime, the girls had weekly phone calls with their mom and, on the rare occasion, Gheynee spoke to her birth father, maybe on a birthday or holiday.

When Nicky was around seven years old, her mom was arrested on a drug charge and sent away for two years. The prison was about a five-hour drive from Mami Gladys's, so they never went to visit her. Instead they sent her cards and letters. The sisters grew even closer during this time, inseparable even, though their personalities couldn't have been more opposite. Nicky was sweet and affectionate and sensitive—she was the one who cried about not having a father figure in her life. "Every girl should meet her daddy," she'd think, then get weepy. Gheynee was less emotional, the kind of girl not willing to open up her heart and say "I love you" or give away free hugs to just anyone, not even her sister. But they always had each other's backs. Since Gheynee was the tougher of the two, "I protected her," she says of Nicky.

Despite being abandoned by their birth parents, the sisters were doing as well as humanly possible. Mami Gladys loved them. They were cared for. They were happy and healthy. Then their mother came home.

She's . . . different, everybody whispered. She'd already had some mental health issues before she was locked up; prison made it worse. It changed her in the way that prison changes people, in the way that those of us who have never been to prison will never understand. Jobless and homeless, their mom needed money quickly, but convicted felons can't just get jobs and homes in the snap of a finger. It's not that simple. But having children does make it a little easier. Having Nicky and Gheynee qualified their mother for public assistance.

One day, out of the blue, Mami Gladys got a call.

"My babies are gonna come live with me," she said.

Gladys was stunned. "Basta ya!" she pleaded. "Stop, no!"

Mami Gladys tried to reason with her younger sister. She knew deep in her heart she loved her daughters, but she was not capable of taking care of them. But her pleas fell on deaf ears.

"Give me my babies back or I'll kill myself!" their mother threatened.

The two battled for custody in court, and Nicky and Gheynee had to tell a judge whom they'd rather live with. Their mom had drilled it into her daughters' heads that if they loved her, they must say they wanted to live with her over Mami Gladys. When Nicky took the stand—out of fear, confusion, and blind loyalty—she told the judge quietly and not at all convincingly, "I want to live with my mom." Nicky could tell by the worried eyes and furrowed brows all around her that everyone knew she was lying. But the damage was done, and the law favored the birth parent. So when Nicky was about ten, she and Gheynee moved back to the South Bronx, into a small apartment on 176th Street, with their mom, who was little more than a stranger. "I was used to a loving family," Nicky says. "She wasn't loving at all."

The beatings started immediately. Nicky remembers first getting whipped with belts, the rhinestones and metal studs leaving visible welts on her arms. Her mom progressed to breaking a cup on Nicky's head, holding a knife to her throat, and lashing her with a wire hanger so many times, she developed a heart-shaped scar on her forehead.

To make her feel better, well-meaning friends would say things like, "Oh, your mom just cares about you *too* much."

"People always say she's hitting me out of love," Nicky says, disgusted. "But I don't accept that. She didn't love me."

Her mother "be violating" Gheynee, too, Nicky remembers. Like the time she smashed a computer keyboard over her head or the time she tried to stab her. If Nicky tried to stop it or protect her sister, her mom came for her. Or she abused both of them at the same time, dragging the girls into the shower for a beating.

Nicky definitely got it worse, probably because she was the oldest, but there was also something more deliberate going on. From the moment Nicky moved in with her, her mom reserved a special brutality for her mini-me. She'd curse her out one minute, pretend to be loving the next. She was an actor and could flip a switch from cruel to kind effortlessly. Anything Nicky did could set their mom off on an explosive, expletive-laced tirade that most often resulted in a shove, a slap, or worse. It could be as harmless as Nicky not being able to swallow her vitamin or as delusional as thinking Nicky stole her money. "The things she got mad over were not things to get mad over," Nicky says. "She needed some sort of help."

Like many abusers, their mom showed remorse after uncontrollable rages. She called Mami Gladys and cried, "Why am I like this?" Gladys told her she needed professional help, therapy, and medication, but her sister refused every time. And then it would happen all over again.

Mami Gladys moved to Florida, so she says she never witnessed her sister's abuse. But it was out in the open. If her mom was mad at Nicky, everyone else felt her wrath, too. Once, she thought Nicky lost her cellphone and shrieked, "I'm gonna beat the shit out of you!" Nicky ran to her friend's apartment next door to hide, but her mother found her. "She literally dragged Nicky by her hair down the stairs, down the street, and up the stairs to their apartment. She didn't even give her a chance to walk," recalls Alcielis, who was not only there but lived in the same building as Nicky and became her best friend in sixth grade. "She didn't even know the lady who lived there. She just walked in and dragged Nicky out. I called the police."

As Nicky's neighbor and closest confidante, Alcielis witnessed Nicky's abuse at the hands of her mother countless times.

Police visited the apartment, as well as the Administration for Children's Services (ACS), who were called about a half a dozen times about their mom's abuse. But the cases were always dropped. Even after Nicky showed up to her grade school, PS 42, with a deep bite mark on her arm and admitted to a teacher that her mother did it. When confronted by school officials, Nicky's mom insisted she had ringworm. Worried that she was contagious, the school sent her home, where Nicky faced another beating for snitching. ACS eventually visited about the bite but nothing ever came of it. Nicky and Gheynee lied to the caseworkers, mixing up the story about their mom and not making her look "psycho" on purpose until it was indecipherable, because they were desperate to avoid being placed in foster care and possibly split up.

Plus, by this time, their mom had given birth to another baby girl with a third baby daddy, and Nicky and Gheynee felt responsible for her safety now, too. The two-bedroom apartment was getting increasingly crowded. Their mom had landed a job working at an auto-repair shop but it wasn't enough to keep a roof over all their heads. So an aunt, who had three kids, had moved in, then another aunt with another three kids moved in. At any given time, there could be anywhere from twelve to eighteen people crashing in the tiny apartment.

Their mother, who was unstable financially as well as emotionally, decided to move into a shelter with the girls, right across the street from their grade school. They showed up to school hungry, scared, and exhausted from sleepless nights at the shelter, due to the fire alarm being pulled in the middle of the night, all night long. Nicky acted like a "loud happy child" at school, but in reality, she was silently suffering. Sometimes she broke down but she hated doing that in public because nobody knew her issues and she couldn't complain about it anyway. It was too risky. "You can't really say nothing to nobody," she says. "I don't trust."

It only took a year after their mom came home from prison to turn Nicky's and Gheynee's lives completely upside down. They'd changed irreparably. Their attitude, the way they talked, even the way they looked was totally different. "They cursed, they talked back, they were quick to anger," Mami Gladys says. "They were not the ladies that grew up with me."

Nicky and Gheynee's relationship changed, too. Gheynee stopped being Nicky's protector. "I didn't feel love for her," Gheynee says. "I just didn't touch her no more. Me expressing myself and hugging, that stopped. I don't know why. When we went back to Mami, it changed for us. It was just different."

It crushed Nicky. "She doesn't show me love," she'd complain about Gheynee. "I be trying and when she does I get hyped. This is why I don't. She give me a hug and I cause attention. She's like, 'Bro, calm down. Don't do that.'"

Nicky and Gheynee morphed from nice naïve kids to stone-cold, jaded old souls, with an armor of self-protection as thick as Fort Knox. Nicky was no longer sweet or social. She didn't like talking to people or even being near them. She hated everyone and acted like she didn't need her mom. "Like for me, you don't have to show me love. I don't really care. All that love is gonna be fake. I don't need it. I got Mami Gladys. She show me love every single day." Gheynee had already been reserved, now she was even more guarded. But there was no going back to Mami Gladys, literally or figuratively. "She's our angel," Nicky says wistfully. "My mom's the devil."

After being returned to their birth mother, Nicky and Gheynee lost who they were and who they might've become. Worst of all, they lost hope.

Chapter Three

A BRONX TALE OR TWO

How do you even have hope when you live in the sixth poorest neighborhood in New York City? Where the unemployment rate is 56 percent higher than the national average and the median income is a dismal $28,038?

That's the South Bronx.

Out of 267 neighborhoods in New York City, the area south of Fordham Road and east of the Bronx River ranks dead last or near the bottom in just about every economic stat recorded. But that's only one section of the Bronx, and it doesn't paint a complete picture of the whole borough. The Bronx gets a bad rap (pun intended, it's the official birthplace of hip-hop), and that's not entirely fair. It's the second smallest of the five boroughs but the Bronx is still massive at forty-two square miles. Yes, it's impoverished, but it also has working-class and upper class neighborhoods, like Riverdale, where Chris went to junior high and John F. Kennedy lived for a short time in his youth.

The Bronx is packed with people; it's the second-most densely populated borough and it's arguably the most diverse. Once a haven for Jewish, Italian, and Irish immigrants, today 56 percent of its 1.5 million population is Latinx and 26 percent is black or African American. The Bronx may be dirt-poor but it's rich in history, education, and culture, and the birthplace/breeding ground of many influential artists, athletes, actors, scientists, and politicians, including Al Pacino, Alexandria Ocasio-Cortez, Cardi B, Calvin Klein, Grandmaster Flash, Jennifer "Jenny from the Block" Lopez, Lou Gehrig, Neil deGrasse Tyson, and Supreme Court Justice Sonia Sotomayor.

The Bronx is gritty but also beautiful. It has the five-mile long Grand Concourse, originally modeled after the Champs-Élysées in Paris and lined with historic art deco apartment buildings, the New York Botanical Garden, the Fordham University campus, and Van Cortlandt Park, which is bigger than Central Park. And yet the northernmost of the five boroughs has always been considered the city's redheaded stepchild, lowlier in status than even Staten Island. "The Bronx/No Thonx," poet Ogden Nash wrote in *The New Yorker* way back in 1931.

Nash later apologized for his cruel words, but he wasn't completely wrong. The truth about the Bronx's questionable reputation lies somewhere in the middle. Its complexity is its biggest strength and biggest weakness. For instance, the Bronx Zoo is amazing and all, but the people who live right next to it might work there cleaning the cages and only be able afford to bring their families on Wednesday's free admission day. It's not fake news that the Bronx, for decades, was a scary, depressing dystopia; "left for dead," as the *New York Times* once reported. In the 1970s and 1980s, for reasons too multifaceted and confusing to go into detail here (but include white flight to the suburbs, a dirty freeway built right through the middle of it, the War on Drugs), the Bronx decayed into an apocalyptic hellscape. About 44 percent of the borough burned to the ground during an arson epidemic, with an estimated 600,000 homes lost, which was unleashed into the pop culture ether when sports broadcaster Howard Cosell spotted raging fires during a Yankees game and allegedly declared, "Ladies and gentlemen, the Bronx is burning." (The veracity of that story has subsequently been challenged, but the quote lives on in infamy.) In 1977, President Jimmy Carter visited blighted Charlotte Street with a camera crew, "projecting a powerful negative image of the Bronx around the globe," according to the Bronx Historical Society. Then Ronald Reagan stopped by, declared that the Bronx looked like "London after the Blitz," and the negative stereotype was cemented. After that, about 40 percent of Bronx residents fled for greener pastures, and the gangs, junkies, and destitute immigrants with nowhere else to go moved into the vacant, decrepit buildings. The rest was history—and a recipe for disaster.

In the last twenty-five years, many parts of the Bronx have been rebuilt, restored, and revitalized with billions in public funds. But the South Bronx in particular—home of Yankee Stadium and Boogie Down Productions—remains a mess, one of the most violent, poverty-stricken, crime-infested neighborhoods in America. You wouldn't dare wander around the South Bronx at night, or even during the day. A simple walk to the bodega can be like playing Russian roulette. Maybe you'll make it back alive. Maybe you'll catch a stray bullet in your head. Or look at somebody wrong and get the shit kicked out of you. Random (gun)fights break out in an instant and don't discriminate—innocent bystanders get caught up in the chaos all the time. On the spot where terrible things happen, locals leave lighted spiritual candles and cardboard signs with the scrawled letters "RIP." It's an all-too-common sight in the South Bronx.

Alexandra Maruri, owner of Bronx Historical Tours, grew up in the South Bronx but she won't walk her groups through its ten-odd neighborhoods, like Mott Haven, Morrisania, or Fleetwood. She drives her clients instead. "The area has always been notorious for mentally ill people roaming around and gang violence," she explains.

The NYPD's 44th precinct, which covers the South Bronx, isn't the largest but has one of the highest volumes of 911 calls in all of New York City. Shootings, stabbings, robberies, arson, domestic abuse, drugs (heroin, meth, crack), runaways, incorrigible teens, and an epidemic of EDP, or emotionally disturbed persons, often young children traumatized by sexual abuse. The local jails can't handle or accommodate the amount of arrests, and could get even more jammed up when Riker's Island is scheduled to close permanently in 2019. But the Bronx actually has one of the lowest conviction rates in the world because they just keep "catching and releasing" the same people over and over again. It's a vicious cycle with no end in sight.

Of course, the biggest criminal crisis is the gangs. A dozen small crews, some affiliates of the Crips and Bloods, operate in the South Bronx: 6 Wild, Mac Balla Bloods, 280, Eden Boys, Sev O, Cholos, Trinitarios, Sheisty Sheridans, and more, which terrorize the blocks they've claimed and recruit its young males and, not as commonly, females. There are girl gangs, but usually the only way to get initiated into one was to have sex with a gang member, or get jumped or stabbed as a test.

Alexa knew all about that lifestyle. She couldn't avoid it. She lived on Morris Avenue and 169th, an area infested with gangs. Getting jumped or stabbed or shot was just a regular part of life. "There wasn't one day that was quiet," she says. "We got used to it. We was immune to it." Her oldest brother swung at a teacher and got expelled, and her other brother dropped out of Taft High School, which once boasted graduates like Stanley Kubrick and Luther Vandross, but devolved into such a morass of failure and violence it shuttered for good in 2008. After dropping out, Alexa says her brothers "did what they had to do to survive." She won't say more, she's no snitch. But they had a lot of free time on their hands, so they put a lot of attention and focus on their little sister. "They were overprotective," Alexa explains. "Too overprotective. They were stalking me everywhere. I couldn't even walk to the bodega by myself, which was right next to my apartment." Her mom and brothers had good intentions and high hopes for Alexa. They wanted to protect her, they wanted her to graduate and make it out of the life. But she suffocated under their smothering and rebelled. "I wanted to be a tough girl."

The gangs were mostly segregated by ethnicity. (But that's not why they fought each other. Their beefs usually revolved around territory and making money moves.) The South Bronx was a melting pot of Puerto

Rican, Dominican, African American, Central American, and West and East African immigrant cultures.

Genesis was born in the Dominican Republic, but when she was seven her mother sent her to live with her grandparents in the South Bronx "for better opportunities." Her mom couldn't get in the country right away, so Genesis didn't see her mother for five long years. "After the second year, she really regretted sending me," Genesis says. Her dad actually lived a half a block away in the Bronx with a new wife and kids, but he had no interest in seeing Genesis. He dropped off and picked up his other kids at school, but not Genesis. She had a half-sister around the same age, but the only time they saw or spoke to each other was at school.

The rejection cut deep and Genesis was profoundly lonely. She barely spoke English and unlike in the Dominican Republic, where everyone was friendly, she had trouble making friends in the South Bronx. "I got anxiety when I was around a lot of people," she explains. She started having panic attacks but was unable to get help because her grandmother was "old school" and didn't understand it. She thought Genesis was just trying to get attention. The truth was Genesis desperately missed and needed her mother. "We talked on the phone all the time but we had no physical contact," Genesis says. "I was going through a tough time."

Johanna, who was born in El Salvador, also didn't see her mother for five long years. Her dad died in a car crash when she was five, then, two years later, her mother, a bartender, was forced to flee the country after drunken gang members threatened her life. She moved to the United States, into an apartment with her own mother in the Bronx but couldn't bring Johanna and her little brother right away. It took five years for the kids' paperwork to come through. When they finally came to the United States and moved in with their mom and grandma, it was major culture shock for a twelve-year-old girl and her brother who'd had an idyllic childhood in the rural countryside of El Salvador. "I couldn't stop crying for a month. I just wanted to go back."

Everything was different: Johanna was used to blue skies and sun. In New York, it was gray and freezing. The city was dirty and ugly and crowded, unlike her beautiful, green, open homeland. In New York, Johanna wasn't allowed to play outside. "There were no kids in the street," she recalls. Back in El Salvador, she played baseball outside with a big stick and a taped up wad of paper, using leaves for bases. She used to live in a big house on a hill, "you could see it from everywhere," and have her own room and a patio to play on. Now she lived in a tiny two-room apartment and shared a bed with her mom and brother. Worst of all, she didn't speak a lick of English. A lot of kids in the Bronx spoke Spanish but it was a different dialect and they couldn't understand her. It didn't matter because they didn't want to talk to her anyway. "The kids were mean," she says. "They'd already formed their own cliques."

All of the immigrant communities coexisted but it wasn't like they lived in perfect harmony like a hippie Coca-Cola commercial. The Puerto Ricans and Domincans mingled a little but they had different value systems, according to Alexandra Maruri. Dominican parents tried to shelter their kids from the streets but were usually working so much they weren't around, while Puerto Rican parents tended to give the most freedom to their children. The tight-knit families in the African communities stereotypically kept to themselves the most and avoided assimilating to the American culture and lifestyle. They also were usually very strict with their children, more so than the Puerto Rican and Dominican parents.

When Grateshka's parents immigrated from Puerto Rico and the Dominican Republic, they were dirt poor but had high hopes of living the American dream. "They came here to have a better life," Grateshka explains. Her parents worked long hours, her mom as a home aide and her dad an Uber driver, and bought a nice house in Patterson, New Jersey. But when they couldn't keep up the payments, they moved to 168th Street and Grand Concourse to save money and be closer to family. "My father felt like he failed us and was depressed," she explains. "He felt like the Bronx wasn't good enough to raise kids."

The new neighborhood also depressed Grateshka, normally a very happy, playful little girl. "It was very stressful," she admits. She was terrified of the gangs and gunshots she heard, and felt bad for the kids who dealt drugs right on her corner. "It hurt me a lot because I just wanted to be able to help them." She constantly worried that her teenage brother might not come home one day. "There was one time I was at the park and five minutes after I left some guy got shot in the chest," she remembers.

Because of that, her parents turned very strict, but that didn't bother Grateshka. "I appreciated the parents I had and thanked God for putting those people in my life. They were strict, but they had their purpose. They just wanted positive things in my life."

Just because the parental figure(s) were strict didn't mean their kids were immune to the streets or getting into trouble. Robin was raised by her Jamaican grandmother, Grandma Redell, after her mom died during childbirth. They lived in a two-bedroom apartment on the Grand Concourse and 172nd Street (right by her best friend Alexa), with Robin's uncle and eight more of her relatives. That did not include her father. He was in jail from the time she was born until she was five years old. Then he moved to Puerto Rico or the Dominican Republic (Robin was never quite sure which one) and had twenty-one more children.

Grandma Redell emigrated from Jamaica and grew up in Charleston, South Carolina. She was that "down south" kind of strict. Robin wasn't allowed to stand in front of her building and play with the other kids unless Redell was present. Robin also couldn't go to her friends' houses unless Redell knew their mothers. "Sometimes I had to lie so I could go to my friend's house." If Robin got caught or got out of line, Redell whooped her butt "with anything she could get her hands on," Robin explained. "I always had a smart mouth but I never talked back to my grandma. You couldn't tell her nothin'."

Robin couldn't help having a sassy attitude and a hair-trigger temper. She inherited it from her late mother, as well as her soft skin, love of long showers, and weird habit of licking the salty sweat off her shoulder. Like her mom, Robin was born a fighter, so when she was young, Redell signed her up for boxing lessons to help get out her aggression in a healthy way. The upside is that Robin never felt like she had to join a gang. "I didn't need protection because I knew how to fight." The downside was that

Robin utilized her new skill in the unhealthiest way. She fought anyone and everyone—male, female, old, young. "You know how black people are," Robin would say. "If someone hit you, you hit 'em back. If someone hit me, I hit 'em back."

Redell, who worked at the DMV but quit to take care of Robin, enrolled her granddaughter in a private Catholic elementary school, and the structure helped keep Robin calmer for a time. But four years later, when the money ran out, Robin had to transfer back to public school and it brought out the worst in her. "I witnessed things I never seen before," Robin explained. "It was more rowdy. Kids wasn't nice. They used to pick on me because I was fat and because of my name. Like, 'Where's Batman?' They fought for no reason over stupid stuff."

Robin did, too. If a kid said anything to her or just looked at her in a certain way, she snapped. She got into brawls every single day and her grandma was called down to the school constantly. "I got so much beef with people because of my mouth," Robin said. "My mouth was reckless but I didn't care. I could talk how I want because I could fight."

Robin may have acted tough on the outside but just below the surface was profound sadness and loneliness. She'd never met her mom, had only seen her in pictures, and her father drifted in and out of her life, showing little to no interest in getting to know her. Grandma Redell became her best friend and her uncle acted like a father figure, but she still felt like an orphan. "The reason I have so much anger is I don't have no parents," she'd tell teachers and social workers.

Robin's situation was not an anomaly. So many households in the South Bronx, especially Puerto Rican households, were run by single parents with a limited income and education. And the absence of, or abandonment by, birth fathers was the norm. There was always a lot of talk about young boys being fatherless, but the effect on young girls was destructive, too.

When Alcielis was six years old, she witnessed "a traumatic thing": her father abusing her mother "really badly." That very day, he left and never came back. For the next seven years, her mom raised Alcielis and her brother and sister, and they saw their dad maybe a couple times a year, at most. "Even to this day, me and my family don't talk about it," Alcielis shares. "I don't know if it was something that was always going on or if it was just that one time but I witnessed him abusing her. While it was happening my older brother wasn't paying attention to it and it confused me. Now that I'm older, I assume it was happening a lot and my brother learned to block it out. I didn't notice because I was so young."

Heaven's father had always been in her life but "there's always been ups and downs." Her parents split before she was born and tried to compete against each other to prove who was best for her. Her dad's new girlfriend also stirred up a lot of drama. "I was always torn between the two," Heaven says, and as a result, "as a child, I was very angry and feisty."

Rashell's anger exploded after her parents split up, too. "It was hard transitioning from mommy and daddy's girl to just mommy's girl," she explains. "Things at home were really bad." Her mom was laid off from her job at a hospital, the money ran out, and the bills weren't cheap. Her brother was a "bad boy," totally out of control, running around in the streets. "Everything was going wrong everywhere. It was a wreck."

Already a "bad young lady," as she called herself, Rashell became even more furious and aggressive after her dad left, her mood set off the minute she walked through the front door. "My dad was no longer there, and my mom was depressed and always crying and complaining." Their relationship deteriorated into screaming matches. Sometimes her mom took her anger out on Rashell. "I'm tired of *you*!" she'd scream. But more often, Rashell would come after her mom. "I was horrible because I had more mouth. Very disrespectful." If her mom even tried to talk to Rashell, she'd go off on her.

"Leave me alone! Mind your business! I don't care!"

"Why are you like this?" her mom would ask, exasperated. She didn't have a clue or a solution. But Rashell knew. First, she missed her dad deeply. She thought everything was fine between her parents; then one day they had an argument and he just up and moved back to the Dominican Republic. When he first left, Rashell refused to talk to him on the phone. "Every time I'd talk to him, I'd start crying," she says. "I told him, 'I'll call you when I'm ready to speak to you. Don't call me because you hurt my heart.'"

Rashell also felt more unsafe without him there. She'd already grown up scared living in their dangerous neighborhood, and she'd been in survival mode from a young age. "That's what really got me into it. If you stare at somebody, they're gonna say something to you. You step on the other block, it's 'What you doing here?' Now we have to fight 'cause you're stepping on my block. Everybody thinks the next person is gonna harm them so they are defensive to protect themselves." Suddenly, with her dad gone, she felt even more unprotected and vulnerable. So she got even tougher and meaner than a junkyard dog. "I'm not even gonna lie," Rashell admits, "I was horrible."

For Yoshie, the same scenario, her dad taking off, had the opposite result. Instead of acting out, she retreated inward into her own cocoon of anxiety and depression. Yoshie idolized her dad. When she was really little, she loved watching him work on cars in the driveway of their two-story Springfield, Massachusetts, house. If he needed a tool, she'd happily run and get it for him. Like Rashell, she was a "daddy's girl," too, but more of a tomboy. She liked to hang out with her dad and uncles, and dress in baggy clothes, even though her mom always tried to get her to do girly things and wear more feminine styles. But that felt too awkward and uncomfortable. She just wanted to be like her Papi. "We were really close," Yoshie remembers. "He took me everywhere."

Yoshie describes the first five years of her life as "fun." Sure, her parents fought, but they were a tight little *familia feliz*. That all changed at her little sister's second birthday party. Everyone was partying hard (her family "liked to drink a lot") but the booze ran out. Her mom went on a beer run and when she got to the liquor store, spotted her dad sitting in his car with another woman. What the actual fuck, he was supposed to be at work. When her mom came home, she was enraged and hysterical.

"What's wrong, Mami?" her sister asked. She'd always been Mami's girl.

"Your father is a liar and a cheater!" her mom screamed.

"Mami, it's going to be okay," her sister cried.

When her dad walked in, her mom "spazzed out," Yoshie recalls.

"Why are you doing this?" her mom wailed. "Who is that *puta*!"

"What are you talking about?" her dad yelled back.

She picked up a table and threw it at her husband. Then, in front of their entire family, he tried to punch her—but missed and hit Yoshie's sister. As her parents went after each other, Yoshie ran to a neighbor's house and called the police.

"Papi hit Mami!" she sobbed to a 911 dispatcher. When Yoshie returned to her house, it looked like a tornado had blasted through their living room. Half of her family had stayed to console her mom, the other half ghosted when it got too hot. Her dad was gone, too—and he never came back. That night, he moved in with his mistress and Yoshie's *familia feliz* was *finito*.

Her mom couldn't afford the house on her own. Before Yoshie was born, she'd survived a brain tumor, but still couldn't work and was on disability. A week after the brawl with her husband, she moved with the girls into her sister's three-room apartment in the South Bronx. It was crowded with the three of them, her aunt and uncle and cousins. At her Massachusetts house, Yoshie had her own bedroom. Now, she shared a tiny room with her mom, sister, and aunt and uncle. Yoshie was a painfully shy, modest child, who didn't like being around other people much. Now, she was forced into a set-up that was loud and chaotic, with everybody in each other's business and jawing at each other 24/7. Yoshie retreated even further into her shell.

A year later, her mom saved up enough welfare money to move with the girls into their own apartment on Grand Concourse and 167th. Their living situation was stable but her mom wasn't. Still unhinged about her husband's betrayal, she drowned her sorrows in alcohol. They'd been together for thirteen years and she wasn't over their painful breakup. "She would just drink and drink with people she knew," Yoshie says. "She wasn't paying attention to us." Sometimes, while her mom partied with friends at an apartment a few blocks away, she left Yoshie at the apartment to watch her little sister for hours. Yoshie would wander down and hang out in front of her building. She knew she wasn't supposed to, unless her mom or aunt was around, because it was too dangerous. But her mom was out drinking, and she was hungry and bored. She'd grab a stick and a paper bag and play baseball with the boys in the street. She loved baseball. It kept her mind off of how much she missed her dad.

Like her mom, Yoshie was still devastated about her dad's sudden, jarring absence, and dreamed that her family would get back together one day. Her dad felt guilty, so a couple years later, he invited Yoshie to spend the summer back in Massachusetts. She was so pumped. A whole summer with Papi? She'd get to be "daddy's girl" again. She jumped at the chance. But it wasn't a summer of fun, it was the summer from hell.

Yoshie stayed with her dad but also went to her aunt's house a lot, and often shared a bedroom with her three older male cousins. "They told me not to go to sleep so they could kiss me," she remembers. For the entire summer, when the adults left for work or went out, two of those teenage cousins took Yoshie down to the basement and took turns raping her. "They took over me because I didn't know what to do or what to say," she says. "I didn't know what they were doing, so I just went along with it."

Like too many other young girls (especially girls of color, girls who live with a single parent, and girls who live below the poverty line), Yoshie's first sexual experience was violent, nonconsensual, and the result of a sexual assault by a "trusted" family member or friend. She had no choice but to acquiesce, no chance to say no, no idea what just happened to her. She was only seven years old.

That whole summer, Yoshie felt weird and awful and jittery but didn't exactly know why. She was too young to understand what guilt and shame were, but she knew enough to tell her mom about the basement the second she got back to the Bronx.

"I think I had sex," she said, having absolutely no clue what sex was.

Her mom flipped out. In disbelief, she called everyone in the family and made Yoshie tell the story over and over to different relatives. Yoshie got really upset. She felt really uncomfortable talking about it, plus she was worried she'd get her cousins in trouble. She could have kept this story to herself her whole life, but she came out to her mom and now she was sorry about it.

Finally, one of Yoshie's aunt's came over, calmed Yoshie down, and told her mom, "Just stop." And that was the end of it. Nobody in her family ever talked about it again. She doesn't know if her cousins even got so much as a whooping. She doesn't remember anyone ever telling her dad. Truth is, after that summer, her dad stopped communicating with Yoshie regularly. She called him but it always went straight to voicemail. It made her mad. Even if his phone was broken, he could still call her on his girlfriend's phone.

"Why isn't he responding?" Yoshie asked her mom.

"I don't know," was all she could muster sometimes. Other times she'd scream, "Just forget about it!"

She couldn't forget about her dad. Yoshie craved having a male figure in her life as a role model. In a lot of ways, she just felt more like a boy. She'd never been very girly but after her cousins sexually abused her, she dressed even more masculine. "I didn't want boys looking at me after my cousins. I didn't want nobody to look at me."

Yoshie couldn't understand why her father didn't want to talk to her or see her.

In 2011, when she was nine, her father and his girlfriend had a baby, and Yoshie asked a relative to drive her to the hospital back in Massachusetts so she could meet her new half brother.

"Why haven't you been calling me?" Yoshie pressed.

"Because you didn't call me," her dad said meekly.

"*You're* the father," Yoshie protested. "*You* should be doing more things than I am."

"Tell me about you," he tried.

"What do you want to know?" Yoshie responded. "There's been a lot of things."

Her papi's feigned interest didn't last long. After the birth of his son, Yoshie and her dad grew further and further apart. He used to call her all the time; then it dwindled down to him only calling her on her birthday or other special occasions.

"Okay, this is what we're gonna do now," she thought, resigned to it.

One time he had the cajones to call *her* on Father's Day, but she wasn't playing that game. She wasn't about to wish him "Happy Father's Day." He didn't deserve it.

"You don't love me any more?" her dad asked.

"Nah, I don't love you no more," she said coldly.

Yoshie wasn't about to chase him anymore. She didn't see her father for another eight years.

Chapter Four

AS SICK AS YOUR SECRETS

Kimberly had no idea who her birth father was. Nobody ever told her. Not her mom, not her stepdad, who'd raised her since she was a month old, not her younger half sister, Claudia. Claudia didn't know and didn't care. They were only a year and a half apart, but it might as well have been fifty. Even though they shared the living room as their bedroom, they weren't that close. Well, sometimes they were. It went back and forth.

Kimberly and Claudia and their parents lived in a one-bedroom apartment on Grand Concourse and 177th, a less dangerous area than most in the South Bronx and a small oasis away from the gangs. Kimberly could walk to the bodega without fearing for her life, and she wasn't surrounded by bad influences. "I didn't see the point of getting in trouble or being disrespectful," she says. She was an excellent student, who excelled in math and science. In first grade, her mom got her the whole Junie B. Jones book collection and she devoured it. "I liked to do homework. I know, I'm weird."

Kimberly liked sports, too, and played softball using plastic balls and bats with her uncles in the street or at the park. Her mom had a huge extended family who got together all the time, renting out banquet halls in the neighborhood for holidays, baby showers, birthdays, graduations, any occasion at all really. When she wasn't eating her favorite foods, rice and beans and Yaroa (Dominican lasagna), you could find Kimberly standing near the dance floor singing Dominican music at the top of her lungs—she was extremely proud to be Dominican—and watching everyone dance to bachata, her long, kinky locks swaying and bouncing in rhythm. Kimberly was too shy to dance herself; she didn't want anyone to watch her. She was an early bloomer and looked almost womanly by the age of nine. Her body had already started to change—her boobs were starting to develop and her butt had shape. She could feel eyes on her sometimes, and she didn't like it.

But Kimberly lived for these parties. She loved kicking it with her aunts and uncles and cousins because, in her own home, Kimberly always felt like an outsider and the black sheep. It was the three of them against her. At least that's how she saw it. "I was really to myself," Kimberly says. "I couldn't talk to my mom about stuff."

This wasn't surprising, since her mom held the key to a huge secret—the identity of Kimberly's birth father—but never revealed it. Kimberly had to figure it out herself. After she got an iPod for Christmas one year, she asked her mom to take her to get a case. First they went to a Western Union to send some money to relatives in DR. Then they stopped by an electronics store on Grand Concourse. When they walked in, Kimberly remembers inhaling that intoxicating smell of new stuff. Her mom asked if Manuel was working that day. He was, and when he walked out of the back office and locked eyes with Kimberly, her stomach dropped. She just knew.

Kimberly picked out a pink case and was a little shocked and a lot suspicious when Manuel didn't make them pay for it.

When Kimberly and her mom left the store, they were both quiet.

"Mami, who's that? Is that my real dad?"

"Yes," her mom said.

Kimberly smashed the pink case on the ground and cried. Her mom wasn't even going to tell her. Even worse, her mom didn't really comfort her or explain much more. At that moment, Kimberly felt like she'd never been loved in her life.

Kimberly and her mom just didn't have the kind of relationship where they'd break down sobbing in each other's arms and talk for hours. It was devastating but not entirely her mom's fault. Kimberly takes some of the blame for their history of bad communication and lack of connection. When she was in elementary school, her mother was diagnosed with lupus, a serious autoimmune disease, and it scared Kimberly so much, she couldn't deal. "My mom couldn't walk. She was in bed all the time. I was so afraid I was going to lose her that I distanced myself," she admits. "Because I was avoiding my mom, she thought I didn't love her." In the meantime, Claudia stepped in and was daughter-of-the-year, cleaning the house and making her mom coffee. Kimberly's grandpa once told her, "If you don't know how to make coffee, your husband will leave you," and it stuck with her. That's exactly what she thought her mom was doing. Leaving her.

Kimberly wanted that mother-daughter connection so badly, but it just didn't flow naturally. As she got older, it only got worse. Kimberly got even more detached and unaffectionate, not only with her mom but everyone. "By eleven years old no one was allowed to touch me," she explains. "I would pull away because it made me uncomfortable. Simple-ass friendly hugs made me cringe."

Part of that was due to her relationship with her mom—there was too much unsaid between them—but Kimberly had another secret she'd been keeping since she was eight years old. She knew it would tear apart their family forever, so she buried it, and kept her mouth shut.

Chapter Five

LOVE & LOSS

Chris idolized his sister Michelle. Though she was six years older than he and they had different mothers, in the beginning, she was always around and the two had a special bond. Before their younger siblings came along, Michelle, a happy-go-lucky kind of girl, always bragged about Chris. She'd say, "That's my only brother!" to anyone who'd listen and anyone who didn't. She had a commanding presence and a big personality. Chris's sister was full of life and sometimes full of shit. Michelle loved to tell Chris stories that were too good to be true because she got a kick out of seeing his reaction. Like after watching the movie *Back to the Future Part II* she told him that the hover boards in the movie were real. Of course, as a gullible kid, Chris believed her.

Michelle never lived at the Astacio's; she lived with her mother a few blocks away by Heath Avenue. As a kid, she seemed so far away to Chris, when in reality, she was right around the corner. It wasn't the best setup:

her stepfather was a known drug user and dealer, and the neighborhood was a cesspool of gang violence. When she was a teenager, Michelle came over to the Astacio house every weekend, but Chris remembers being scared to go pick her up with his dad. Her apartment building was terrifying. Chris's grandmother lived in the projects and this wasn't much better. It just seemed so menacing. Prison-like hallways that reeked of urine. Elevators covered in graffiti. Too many hidden, dimly lit corners. Michelle wanted to be away from all that. Chris didn't want to be around it either.

"Can I stay in the car?" Chris would ask June.

On family game nights every Friday, Chris and Michelle played Monopoly and The Game of Life late into the night, and it was war. Chris threw the game in the air if he was losing, scattering the pieces all over the room. They had some drag-out fights, like the time on his birthday when she smushed Chris's face into his chocolate cake. But most of the time, it was all in good fun and they were really cool with each other. She was always there for him and always gave him good advice, like begging him not to do drugs. She was also so proud of him, even when his confidence was so low he felt like there was nothing for anyone to be proud of. She showed up when Chris graduated elementary school and also the fancy Riverdale junior high, and cried at both. "What the hell is she crying for?" Chris wondered.

By the time Chris was a teenager himself, he and Michelle had drifted apart. They talked, but not as frequently. Michelle enrolled at Lehman College in the Bronx and stopped coming over to their home as much. Plus, both were in rebellious stages at the same time. Chris was in fake gangsta mode after being attacked, while Michelle was becoming more carefree and wild. She told Chris she broke into the Van Cortlandt Park public pool and went skinny-dipping. ("Didn't need to know that," he thought.) She'd always been smart and outgoing, now she was channeling that energy into some positive things, like political activism at school, but also negative, risky behavior, like dating shady guys. June thought Michelle was spinning out of control, so whenever they got together, it ended in a screaming match.

June felt in his gut big trouble was coming and he was right. During a protest on campus about high tuition, Michelle barricaded herself in a classroom and threw chairs at some professors and administrators. She was expelled and the incident landed on the front page of a local newspaper. She came to the Astacio house, all proud of herself.

"Look, I'm in the paper!" Michelle beamed.

June smacked her across the face.

"You're proud of that?"

That was the turning point. Without college as her anchor, without purpose or direction, Michelle's life spiraled downward fast. She'd never had the best taste in men, but after she got kicked out of school, she hooked up with a really bad dude, who was abusive and extremely controlling. He isolated her from the Astacios and she went MIA.

Chris barely noticed—he had his own shit to deal with. Anxiety ruled his life. He knew he didn't want to end up like the kids in the streets, but what could he do when he was paralyzed like this? When Chris dreamed of "getting out," it wasn't to be a doctor or lawyer or an MLB player. He dreamed of being "normal."

After graduating high school by the skin of his teeth (including the blackened dead one), Chris was accepted to Lehman College, following in Michelle's footsteps. He'd finally made it out, the first male Astacio to go to college, but nothing changed. He still couldn't function. He was overwhelmed in the big lecture halls—it felt like everybody was staring and laughing at him. In his warped mind, the professor talked in slow motion and the walls were closing in on him. He once ran into the restroom and cried in front of the mirror, "What is wrong with me?" Out of class, he walked around campus in a daze. He couldn't breathe. He couldn't eat and was sick to his stomach all the time. To feel better, he exercised obsessively, passing out once after lifting weights that were too heavy. It didn't help. His anger was so severe, he yelled at his mom and punched walls just to feel something, anything, even pain. His hands were all bloody and scarred up but he felt nothing. He was numb.

Chris was suffering but he didn't know why.

One night out with friends, he could sense something bad was about to happen. His heart and mind had been racing for two hours straight and he knew he needed to release the anger that was suffocating him. Around midnight, one of his buddies said something that pissed him off and Chris blacked out in a blind rage. He screamed that he was going to kill his friend then jumped him. It took three people to pull Chris off the guy. Chris fell to the ground, gasping for air. He watched his friends hover over him but couldn't hear anything they said. All he could see was their mouths moving in slow motion. Then he passed out.

Chris had a massive panic attack. When he came to, his friend told him he'd never been so scared for Chris in his life. Everybody was looking at him like he was crazy. Chris didn't want to feel crazy angry anymore. He looked at his hands and saw those horrible scars. His anxiety had turned into violence and that was not who he wanted to be. Chris was nineteen years old when he came to the realization that he could no longer hide from the world.

The next morning, he went to his mother and cried. He told her that he hated himself and needed help. He told her that he had been suffering for years. "Fuck, I can't deal no more!" he sobbed, his head in his hands. Cecilia took Chris in her arms and held him, as if he was a baby. "Everything is going to be okay," she said, rocking him gently.

Even though June was old school and didn't believe in headshrinkers, he took Chris to a psychiatrist. It took every fiber of his being to admit to the doctor, "My son can't function in the real world."

The psychiatrist said he wanted to commit Chris for six months.

"Hell no, I ain't committing him!" June barked. "Thanks but no thanks."

In the car ride home, June stared straight ahead. "You're gonna do this on your own," he said quietly. "A good therapist can help you."

Chris dropped out of college and started seeing another doctor as an outpatient. The doctor prescribed Paxil to treat his anxiety. Unable to work, Chris usually slept until 1 P.M. and admits, "I thought I was a stupid and lazy bum." He tried working with kids at an after-school program but could only manage his anxiety for three hours at a time. Those three hours had a huge impact on him though. Working with young minorities opened his eyes to all the pain he'd been harboring within himself. He refused to allow them to be held back by teachers like Vincent Cuomo or anyone else based on the color of their skin or the neighborhood they grew up in. He wanted them to become the bright young minds he knew they could be. He was passionate and dedicated to guiding them to break stereotypes and prove everyone wrong by being great.

When he wasn't at the after-school program, Chris spent the rest of the day zoned out watching TV, playing video games, and surfing the World Wide Web (as it was called in the early days). After the movie *You've Got Mail* came out, online dating exploded and Chris checked it out, tooling around in AOL's popular chat rooms.

Anxiety had stunted his love life, too, and unconditional love had evaded him. He'd dated one woman with a young daughter, who he'd come to think of as his own. But his girlfriend cheated on him, and when they split up, he was devastated. Not because of his ex, but because he missed the daughter like crazy. He'd been burned badly and wasn't about to get hurt again.

In April 2001, he got a message on Love@AOL from Charisse Cruz asking him the usual a/s/l (age, sex, location). From her profile, he could tell she was beautiful and sexy and smart, and she also went to Lehman, but he scrolled by her message. Charisse was not the kind of girl who would be ignored, so she wrote him again and made it clear that she had tried him once before and this would be the last time she was going to try.

"You're a hard man to get a hold of," she wrote. "I'm about to give up on you."

Chris laughed at the message and answered. They instant messaged about their lives, and Charisse thought Chris was "cute and interesting and sweet," the exact opposite of the rough guys she'd been seeing, including a couple drug dealers. They had a lot in common besides college: they lived on the same block at one point and both hung out at Fieldston Billiards. "We crossed paths but never saw each other," she says. Charisse could also tell he was going to be family-oriented. "He was really torn up from being separated from his ex's daughter, even though she wasn't his biologically. I just knew then he was going to be a good father."

On their first date, Chris took Charisse to see the movie *Along Came a Spider* because she was obsessed with James Patterson novels, and they held hands during the scary parts. Their chemistry was off the hook but Chris was nervous to open up about his flaws and weaknesses. He didn't work, he lived at home with his parents, and he had crippling anxiety. Not exactly dreamy. Charisse, on the other hand, had it going on. She'd grown up in the Bronx in a rough neighborhood infested with Crips and Bloods, but her parents had put her in private Catholic school to shelter her from the bad stuff as much as possible. Though she still had a rebellious phase and hung out late with the "wrong crowd," she managed to make something of herself. She was putting herself through school and had made new upstanding friends with goals and real careers.

A week after they started dating, Chris took the plunge and told her the truth. "I was like, 'fuck it.' She was dating assholes and I was the first nice guy who wasn't an asshole. I told her I had anxiety issues but understood if she didn't want to keep dating me." Charisse saw potential in Chris, but she also insisted he confront his anxiety head-on. "She shook that all up. She said, 'I'm willing to work with you and help you get over it.'"

With Charisse by his side and the Paxil finally kicking in, the heavens opened up. Chris had been in a mental prison for fifteen years, but now, finally, it was like he was given the key to open his cell. He was *free*. He'd never known the meaning of "normal." He'd gone through life believing he was different and that normal was this elusive concept that was unattainable. But with Charisse, he began to enjoy the world. He found himself within her and that's where his normal was, even if he was still "crazy." For the first time in his life, he was okay being different. Accepting himself was his first step to being "normal." Chris had dated and been "in like," with other girls, but Charisse truly opened his eyes to what real true love looked like.

The first four months of Chris and Charisse's relationship were hot and cold. They kept a couple's diary that they traded back and forth. Chris would leave it with her, she'd write something romantic to him, and then he'd get it back and write something romantic to her. That was the good stuff. On her dating profile, Charisse said she only smoked "occasionally," which wasn't true. Chris had told her the story about June and his baby sister Christina but he kept finding packs of cigarettes in her purse. He told her if she didn't stop smoking, they were done. So she quit. Charisse had major issues with him, too. Chris was still not really working, making child's pay at the after-school program, and it worried her about their future. She dumped him, a few times actually.

Then, on September 11, 2001, the World Trade Center came crashing down. Chris saw it on TV and, like the rest of the world, freaked out. "Yo! Holy shit! What is going on?" he yelled, worried sick about Charisse. She worked in downtown Manhattan and walked for hours all the way home to the Bronx covered in toxic dust. The tragedy brought the couple back together, and a month later, she got pregnant. She wanted to get an abortion, but Chris wasn't having it. "I believe in a woman's choice but I also believe I have a choice, too. That's my child, too. We at least needed to have a conversation about it. I would have been supportive if she did it but I wouldn't have stayed with her." They decided to keep the baby.

The Astacios were thrilled about the baby news. June grabbed Charisse in a bear hug and Cecilia shouted with glee, "Well, it's about time!" The announcement did not spark as much joy at Charisse's house. Her father was infuriated, he hated the idea that she'd gotten knocked up by a bum like Chris. The Astacios invited the Cruzes over for a meet and greet, and it was tense. As they argued back and forth, Chris and Charisse sat in silence, letting their mommies and daddies dictate their future. "This is not appropriate," Mr. Cruz fumed. "A real man would step up and marry my daughter." Both families ultimately agreed it was against God that they live together as an unmarried couple having a baby.

So, they got hitched. Dead broke, Chris had Charisse move in with him at his folks' house, then two months before she gave birth to their son, Justin, on her birthday, they got married at City Hall. No wedding, no party, no nothing.

Something clicked in Chris's head after the birth of his firstborn that propelled him to action. He was no longer living just for himself—he had to get a real job, pronto. He didn't want to, and he wasn't sure he could handle it, but he didn't have the luxury of avoiding it anymore. "I'm having a kid," he thought. "I have to give up whatever fears I have. I want to be a man."

He worked anywhere and everywhere that would pay him. He got a dreadfully boring job shelving books at the New York Public Library. He was a doorman at a fancy Bed Bath & Beyond in Manhattan. Tips from B-list stars like Rick Moranis and one of the Baldwin brothers (who knows which one, they all look alike) were good but the hours not so much. Plus, that signature smell they pumped through the air ducts made him queasy. So, he sold shoes at Macy's, like Al Bundy, and clothes at Syms, like his old man. Finally, he became a cashier at Stop & Shop. All of these jobs paid the minimum wage of $7 an hour. None of these jobs made him happy.

After Justin was born, Chris's sister Michelle reappeared from her secret life to meet her nephew. She was married now to the control freak guy and had her own kids, but something was off about her. She wasn't herself, seemed out of sorts and frazzled. Was it drugs? Chris couldn't tell. Still, he was her baby bro and, as his big sister, Michelle still doled out advice, even though it was obvious she wasn't practicing what she was preaching. She was disappointed in him and judgmental about his marriage. "You got forced into it," she insisted. She also didn't like all of the odd jobs. "You're better than this," she scolded. "You've got so much potential. What's wrong with you? Be a better role model for your son. Go back to school."

Chris laughed at the idea and said he was already a dropout. Plus, he couldn't handle it. She shook her head. "That was a long time ago," she said. "You've changed. Stop making excuses."

Michelle encouraged Chris to work with kids. "You have a gift," she said. "You connect with children, you understand the world they live in. You should be a teacher. You could do it."

He had just gotten control of his anxiety and he was scared. "Maybe I *can't* do it."

"You have a brilliant mind. To not use it would be blasphemy."

"What if I fail?"

"Then you have the opportunity to fail. I don't even have that opportunity any more. I can't go to college anymore. You can. Be the person I know you can be."

Less than a year after Chris became a dad, Michelle had a stroke and died on Mother's Day. At the time of her death, she was alone at a shelter, without her children. She was only thirty-one years old. Chris didn't know why she was at the shelter and was too distraught and angry with her husband to ask. But he remembered that Michelle had called him a few weeks before and gotten really sappy.

"You know I love you very much," she said.

"What the hell is wrong with you?" Chris joked. "I'll see you next week."

At Michelle's funeral, Chris witnessed an overwhelming amount of young teens from her church and her neighborhood profess how much she had helped them. Chris didn't even know she was helping anyone. He'd been too wrapped up in his own world to notice.

When Michelle and Chris first talked about him becoming a teacher, he'd brushed it off. After she died, Chris vowed to make it a reality. At the funeral, he walked up to her casket and held her cold, lifeless hand.

"Don't worry," he whispered. "I will see you again. And I will be the person you wanted me to be."

Chapter Six

THE ANGEL KID

When the screaming started again, and it always did, Angie knew the drill. She ran into her room, shut the door behind her, curled up on her bed, put her headphones on, and blasted Chris Brown. No matter how loud she turned up the volume, she could still hear her mom and dad cursing at each other, smacking each other around. Their fights happened so frequently it was almost white noise, except it wasn't relaxing like a running brook or gentle rain. It vibrated their apartment like a chain saw. As it escalated, and it always did, Angie got a sick feeling in the pit of her stomach and cried. She prayed for it to be over but knew all the praying in the world wouldn't make it the last time.

Her parents' fights happened every single day and could go all night long. They usually started when her mom got home from work and her dad, who worked in construction and was more often than not unemployed, hadn't done the household chores, made anything to eat, or put Angie, her brother, Isaiah, or her little sister, Nece, to bed.

Angie's mom was a damn hard worker. She always had a job—whether working at the pharmacy, the Bronx Zoo, or an old folks home. She was gone from morning until night, making sure their kids had food on the table and a roof over their heads. So when she walked into their apartment after a long day, and the place was a mess and her un-bathed children whined, "Mommy we're hungry!" well, that was a problem. That's when they'd start throwing jabs at each other.

"Why is the house still dirty?" Angie's dad would taunt, and her mom, exhausted, would flip out.

"I'm the one who worked all day!"

They didn't need a bell to ring or an announcer to proclaim, "Let's get ready to rumble!" It was on, and it was ugly. There were times when little Angie, all five feet of her, had to physically step in and try to stop her dad from killing her mother. "Don't touch my mom!" she'd shout. Angie tried her best to "keep it sane," because her brother got too hyped up to be helpful and her sister sobbed until she had asthma attacks.

Her parents' fights broke Angie's heart, because she loved them both so much. Some kids with volatile parents deal with the stress by acting out themselves. That was Angie's siblings: her brother turned "hard" and her little sister got "reckless." But she was the exact opposite. Angie was the golden child, or "the angel kid" as her mom called her, and probably subconsciously believed if she was a good girl, the peacekeeper, the one who made everyone smile, her parents might call a ceasefire in their never-ending war.

They didn't.

The fights went on endlessly, day after day, all day long and through the night. Sometimes her dad would call her mom at work, just to keep arguing. Angie's mom threatened to throw her husband out countless times, and literally tried to push him out the door more than once, but she never went through with leaving him for good. Angie believes her mom was desperate to have a nuclear family, the kind you see on a Christmas card, because she never had that herself growing up. "I wanted it to be better for you," she'd tell Angie. "I wanted you to have a dad."

Angie was puzzled when her mom said that—their family was far from picture-perfect—but also because the official story of her early childhood never made sense to her. Angie's mom had her young, at age seventeen. She has no memories of her father before the age of three (who does?), but distinctly remembers that she and Isaiah lived with her grandmother, who made the best Spanish food on the block. When her mom got pregnant with her little sister Nece, she moved with Angie and Isaiah into a shelter in the Bronx. After the shelter, her mom and her dad finally moved them all into a three-bedroom apartment on Grand Concourse and Weeks Avenue. She never really got a good explanation about where her dad was the first few years of her life, but she didn't dwell on it or overthink it. "I accepted everything for what it was."

Between them, her parents had eight children. Angie, Isaiah, and Nece lived with them on Grand Concourse. Her dad had five more children, Alex, Amber, Joey, and twins Justice and Justine, who lived with their moms but came over for sleepovers a lot. Angie's apartment was always "real rowdy," and her room was her solace away from the noise. She'd read a book or tool around on her iPad. "I was in my own zone and not really in the mix," mostly to stay out of her family's drama. "I wish I could say we were that family where everyone all got along but it wasn't like that," Angie explains. "My family isn't really all the way connected. There were some problems in between family members that were just so beyond."

Angie got along best with her oldest brother, Alex, whom she idolized. "We really connected a lot, I was so attached to him. He was my go-to person. He always made sure I was on track with everything and he always knew when something was wrong. He read through my silence."

Angie craved alone time, but that wasn't the only way she was different from the rest of her family. She didn't exactly look like anyone else, and she didn't have the family's signature features, like their prominent noses and lips. Isaiah teased her about it. "Do you find it weird that you look like yourself?" he'd say cryptically. "Like, you're unique. You don't look like us. You look like you."

Angie hadn't really noticed it, she thought she kinda looked like her dad. But she *was* aware that her personality was different. Her family was high-strung, but Angie was the laid-back, responsible one, the one who might shake her head and say, "C'mon man, that ain't right," she says. "I never caused any trouble, that wasn't my intention growing up. Yeah, I definitely knew what was right from wrong."

A bright child who loved going to school, Angie says she was always "in my books" and got straight As. "Even when I slacked off, I was picking myself up. Mommy and Daddy didn't have to tell me like, you know, 'get it together.' But I had to be perfect. If I didn't write neat and correctly my dad would rip it up and say do it over. If my math homework wasn't right, I'd sit at the table for hours and do it. I had to do this not only to satisfy me but everybody else."

She was good at English and math but loved PE the most because she was a natural athlete. "I was into everything sports," she remembers. Angie was a joiner and she had no fear. She joined the boys' baseball team but quit when the coach refused to play a girl. She was in the band and tried out the trumpet and guitar before settling on the drums. "I was the only female who played snare. All the other girls played the cymbals. I was really small, carrying around that big drum."

Angie was a tomboy, and she knew from an early age that she was gay. Everybody pretty much knew, it was kind of obvious, but she didn't get bullied. It's easy to see why. Angie could win over a lamppost with her infectious personality and sense of humor. She could be introverted, locking herself in her room for hours to sing Michael Jackson songs and dance in front of the mirror but also easily be the life of the party when she wanted to be. She also had a strategy when going into new situations that helped her in the 'hood. She introduced herself to people right away, so they'd like her and be less likely to jump her. It worked because Angie never got into a fistfight in her life, not an easy accomplishment in the South Bronx.

Growing up, Angie had two dreams, and one had to be pragmatic. Plan A was to be a psychologist, because her friends always came to her when they had problems. "That was my role. I guess it's because I've been through enough things but still always have a smile on my face," Angie explains. "I'm understanding and I don't judge, even if it's a bad decision. You can come to me with anything and I just give motivational advice. If you're having a bad day, I'll be there all giddy and I'm gonna put a smile on your face. I'm like the light." Her other dream was to be a singer/rapper.

Angie was so respected and liked, nobody messed with her about her sexuality. Angie's mom found out she was gay in sixth grade, during her first year at Jordan L. Mott JHS, after she scrolled through her daughter's phone and stumbled on pictures of her cuddling with her boo. When her mom confronted her, Angie at first denied it, but then came clean. "Listen, Ma, I'm gay," she said bravely.

After a long pause, her mom finally said, "So you like this girl?"

Coming out brought Angie and her mom closer: "My mom is my best friend and my role model. I can tell her everything and she's there to listen." Also, one of her older half-sisters was gay, so it wasn't a huge deal in her house. The only issue Angie and her mom ever had about the whole LGBTQ thing was Angie's style. Her mom, worried what other people would think, didn't like seeing her daughter in do-rags and saggy pants. She preferred her in nice dresses. Once on Halloween, the whole family dressed up and Angie's mom forced her to wear a Little Red Riding Hood costume with a skirt. "Can't I just wear black pants or something?" Angie begged. Nope.

Worst of all, Angie wasn't allowed to get a Shape Up, a trendy haircut for boys at the time. "You're still a girl," her mom would say. "I don't want people to talk about you and then you feel bad about yourself." If there was one thing Angie didn't lack, it was confidence. So she was frustrated when she couldn't wear what she wanted or get swag shaved hair designs on the side of her head. It caused a bunch of arguments and more tears. "That's how I want to be presenting!" Angie would protest. She couldn't understand why she couldn't just look the way she wanted. It made her feel like a clown to wear really girly clothes.

Bottom line, though, her mom accepted and loved her. Angie actually got in more trouble for making a secret Instagram account behind her mom's back than being gay. Her mother was super-strict and had eyes on her kids at all times. She always told them, "If I catch you doing something you're not supposed to, it's going to be a problem." She also had a secret Spidey sense when her children were not where they were supposed to be. Once, Angie's brother announced he was going to the library. After he left, her mom told Angie, "Let's go to the library." When they rolled up, sure enough, the library wasn't even open and her brother was in the park with his friends. Busted.

That's another reason Angie kept on the straight and narrow, and never really got mixed up in gangs, drinking, or drugs. Her mom put the fear of God in her. The one time her mom let her guard down and got lenient, tragedy struck their family.

One night, when Angie was in sixth grade, the brother she adored, Alex, went to a party in Queens, despite his father's objections. He told him his birth mother, who lived in Florida, was supposed to be there and she really wanted to see her son. Angie's dad was against it, but her mom said, "Stop being so hard on him. Let him go."

According to Angie, during the party, a gang busted in and started a huge brawl. They killed an eighteen-year-old kid right in front of Angie's brother, beating him to death with a metal pipe. Alex, sixteen at the time, grabbed the pipe, trying to break up the fight. When the cops came, Alex tried to run but was arrested. His handprints were on the pipe and he was charged with the murder.

Multiple news reports tell a different version of events. According to the District Attorney of Queen's County, at the party, Alex hurled an antigay slur at the boy, who was straight, then six teens, including Alex, chased him down the street, stomped on him, and beat him to death with a metal pipe, a cane, and lattice fencing.

Alex eventually admitted punching the victim but insisted he did not kill him. His lawyer convinced him to "take the years," a plea bargain of eighteen years behind bars in exchange for dropping the hate crime charge.

"He was a great kid," Angie says. "He had his stuff together. It was never fair." Angie's dad told the *New York Daily News* that Alex was an A student who was "in the wrong place at the wrong time."

Alex's arrest tore Angie up and, at first, she visited him every weekend on Riker's Island. She'd put on clothes with no rips, take her hair down, and take off all her jewelry—because those were the rules at Riker's—then take the Q101 from Queens to the Visitor Control Building. It took nearly all day going through three big security checkpoints, getting searched invasively, as if she was a criminal, just to be able to see her brother behind glass for one measly hour. When he got moved to a maximum-security prison upstate, she stopped visiting him.

Between her brother's incarceration, her coming out, and her parents' endless fighting keeping her up all night, Angie struggled in sixth grade. She tried to smile through it all, but "I'm not going to lie, it affected me," Angie says. "I had times where I broke down in school, but I didn't open up to anybody. They always told me like if you need anything let me know. But I always been an insider, bottled everything up, had a tough exterior."

"Everybody would tell me, 'Oh, we're here for you, don't worry. I got you,'" she adds. "And I was just all, 'I'm here for myself.' I didn't feel like I had anyone to go to."

Chapter Seven

GUT PUNCH

In June of 2009, six years after his sister died, Chris graduated cum laude from York College with a bachelor's degree in physical education and a 3.54 grade point average.

He'd worked so damn hard at school, at his job, and at home helping take care of his son—often skipping meals, sleeping in class, and bringing Justin to class as a toddler—he'd made himself sick trying to balance it all. One time, he even fainted in the middle of the street in Queens. That morning, he threw up violently but mustered enough energy to drive the hour to class. When he arrived at the college, he felt too sick to go in, and decided to drive back home. He didn't make it. A few miles from the school, he felt a surge of heat, forcing him to park his car at a hydrant. He stepped out of the car and collapsed. A random stranger found Chris passed out in a puddle of his own vomit, his lips cold and blue.

Chris spent a lot of time in the ER during that time, because Justin was also severely asthmatic. He'd sit in the hospital overnight with his son knowing he had to be at work in a few hours and hadn't finished his schoolwork.

Somehow, with grit and perseverance, he made it through school. On graduation day, Chris felt really sick again but nothing was going to stop him from walking down that aisle. Burning with fever, he received his diploma and felt like he could finally ease his foot off the pedal. He'd been going, going, going; now everything was finally going to fall into place. He'd done it! Next up, a master's degree in education, so he could fulfill Michelle's dying wish and become a teacher. He applied for a job with New York's Department of Education, but they were in the midst of a hiring freeze for full-time teachers. In the meantime, he accepted a position as an assistant teacher, making $20,000 per year plus benefits, at PS 86, an elementary school in Kingsbridge Heights in the Bronx. It was the school his mother worked at as the school secretary. Was it nepotism? Maybe. His mom may have gotten him the job, but he would make sure he'd keep it. As soon as he was hired, Chris quit his job at Stop & Shop. Now he just had to wait patiently for the freeze to lift.

In October, Chris and Charisse welcomed a bouncing baby girl, Cristina, named after his late baby sister, and it felt like this could be the best year of Chris's life. "He always wanted a girl," Charisse says. He was reaching his professional goals and had a beautiful wife and two children. He wasn't making a ton of money, it felt like "chump change," but he could provide for his family. He wasn't a bum anymore. He was on his way.

The only problem was that he couldn't kick this damn sickness. He'd been nauseous for months. He'd feel better for a few weeks, then get sick again. And again. Charisse thought being around kids all the time could be the reason. He went to see his primary doctor, who referred Chris to a gastro-intestinal specialist. "It's probably just acid reflux," the doctor said, unfazed.

In December, Chris underwent a routine endoscopic procedure. A tube was lowered down into his stomach through his mouth, and a camera took pictures of his intestines. Directly after his procedure, Chris was told he had a bleeding ulcer in his stomach, which concerned him a little, but at least he finally knew what was going on. "I got this," he thought. He went home feeling optimistic.

Later that week, on Christmas break, Chris took care of the kids while Charisse worked. Cristina was only a few months old and fidgety, so Chris carried her around a lot. The landline rang and Chris answered, Cristina cradled in one arm, the phone in the other. It was the gastro doctor.

"Mr. Astacio, are you sitting down?" he said, in the most depressing tone ever.

Chris squeezed his daughter tight.

"I would rather stand," he said.

"Upon more investigation of the ulcer, we found bad cells."

A pause to digest.

"What do you mean by 'bad cells'?"

"I'm sorry to tell you this over the phone, but you have stomach cancer."

Chris looked at his daughter, who had yet to speak, and pictured her life without him. He saw her walking down the aisle wishing her father was there. He saw her blowing out the candles of her sweet sixteen birthday cake wishing her father was there.

Chris had just been given his death sentence and it wasn't fair. To him. His wife. His children. He felt hatred toward God again. Why did He make him go through six years of stress only to take it away? He felt betrayed, confused, overwhelmed, and scared for his family. He desperately didn't want his children to grow up without a father.

"Hello . . . hello?" The doctor didn't know if Chris was still on the phone.

Chris was in shock and couldn't speak. He placed Cristina down on the couch.

"Mr. Astacio, to repeat, we found cancerous cells surrounding the area in question. The extent to which this cancer has spread is unknown so we need to do more testing immediately, do you understand?"

He didn't understand. Why was this happening to him? His son was still so young. He needed him. He needed to be taught how to be a man that respects women and his daughter needed a father that cared.

Chris hung up and immediately called Charisse.

"I don't feel well, can you come home?"

Charisse was annoyed. "You're sick, *again*? Can't you just wait until the end of the day?"

"I have stomach cancer."

It sounded like Charisse dropped the phone.

"Say that again," she said quietly, as if he might say something different. He could tell she was trying to act calm but he knew her too well. Her voice was full of fear.

"I have stomach cancer."

For the next few weeks, Chris's health dramatically deteriorated. He was referred to an oncologist who specialized in stomach cancer. After several exhausting tests involving PET scans and drinking nasty solutions, he waited for what seemed like an eternity in a waiting room. Finally, a doctor came in and told him nonchalantly, "Well, you definitely have stomach cancer. But don't worry, we can prolong your life for a few more years."

"What does that mean?" Chris cried.

He was assured he could live anywhere between three to five years, but that technological and medical advancements were made everyday and he could possibly live "a bit longer."

Chris had waited five hours in pain, feeling sicker than sick, for this unsympathetic, uncaring jerk-off to tell him what he already knew. He was going to fucking die. Chris left the hospital feeling hopeless and ready to give up.

After telling Charisse what had happened, she was enraged. How could any doctor talk to a cancer patient in that manner? She immediately contacted Memorial Sloan Kettering Cancer Center, the best in the city, to inquire if they could accept his case. They did and Chris met with Dr. Strong, whose name alone made him feel more confident. She told Chris her team would do everything in their power to make sure they'd eradicate his cancer. She told him not to give up hope.

On April 20, 2010, just a few weeks shy of the seventh anniversary of his sister's death, Chris underwent laparoscopic stomach surgery to remove the cancerous mass. He was thirty-one, the exact same age Michelle was when she tragically passed away. It was a scary coincidence, and Chris was terrified that maybe it was his time to die, as well.

He also worried about the length of the surgery. He'd be under for six hours, and, as with any surgery, there was a small percentage that things could go sideways. Most concerning, he could develop an infection that would kill him. The plan was to remove one third of his stomach, a portion of his small intestines, and a portion of his esophagus. In order to accomplish this, his esophagus and small intestines had to be severed and reattached in different places in the hopes that they remained adhered to each other. His stomach had to be inflated to the size of a basketball so that all of his internal organs could be suspended "in air" to make the surgery easier. The surgery was done using a joystick that controlled a machine with six mechanical arms, which were inserted into his stomach.

The surgery was scheduled for very early in the morning. Chris's wife and parents accompanied him to Sloan Kettering. As he lay in the hospital bed waiting for the anesthesiologist, Charisse stood by his side, assuring him that everything was going to be okay. Little did he know, she was holding on by a thread. As soon as they took Chris away, she broke down in tears. She was afraid he'd never wake up.

"I was petrified because Cristina was just born," Charisse remembers. "I kept thinking he wasn't going to be here to enjoy his time with her. He didn't deserve that. I just kept praying and saying, 'He can't leave me now.'"

A nurse wheeled the bed halfway down a gigantic, freezing hallway. Dr. Strong met Chris halfway and asked if he wanted to walk the rest of the way to the operating room. Though feeling very weak from all the surgery prep, he got up.

"You're in very good hands," she said, as they walked as if strolling in a park on a beautiful summer day. In the operating room, Chris met the team who would try to save his life and lay down on the operating table. Soon anesthesia flowed through his veins and the last thing he remembered was someone saying, "Happy dreams."

Chris had no dreams for the next six hours but woke up to an inescapable nightmare. The pain was indescribable. Unbearable torture. Any slight movement set off a cataclysm of unimaginable agony. Chris pleaded for pain medication but the nurses said he'd already been given the maximum dose. Any more could stop his heart.

"They're lying!" he screamed inside his head. "They just want me to suffer!"

He looked down at his stomach and it looked like he was six months pregnant. Tubes crisscrossed all over his body, he wasn't even sure where they led or what they did. Chris asked God over and over, "Why is this happening to me?"

Chris's mouth felt like the Sahara and Charisse placed single ice cubes on his lips, all he was allowed. From that point on, his time in recovery became a blur. He was pumped with heavy pain medication that finally took him into another world. He no longer recognized voices or faces. The next morning, he woke to pulsating sleeves on his legs, which were used to prevent blood clots. A nurse instructed him to get up and walk.

"You want me to do what?" he thought incredulously.

He walked for a few seconds before feeling like he was going to pass out. Every hour on the hour, he was forced to get up and walk, even if just a few steps. Each step was excruciating. He limped by a room and heard a doctor tell a family that their father might not make it through the night. It was at that point that he felt grateful for feeling this horrible pain, since it meant that he was alive.

Two weeks in the hospital felt like two years. Charisse came every day to visit and slept overnight in an uncomfortable chair next to him. Back home, Chris's recovery was a long, painstaking process. "Charisse became like my caregiver," he recalls. Chris couldn't do "anything at all" for six to eight weeks, and everything fell on Charisse, who also had a toddler and a newborn to take care of by herself. "I felt more like a burden on her than anything." But Charisse stepped up and became "super mom" and "super wife." She made all of his appointments and made sure he never missed one. She researched foods on the Internet that would be safe for his stomach.

She altered her diet, cutting out red meat, so he could remain healthy. She even bathed Chris like a child, definitely a humbling experience. "I don't think I could have gotten better without her," he admits.

The one regret Charisse had was that between Chris and Cristina's needs, Justin may not have gotten the attention he needed, too. "It really affected Justin," she says. "I never really sat down with him and explained what was going on. I was overwhelmed."

Justin didn't need to be told that something was wrong with his dad, he could see it with his own eyes. Chris experienced a radical weight loss, dropping from 175 pounds to an emaciated 110. "He basically had to learn to eat again," Charisse adds. At first Chris wasn't allowed to eat anything, then slowly, liquids and fruit were introduced back into his fragile stomach. He remembers he ate one small grape and felt so full, as if he'd eaten a large steak. He basically had a stomach the size of a child's and could only consume tiny portions or he'd throw up.

Dr. Strong told Chris the first six months were going to be tough. That was an understatement. "He was constantly sick," Charisse says. Chris didn't want his wife to end up resenting him so he worked hard to build up his strength. At first, he couldn't lift anything heavy, which included his daughter, who always wanted him to carry her. Instead, he would sit on the couch and Cristina would sit on his lap. He used a cane since walking really hurt. It felt like his stomach was attached by strings and with each step, was about to drop to the ground.

Fortunately, he did not have to go through chemo, but the couple spent countless hours traveling back and forth to Sloan Kettering for follow-up appointments to make sure his stomach was still attached and to deal with the side effects of a medication called Reglan, which caused his whole body to contort in opposite directions, causing even more pain.

By the sixth month, in the fall, Chris finally felt strong enough to go back to his teaching assistant job. Well, he acted strong but inside, he never felt like he was going to "make it." He was scared. He believed that each day he was alive was a gift and made sure he didn't squander any time on foolish endeavors. Chris became the best damn father he could possibly be. Cristina had been having some developmental issues and they took her to a specialist to be evaluated. "She wasn't talking, she wasn't responding to her name, she wasn't giving eye contact," Charisse explains.

Chris and Charisse thought maybe she was just taking her time and she would speak when she was good and ready. But other things started to cause concern and raise red flags. They noticed that a lot of sounds really bothered her to the point that she cried nonstop. She didn't like to be touched and just kept to herself in her own little world. Even when they dropped her off with a babysitter or when they visited people with small kids, she found a corner and isolated herself.

They focused on Cristina constantly, consistently calling her by her name over and over. It was as if she was just ignoring them, even though doctors insisted her hearing was normal. They noticed that she didn't play with her toys like other kids her age. Rather, she'd line up her blocks or dolls in perfect size-order. Chris sat with her and modeled how to "correctly" play with her toys but she'd just grab them from his hand and line them up again. When he'd try to get her to speak, just to say "Papi" or "Mami," she screamed and threw a tantrum. Then she started to bite Chris when she wanted something or to get his attention. Sometimes there was no consoling her.

Chris and Charisse both knew that something was wrong. Their pediatrician recommended they make an appointment with a child psychologist. Chris couldn't miss work, since he'd taken so many days off for cancer-related appointments. So Charisse took Cristina to get evaluated in the city, dragging the baby carriage on public transportation. She called Chris as soon as the appointment was over.

"I didn't even say, 'Hi, honey,' just went straight to the point. 'What happened with Cristina?'" Charisse sounded very upset.

"It's pervasive developmental disorder, on the spectrum of autism," Charisse explained. Chris's heart dropped into his stomach because he immediately saw the hard life his daughter would endure for years to come. But he spun it positively for Charisse. "Now we know and now we can help her."

Thank God Chris could help at home again. Charisse bought a lot books on autism and Chris researched it heavily on the Internet. They took her to an early intervention agency called Los Ninos, which provided physical and behavioral therapy, as well as helped the couple communicate better with Cristina. They'd been trying to force her to live in their world. But the therapist said, "Now it's time for you to learn how to live in Cristina's world."

First, they had to label everything in the house: the bathroom, kitchen, her room, the TV. At one point, the whole house had pictures and labels all over the walls. Cristina had a little flipbook with pictures of important members of the family with their names labeled. They had to go through that book every day with Cristina, even if she didn't repeat what they said. Charisse's job at the time donated an iPad to the family and they downloaded every app that catered to autistic children, which was not only a huge help but replaced the flipbook. So now when Cristina clicked on Chris's or Charisse's picture, their voices would say, "Hello, Cristina, I am your papi" or "I am your mommy." They also could not allow Cristina to point or grunt at things that she wanted. They had to force her to speak, even if it was one syllable of the entire word. When they spoke to her, they had to gently guide her face so that she looked directly at them, which was difficult, because Cristina did not like to be touched.

Chris felt guilty that Cristina kicked and smacked her therapists but they were pros, they sat there and took it. He attempted to intervene but the therapists shooed him away. "No matter how bad it gets," they said, "do not try to swoop in and save the day." That was a hard thing to do as a parent. Sometimes they had to sit in the other room and listen to their daughter scream and yell. And they could not give in to her demands even if she threw herself on the floor. One time, Cristina wanted her juice, and she tugged and pointed at the fridge. Chris knew what she wanted but she had to tell him herself.

"You want your juice, say 'juice,'" Chris said slowly. And she would get so angry and smack him. He needed to hear some kind of sound from her mouth. After about thirty minutes of her screaming and hitting him, she finally uttered a sound that didn't sound like "juice" but because she had tried so hard to say it, he rewarded her with her sippy cup. She drank it and fell asleep from exhaustion.

During that time, Chris and Charisse didn't go out with Cristina because any loud noises would automatically put her in tantrum mode and she'd cover her ears. They tried eating with the family at a restaurant and Chris and Charisse had to take turns sitting outside because all she did was scream. The world was just too much for her and they had to carefully introduce her to new stimuli. Cristina learned to speak about twenty words after the first several months of therapy. Her first word was "Papi," which was understandable since she spent a lot of time with Chris. Every day, he put his daughter to sleep and said, "I love you Cristina." And one day Cristina finally said back, "I lub you."

Chris thought he was hearing things. He'd accepted the idea that his little girl may never put together clear sentence structures but then she said this! He ran to Charisse to tell her, but she thought he was lying to her, just like when he told her she said "Papi." Charisse wanted Cristina's first word to be "mommy," of course. She walked over to her crib and Cristina said the phrase again to her.

"I lub you."

"We love you too, honey," they said, tears streaming down their faces.

As part of his commitment to being the best father he could be, Chris got a tattoo on his forearm of a blue puzzle piece, the symbol for autism. He also became the best damn teacher he could possibly be. He worked with special needs kids who came from rough backgrounds. Any time the main teacher let him, he taught class. He stayed extra hours after school and taught the kids how to write poetry, after noticing their interest in rap music. Chris worked his butt off as an assistant teacher and won an award, the Paraprofessional of the Year, from the United Federation of Teachers.

Two years after his surgery, two fateful events intersected. The DOE hiring freeze was lifted—and Chris's cancer went into remission. He went for a routine endoscopy and his oncologist said the magic words: "There is no sign of the cancer returning. I think soon we could say that you are cured." Chris was hesitant to believe it. "To this day, I still don't believe that I will be ever out of the woods."

Despite his skepticism, it was a huge turning point. Chris believed God had given him cancer to make him realize that nothing had control over his life. He felt no fear anymore, just empowered. He'd been an assistant for long enough, it was time to take a leap of faith. He submitted his resume to every school in the city that had an opening—"a million places"—and trusted fate. If it was meant for Chris to become a teacher, then the heavens would make it so.

At first, none responded and he was crushed. He figured if he didn't have blue eyes, long blonde hair, and traveled to Africa in the Peace Corps he had no shot. But during the summer break, Chris received a call from Jordan L. Mott Middle School. They had a PE opening. It was his first and only interview.

"If they offer you a job, don't accept it right away!" Charisse commanded.

Chris drove up to the school on the corner of Morris and College Avenues in the South Bronx. It looked like a prison and just like when he picked up his sister Michelle from her scary apartment building, he didn't want to get out of the car. But he wasn't about to pass up this opportunity. Beggars can't be choosers. Chris walked into the school and it was empty, since it was the beginning of summer vacation. There were a lot of other candidates waiting to be interviewed, as well.

Chris was finally called into the principal's office and was surprised to see a hiring committee, about six to eight individuals. He recognized one woman from a teacher's seminar he'd recently attended. He'd asked her if she could help him locate a physical education teaching position. She basically laughed in his face.

"You picked the wrong field, you should go back to college and do something else."

Now, here she was, about to determine if Chris was qualified for a physical education position. Oh boy, was he fired up now! The principal gave a spiel about the school's history and how it was currently failing. That she needed teachers who were willing to devote all of their time and energy. She asked Chris to tell the panel why he would be a good fit for this school. Chris stood up from his seat, ready to "teach" the panel. He turned to the woman he recognized.

"Do you remember me from a few weeks ago? I had asked you a question."

She pretended to not remember who he was and then with a smirk said, "Oh yeah, you're the guy from that elementary school who wanted to be a PE teacher!"

Adrenaline surged through Chris. He spoke for ten minutes straight about his experiences in education. He told them that even though he was an award-winning assistant teacher, he didn't let that define him. He told them that he was a teacher at heart and no one could tell him otherwise. He turned his gaze toward the Negative Nelly who told him to choose another field and said, "Even through discouragement and adversity, I will never stray from this path because I am destined to be a physical education teacher."

When Chris was done, the principal said, "Follow me." Chris thought he was getting kicked out of the building but instead she walked him over to the secretary's office and said, "Please print out an acceptance letter." She grabbed the letter and handed it to Chris. "Congratulations. You can accept the job now or give it some thought, but I can't guarantee the job will be available tomorrow."

Without hesitation Chris said, "There's no need to think about it," and signed the letter. Charisse was going to be so pissed.

"Welcome, Mr. Astacio," the principal said. "Do you believe in miracles?"

Chris didn't hesitate.

"Of course. I am a walking miracle."

Chapter Eight

A TEACHER GETS SCHOOLED

An X marked the spot where Jordan L. Mott Middle School stood on the crisscrossed streets of 167th and College Avenue—but it might as well have been a bull's-eye. The intersection, and the ten or so square blocks surrounding it, was the epicenter of violent gang activity in the South Bronx. A simple stroll around here put a target on your back and put your life at risk.

A bodega opened directly across the street from the school entrance, but students didn't dare loiter there. They bought their Arizona Iced Tea and Flamin' Hot Cheetos and got the hell out because one short block away—on College between 165th and 166th—was 6 Wild turf, a "hot" area for drug dealing and robberies. Not far, near Grand Concourse, there was a bakery and a McDonald's and a pizza place, but it's not like kids hung out there either and socialized. Around the corner, the 280 crew terrorized the blocks between 167th and 170th, between Morris and Teller. Within spitting distance, you had pockets of Sheisty and Sheridan Gunnaz and Violating All Bitches and Sev O and Eden Boys. The Dominican gang Trinitarios and their girl gang the Bad Barbies, aka One Seven Hoes, who hacked their enemies into pieces with machetes, were also a looming presence. If that wasn't enough (and trust that wasn't even all of them), two competing methadone clinics faced each other five blocks away on 161st at Morris.

So, imagine the walk to and from school for ten- to thirteen-year-old girls. Despite an NYPD "Eye in the Sky" surveillance tower, attached to a mobile command center van manned twenty-four hours a day and parked right outside 22's playground on College Avenue, "safe space" was for privileged white kids. It just wasn't in the South Bronx vocabulary. Random gunshots around MS 22 were regular. One year, the first day of school started with a machine gun battle between two gangs at eight o'clock in the morning on the corner. ShotSpotter sensors placed all over the neighborhood could pick up gunfire and pinpoint the origin in seconds, but by the time cops arrived on scene, it was usually too late anyway.

"If you walk down College Avenue, you can get shot at any point," a 44th precinct police officer confirms. "That's a fact." Kids, adults, whoever, got gunned down or killed near the school all the time. In fact, he adds, one recent summer, a shooting or stabbing happened every single day within blocks. "This is not Mickey Mouse shit, it's the real deal."

MS 22's 800 students shared a cramped two-story building with the Bronx Writing Academy's 500 students, creating yet two more warring "crews." From the outside, the façade looked like a prison and was covered in competing gang graffiti. From Crip warnings like "Blood killer slobs," "C's up," and "Slob killer" to BWA students threatening the Mott kids with messages like "22k" (I'm gonna kill 22) or the more straightforward "Smile now, cry later putas [sluts]."

The neighborhood was bad enough but nobody, not even the NYPD, could control that. You'd think someone could create a sanctuary inside the school for the sake of the children. You'd be wrong. The inside of MS 22 was just as dangerous and chaotic as the neighborhood outside. One step inside its bright orange doors and it was crystal clear that Mott Junior High School was totally out of control. "It was a zoo," one former staff member confirms.

The hallways were dark and dingy, like a sanitarium. Every window, doorknob, and light bulb was broken or smashed. Food and garbage was strewn about on the floor, and roaches crawled out from the walls to feast on the leftovers. Containers of milk had been poured down the sticky stairwells, which already smelled skunky from weed. At any given time, even during class hours, there were 80 to 100 kids roaming the halls unsupervised.

Mott JHS was a dangerous place to be, especially the basement, a common area for both 22 and BWA that included the gym and the cafeteria. Kids were literally scared to go down there because on a daily basis somebody got beat up badly. Like the time a kid was surrounded by two dozen boys, and they broke his kneecaps. The basement was a bacchanal den of sin—drinking, drug dealing, drug using, even blowjobs, all happened out in the open. Hungry students didn't think twice about throwing a chair through the candy machine glass to get a Twix. The students didn't care that they were being watched on security monitors. They'd just look up at the camera and give it the finger.

At intentionally random times, the local 44th police precinct came to the school to set up temporary metal detectors and searches, since it was so overrun with gangs and drugs. That didn't work. Kids hid weed and crack and pills in their sneakers, then ran up the staircase laughing, "Told you they don't check shoes!" Kids who brought weapons to school just left them outside the building when they saw a police presence at the school.

The cops always set up security checkpoints on Halloween, the most dangerous day of the year. Picture the movie *The Purge* and that was basically 22 on October 31—a violent free-for-all by anonymous students hiding behind masks (which eventually were banned). "Everybody brings something, just in case," Alexa explains. Gangs also used the holiday to initiate members—slice someone and you're in the game that day. "I came prepared," Alexa says. "I had a big ass blade but I had to hide it outside."

Metal detectors were merely a temporary deterrent. As soon as the cops left, it was business as usual. Business as usual didn't mean going to class. The classrooms were a joke. There might be a handful of kids up front, like Kimberly or Grateshka or Yoshie, actually listening to the teacher's lecture, but in the back of the room "it was a party," says Heaven. "Kids be laughing and listening to music and pushing each other around and throwing things."

Students came in and went out as they pleased, like it was a nightclub. "I never went to class," Rashell admits. "If I did, I would sit there like, 'Why am I here again?'"

She'd head down to the basement. Robin was also there from "early morning to dismissal" with forty of her closest friends, smoking weed. "To us, that was like the block, our chill-out spot. If the security guard told us to move, we wouldn't move. Sometimes we'd play tag with them. Come chase us! We was so bad."

Nicky and Alcielis were regulars down in the basement, too. "I was one of the worst," Alcielis admits. "I was the one with the attitude and the one influencing my friends, 'Oh, let's do this and let's do that.' I was really bad and not well behaved. I cut class and cursed at teachers. I had pretty bad grades. I was a fighter."

"I wasn't into school and I just wasn't going to class," Nicky adds. "I was reckless. I was always in detention. A lot of that was because of how I was feeling at home. To release that anger, I was arguing and fighting with people." She'd hang out in the stairwells with her friends from 22 and BWA, listening to whining music by Gyptian and Popcaan. Her friends smoked weed and grinded on each other, and even though Nicky was a "little bad girl," she wasn't about to do that in the middle of the day. "Oh no no," she says. "That's just odd."

No, she was more likely to get into a fight, for any little reason at all. "Just the way people would look at me. Don't look at me in that type of way. Don't do that. That's just how New York people are. If you look at me, I'm gonna feel some type of way and gonna wanna approach you. It's crazy how us New York people are. Little things will make us go insane. I don't like people looking at me. People like to argue with me. Don't look at me a certain type of way and we won't argue. People be asking for it. If they lay hands on you first, course you gonna have to do something. You can't just stay touched."

Angie was one of the good kids—but even she could be found wandering around in the hallway during class. "Don't get me wrong, I used to take walks, be in the hallway for a little bit. But I'd be like, 'Bro, let's go back to class now.' I'd walk out but I'd always come back."

At least twenty kids a day randomly walked out of the building. This was before schools were on mandatory lockdown because of Avonte's Law, named after an autistic student who wandered out of a New York City school and drowned in the East River.

Back then, if a teacher tried to stop 22 kids, they'd just say, "I'm leaving."

"No, you're not."

"Fuck you. What are you gonna do?"

Disrespecting the staff was endemic and status quo.

"I'd tell teachers, 'Suck my dick,'" Heaven admits. She argued with teachers and always got in trouble because she was hardheaded and proved her points with her signature rapid-fire way of speaking. "Just 'cause you have higher authority don't mean you get respect. We both bleed, we both human. I don't know you and you don't know me. You have to give respect to get respect."

Rashell threw a chair at a teacher and Robin got into a fistfight with a female security guard. "She told me to stop bouncing a basketball all hostile. I didn't stop bouncing it so she said, 'I'm tired of your smart mouth, you little bitch.' My friends were laughing and saying, 'Don't talk to Robin like that!'" Next thing she knew, the guard put her in chokehold and slammed her head into the wall. Robin fought back. "I just kept hitting her and hitting her. I spit in her mouth."

"That bitch spit in my mouth!" the guard screamed.

Robin got handcuffed and ended up in juvie. "That was my first time being arrested." She spent a week in Horizon Juvenile Center and that whole scared straight thing worked. "Damn, some of those girls were in there for so long. I just learned so many different things from them. It was heartbreaking to me and I never wanted to be there again. Who wants to keep going in and out of jail for the rest of their life? That's no good. If you want a good job they look at your record. I knew I gotta change the way I acted."

Students attacked the staff at 22 with abandon. The teachers feared for their lives. It used to be the other way around—in the past, the staff knocked around the kids. Forty years ago, 22 was one of a handful of New York City public schools under investigation for secretly doling out corporal punishment. In 1970, a student named Althea Morris claimed that two deans at Mott whipped her with a leather belt and a thick wooden paddle, giving her "five licks with the smoker" because she was late and forgot her books. She described the sadistic teachers as having "fixed smiles on their faces, it seemed like they were doing it for entertainment," the *New York Times* reported.

The history of Jordan L. Mott JHS, named for a famed inventor/industrialist, is a case study on the epic failure of public education in the inner city. The school has had brief periods of hope and change. For example, in 1971, former Boston Celtic basketball player Bill Green became the principal and was hired to clear out gangs like the Savage Skulls, the Ghetto Brothers, and Young Saigons, who roamed the hallways freely, according to *Celtics Life*. He also started a program of intellectual competition, and the students' reading scores improved dramatically. Maruri was a student at Mott back then and remembers his method being "very effective. I was in the Special reading Sub-school, which highlighted as the smartest group of kids in the school. We were referred to as the Bronx nerds or Bronx rejects. There was a lot of shaming and bullying in being studious." Green won awards for his work at Mott, but Maruri notes that he was suspended for covering up a teacher's sex offender status, then, at the age of fifty-two, he had a heart attack and died.

In 2004, Mott hired a new principal with great expectations. Shimon Waronker, a Harvard-educated Hasidic Jew and former marine, received much media fanfare but his biggest claim to fame was inventing 22's infamous Academies—UConn, John Jay, and Columbia—so teachers could "concentrate on manageable clusters of students," the *New York Times* reported. He basically created three more gangs in the neighborhood. When Waronker got there, reading and math scores were in the single digits, and he fired half the staff. He implemented etiquette lessons and a "take back the hallways" program. When he left, attendance was over 90 percent. He made some improvements but took off four years later. His rep for fixing low-performing and violent schools, earned or not, landed him the superintendent gig for a troubled district on Long Island, with a yearly salary of $265,000. According to a report in *Newsday*, Waronker was ousted a few months later after that school board levied forty-one charges, including bid-rigging, neglect of duty, and misconduct, against him (which he denied). It's a typical scenario for schools in low-income areas, that politics and corruption impede any possible progress.

After Waronker left, Mott backslid into its old behavior. Sure, 22 has had brief moments in the sun—when altruistic, naive do-gooders vowed they would finally be the chosen one to make a difference—but more often than not, 22 was neglected and left to rot and decay, because nobody gave a damn. Not the DOE, not the principals (for long), not the parents, not the students, and certainly not the teachers.

Chris Astacio accepted the job at 22 because he was desperate. It's not like he wanted to work at a school on the city's "12 Most Dangerous" schools list. Around that time, Mott was the only middle school in New York City deemed IMPACT, a designation given by the NYPD and DOE based on crime statistics, including suspensions and arrests for seven major felonies. When Chris got there, the school had approximately 33 arrests and 278 suspensions per year. Out of 353 total incidents, 163 were considered level 4 out of 5 on the danger scale for violence, weapons, or injuries.

So, yeah, nobody wanted to work at 22. Almost all of the teachers, like Chris, were there because they couldn't get anything better or couldn't work anywhere else because A. They weren't qualified or B. They sucked at being a teacher. There was one staff member who had been at the school for more than ten years, an eternity at 22, and that was Eydie Holloway, the office manager known for her signature fancy glasses, her sweet voice, and her sassy personality. For some reason, she was able to remain calm in the midst of the storm and was beloved by all, faculty and students. "She'd seen it all but was still very kind and loving," Chris says. "She really cared about those kids. She called them her 'babies.' She always had compliments for everyone, like 'I love your hair!' or 'Look at them shoes!'"

Unlike a lot of teachers, she was on the students' side. During random hallway sweeps, she rounded up the stragglers and hid them in the girls' bathroom. "Stay there and be quiet," she commanded with a smile. When it was safe to come out, she'd curse at them and scold, "Now get where you have to be!" or "You need to get your shit together, you want to be in middle school the rest of your life?" Then she pulled them by their ears to class.

Mrs. Holloway was a fixture at 22, but she was an anomaly. Not surprisingly, 22 had one of the highest staff turnover rates in the New York City school system. In the twenty years before Chris arrived, eleven principals had come through the doors. When Waronker showed up, he was the school's seventh principal in two years.

High teacher turnover and low standardized test scores go hand in hand. In 2012, Mott's eighth-graders had a 14 percent pass rate according to the *New York Times* report "New York Schools Test Scores"; 37 percent of its seventh-graders scored below "basic standards." The decade before that, during Mayor Michael Bloomberg's reign, the administration doled out school ratings. Mott received an F multiple years in a row and was on another list of school shut downs several times. But somehow it always slipped through the cracks and remained open.

Chris had been warned that 22 was a failing school and the principal was searching for teachers willing to miraculously turn it around. He spent one week training on what to expect from a population of students who came from broken homes, suffered from depression, and were exposed to drugs and gang violence. Chris left the training session hopeful and optimistic. It was short-lived. In reality, nothing could ever have prepared him for the onslaught he would encounter during that first week of school in September.

"My first day was frightening," Chris admits, "due to the fact that I was a new teacher. I was fresh meat."

A young, white co-teacher, who had made it to his second year teaching PE at the school, instructed Chris, "Don't let them see you sweat. Stand your ground and be firm." At the beginning of the first class they taught together, the co-teacher introduced himself as well as Chris to the class. He asked if Chris had anything to say.

"Nah, I'm okay, you said it all."

Chris heard one smart-ass voice in the gym sarcastically shout out, "Awwww, he's scared!" and the whole class erupted in laughter. Chris had barely even opened his mouth and already the kids felt the need to disrespect and taunt him.

Chris was hired as a physical education teacher but had to double up and also teach poetry. In his first poetry class, on his first day of teaching, he welcomed each student one by one, shaking their hands while greeting them with a smile. In training, he'd been told not to crack a smile until Christmas, but he didn't want to be one of "those" teachers. One girl walked through the door, and Chris noticed she was waddling. She was nine months pregnant. He wasn't expecting a pregnant eighth-grader in his class. She was his first; she wouldn't be the last.

"Mister, could I get out of gym class?" she asked.

The question baffled Chris. What teacher in their right mind would endanger such fragility?

"Yes, of course, you are excused," Chris said.

At least she asked. The level of disrespect by these children was off the charts. During his first assembly in the auditorium, Chris understood immediately why it was never a good idea to put too many of them in the same place at the same time. He felt like he was in the movie *Lean On Me* but without the smoking. The students never listened to a word. Kids just laughed, threw paper at each other. A fight broke out. The only time they paid attention was when there was a musical performance by their peers. Other than that, they couldn't care less about who was speaking. And when the teacher tried to settle them down, he got bombarded with a chorus of "fuck you"s and "shut the fuck up"s.

Another time, on a nice day, the dean made the questionable decision to let all of the students go outside in the fenced-in playground at the same time. The three academies—John Jay, Columbia, and UConn—self-segregated, then retreated into the corners of the lot, leaving the middle wide open. A few knuckleheads strutted into the center, like bait on a fishing line. Sure enough, within minutes, a rumble broke out, and the police had to break it up and restore order.

One major problem at 22, among many, was the population of "over-aged" students. Mott had a sizable number of older teenagers who'd been held back for various reasons, none of them good. They were a bad influence on the younger kids, who actually belonged in middle school. Chris had one overage female student, who was eighteen years old and simply signed herself out of school every day. He had another overage student in his class who'd just been released from juvenile detention and had a parole officer assigned to him. He was 6 feet tall and 200 pounds and had a scary, intimidating demeanor. He walked through the hallways like he owned them and disrespected almost everyone. For some reason, he liked and respected Chris. He would say, "Astacio, you real, not like these other fake-ass teachers in this building." Maybe it was because Chris chose not to let the fact that he was labeled a "delinquent" effect the way he spoke to him. Chris told him that everyone was capable of change and that he believed in him.

One morning, as Chris walked down the hallway, he saw this student get stopped by one of the deans. The dean simply reminded him to go back to homeroom but this kid was not having it. "Move out of my way or I'll move you," he barked, then shoved the dean out of the way. The dean circled back in front him of him, blocked his way, and put his hands on him to keep him from advancing.

"Don't you fuckin' touch me, old man!"

Chris ran over because he read his body language—he was about to knock this dean out.

"I got you, meet me outside, let's see if you keep talking shit, meet me outside!" the student yelled. Chris threw himself in between them and pushed the student away as he tried to swing and punch the dean from over his shoulders. Chris held him against the wall, as he kept whispering, "Let me go, Astacio, I don't want you to get hurt!" Chris diffused the situation and, later that day, the student thanked Chris for stepping in. "You're crazy, Astacio, I was about to kill that white prick, and when I get like that, I black out." He reminded Chris that he was on parole and there was no way that he was going back to jail. Unfortunately, he did violate his parole in the following months and Chris never saw him again.

The teachers were immersed into a chaotic environment of unruly disruptive behavior. Students seemed unwilling to learn and appeared to not care about anything. Violence from the streets spilled into the classrooms and it seemed like teaching was barely part of the job description anymore. Getting kicked in the face? That came with the territory. Chris saw it happen to another teacher and wondered when it would be his turn. After the first week, several teachers abandoned ship—it was too much for them to handle. Like the pregnant teacher who was taunted mercilessly by the students. Kids called her "the slut" and laughed at her. The final straw? A female student shoved her really hard and told her she hoped she lost the baby. That teacher did not come back to work.

As for Chris, he couldn't bring himself to quit. "I have never been able to comprehend such a word," he says. Just like when he was in high school, Chris's main goal was "to survive," even if only for one year.

Making that nearly impossible was the fact that most of his classes were in the dreaded basement gymnasium. Everyone who cut class either hid in the staircase, the bathrooms, the cafeteria, or the gym. Every day, on the dot, the "Cutters" as the staff called them, waited for Chis to open the gym doors for his scheduled PE classes. He did his best to stop these kids from coming in but they rushed him as soon as the gym doors flung open. Chris asked assistant principals, deans, and safety agents to escort the Cutters out of his PE class. Of course, they would return no less than five minutes later, banging on the gym door, threatening kids on the inside to let them in or else, which they did. It was a vicious and exhausting cycle.

There was an overwhelming number of Cutters who hung out in the gym all day, sometimes up to one hundred of them. Locking the doors was not an option. The lock had already been busted by the Cutters and had been left broken for years, so the likelihood that it would ever be repaired was bleak.

Chris did his best to ignore the hooligans who didn't belong in the gym while he taught but it became increasingly difficult when more groups of Cutters would barge into his classes only to cause trouble. Brutal altercations happened almost every day, since students "scheduled" fights via social media and/or text messages. Achelin and Alexa and their crew often videoed brawls and posted them online. The fights were not necessarily segregated by gender, either. Boys laid hands on girls and vice versa. "I had beefs with boys and girls," Robin admits. "There was no line. My ex-boyfriend got jumped for his baby blue iPhone 5C and I jumped into the fight. I hit one of the boys and I had mad problems every day after that for a month."

Technically, teachers were not expected to intervene during any student altercation. Chris was supposed to immediately contact school safety agents and attempt to "control" the class while staying clear of the fight. About midway through Chris's first year, 22 hired Richard Frederick to be the assistant principal of security. Frederick, a beefy Brooklyn-born safety expert, had a rep for doling out tough love in the very toughest school districts. "I was told, 'This school is absolutely out of control,'" he recalls. A school that size should have three school safety agents. Mott had eight, including a young tough guy named Mr. Rafael Toro, who wore a suit every day so everyone, including the teachers, figured he was a narc. Plus, there was an

NYPD mobile command center right on the corner. "If we needed to call the cops, we'd just knock on the van window and say, 'Come on over,'" Frederick explains.

As a father and human being, Chris could not fathom the idea of watching two or more kids beat each other senseless while someone else ran for help. Especially considering where the gym was located in relation to the location of school safety (a far distance). It was illogical to expect safety officers to arrive immediately. He had no way of communicating with these agents since it meant he had to leave the class unsupervised in order to use the phone in his office, which often didn't work. And how long would it take before they actually came to the rescue? Not as a teacher, but as a human being, Chris could not allow kids to tear each other apart in front of him while waiting for help. He could not do it.

And because of that, he often intervened in fights and got hurt. Chris was pushed, punched, and kicked in the groin. He remembers trying to break up a fight between two girls and getting punched in the back of his head. On another occasion, while breaking up two male students, he was shoved against a door and a metal screw sliced his arm. Not paying any attention to the pain, he continued breaking up the fight and eventually safety agents arrived to take one boy away. As Chris checked to see if the other kid was okay, he saw blood all over his shirt and automatically got worried for his well-being.

"Mr. Astacio, this is not my blood, it's *yours*."

Chris looked down at his arm to see a six-inch vertical gash on his forearm. Luckily, it didn't require stitches, just some surgical glue and a tetanus shot.

At one point, Chris tried another tactic. He welcomed the Cutters and utilized them in his class. He'd gotten tired of trying to kick them out. "If you're going to be here, then you're going to help me out," he told them cautiously.

"You can't teach when you have a hundred kids in the gym," Frederick says. "Here's some balls, don't kill each other? I offered to stand at the door like a security guard so nobody could leave. I felt for him and always gave him as much support as I could. An extra body to be eyes in there. I made sure he had Walkie Talkies but they didn't work much in the basement of a gym where there's no cell service."

At first, the Cutters assisted him with his lessons. But the mutual arrangement soured quickly. There were too many different gangs in the school, as well as in his class. One day, some Cutters and some kids in his class were playing basketball. One boy unintentionally threw the ball into the face of another male student, who was part of a rival gang. Chris tried his best to diffuse the situation but a fight was inevitable. As he tried to hold the kid who was hit with the basketball, he began getting violent with Chris, taking a few swings but fortunately missing his face.

The last thing Chris wanted to become was a target. But it was unavoidable. These kids didn't know him or trust him in the early days so they tried to intimidate him. One time, a bunch of students were running around the school, hiding in staircases and behind the stage in the auditorium. Chris was called on that day to help clear out those hiding on the stage. All of the students dispersed, except one who thought he was somehow invisible.

"I know you're behind the curtain," Chris told him.

No response.

"I can see you," Chris repeated.

No response.

Chris swiped the curtain out of the way, and the kid stood there like a deer in headlights. He didn't budge. When Chris gently placed his hand on his shoulder to guide him out, he hit his hand away and shouted, "Don't you fuckin' touch me, I'll fuck you up!" As he exited the auditorium, he yelled over and over, "You don't know me, I'll kick your ass!" Then he turned back toward Chris, formed his hand into a gun and said, a little too seriously, "Boom."

Living in a constant state of looking over his shoulder drained Chris, physically and mentally. "There was no such thing as a calm day," he recalls. "It was always 'turnt up,' like the kids would say." He was supposed to be on a special diet for his stomach and he wasn't eating right at all. Chris was in remission but under a lot of stress. On top of that, during his first year at 22, he was still finishing up his master's degree in health education. He wrote a 120-page thesis, which took a few months of research, blood, sweat, tears, and sleepless nights to complete. But he did it and graduated magna cum laude with a 3.7 GPA. All while enduring hell.

He'd filled Charisse in on his daily drama—how hoods constantly cursed him out and threatened to follow him after school and vandalize his car or kill him—but when he told his wife the finger-gun story, she finally had enough.

"You need to quit immediately!" she pleaded. "Just walk away! You're supposed to be keeping it easy and you're gonna have a relapse. A highly stressful environment is not conducive to your remission," she reminded him. "To be honest, I'm scared."

Charisse wasn't sure if Chris was putting on a front, but he didn't seem as worried as she did. Secretly, he was, but more than that, he was stubborn. He refused to let anyone in that school get the best of him. The kids didn't know him yet so he couldn't get a handle on them. He knew he could and he would, with a little more time. "I want to stick this out," he said. "I want to be a teacher."

"It's not worth it—this is your life," she shot back angrily. "God forbid anything happens to you. You have children to think about. Do you want them to lose their father? It already almost happened once!"

God forbid his children ever have to go to a school like 22, he thought. Especially Cristina. He couldn't imagine his beautiful daughter being trapped in a school like Mott. Out of all of the horrible things he'd witnessed so far, it was the female altercations that bothered him the most. They were, by far, the worst and most disturbing.

The majority of beefs between the girls were over boys. They'd scream, "You're a thot!" slang for "That Ho Over There," or "You're a slut, you stole my man, ho!" before trying to yank each other's hair out. But it could simply be over a look or anything at all. Achelin constantly battled with other girls, and even scrapped with her best friend Alexa over something really stupid. "I had a lot of anger and I just couldn't let it go," Achelin admits. "I was so bad. My mom used to not pay attention to me because I was such a troublemaker. We never got along." Rashell and Robin were warriors, too, they'd fuck anybody up at the smallest slight. "I was fighting for unnecessary things," Rashell admits. "A girl would say something or look at me and boom, I'd automatically start swinging."

The girl fights were designed to brutally maim their victims. Chris heard one female boasting she had her nails filed to look like daggers a day prior to a fight so she could "claw the other girl's eyes out." Indeed, after the fight, her victim looked as if an animal had attacked her, as she gushed blood from multiple deep scratches on her face. Rashell remembers girls wearing rings on purpose to better slice up enemies' faces. To defend from attacks, they smeared Vaseline on their faces and put their hair in scarves, so it was harder to pull. Robin started plenty of fights herself, got jumped twice, and was stalked by a female with a knife once at school, but even she followed an unspoken code. "Carving somebody on their face, that's just messed up. Don't scar somebody up for the rest of their life."

Social media caused a lot of the drama. Girls would jaw at each other online overnight, about boys but also material things, like backpacks or clothes they bought at shops like Jimmy Jazz, Pretty Girl, or Easy Pickins on Fordham Road. "I have this phone, what kind do you have?" "I have $300 sneakers, yours only cost $70." Everybody would comment on it, and a fight would be scheduled for the next day. "Everybody's like, 'Wasn't you arguing on Facebook last night? What you gonna do about it?'"

The most upsetting fight Chris saw that first year involved a teen that may have been pregnant. Her aggressor stated that she didn't care about the "bastard" growing in her belly, she was going to punch her so hard over and over in the stomach that she would lose the baby right there. "I'm gonna fuck you up!" she screamed.

"Yo, stop, stop!" Chris pleaded.

"I don't care if I'm pregnant, I'll fuck you up!" the "victim" yelled back.

"I'll kick you in the stomach and make you have yo baby right here!"

Having a daughter himself, his heart sank into his stomach. "It was just so sad to hear a young female say that to another female," Chris says. All these girls desperately needed an intervention but he just didn't know how or where to begin.

So many of these girls never showed up to class. They wandered the halls and hung out in the staircases. He'd ask them nicely, "Hey girls, don't you have class now?" and get back, "Fuck you, mister. Don't fucking look at me. Who you talking to?"

He decided to start a poetry slam club and invited a lot of the troubled girls to check it out. Their poetry was eye-opening and heartbreaking, a lot of it revolved around rape, violence, suicide, or drugs.

Faces
By Ashley Victor
Feeling alone in a crowd
full of people is a feeling she's use to
She gets scared when
you raise your hand at her
because she's use to the abuse
She cries when you yell at her
but she's heard it all before
She pretends to be strong
but on the inside
she's nothing but broken
How do I know?
Because she's me

R.I.P. Frankiee
By Cathryn Carmichael
I swear bro if I was there,
I would have took those two bullets for you that's word to Mami.
When I got that phone call telling me you was shot . . . I stopped

everything I was doing and my heart dropped . . .
There's not a day that goes by that I don't think about you . . .
and there's
not a day that I don't have flashbacks about that one day
April 26 2011 . . .
I was there at Jacobi hospital, sitting at the edge of my seat, crying my
eyes out, praying to God that you'd come back to life
and walk out the hospital room.
It wasn't long before the doctor came out and announced you were
dead . . .
I lost my one and only best friend . . .
I will miss you bro, my one and only true friend.

The World
By Johnniel Reyes
This world is nothing but a lie
I hate it
because all you see
is how much people cry
and get hurt.
To me this world is hell
Because when you have something good
it is not going to last long
and in the end
all you are is a person
that is hurt.

Chris compiled the poems into a book called *Lyrics of Life*. He raised funds to buy a book-making machine and printed it out, turning their beautiful pieces of poetry into a work of art. He also plastered their poems all over the school, on walls and in the bathrooms, so they could feel pride in an accomplishment. Chris hung up his own poem, too, about his late sister Michelle, in the hallway for everyone to see:

Someday
My sister found herself homeless, living under streetlights.
She kept this a secret from everyone she knew,
She was a good liar because I never even had a clue.
From a payphone one day, she called me to say,
"I love you brother, every second of every day"
"Of course you do, you don't really have a choice"
We laughed, hung up and that was the last time I heard her voice.
Two o'clock in the morning as I laid in my bed,
I received a phone call saying that my sister was dead.
Maybe she knew that she was going to die,
I wish I could have helped her, why did she lie?
As I walked by her casket and stood by where she laid,
I held her hand and whispered in her ear
"I will see you again . . .
someday . . ."

Charisse remembers the poetry class a little differently and she wasn't pleased about it. "It came out of his *own* pocket. He was buying notebooks and things and I was like, 'Are you kidding me? What are you fuckin' thinking about?' We weren't rich, and I had to re-budget to make room for all that." Despite her frustration, she couldn't deny that Chris had a way with these kids. "He just had this aura about him and they would just come to him." She reluctantly supported him.

One afternoon, after poetry slam club, Chris was stopped in the hall by the principal. She commended him on developing good relationships with some of their most difficult and violent students. She confided in him that she was worried about the fate of the kids and the school. She hadn't given up but felt like she was running out of ideas on how to save these kids.

"What can I do to help them?" she asked Chris, as if he knew. He empathized with her but offered no solutions because he really had no clue himself. She'd come up with the hair-brained idea to change the name of the school to the College Avenue Academy, like that would do anything at all.

Ultimately, she just gave up, just like so many principals before her. Later that year, she announced to the staff that she was leaving 22. Chris's co-teacher in the gym also got another job. Who could blame them? Chris survived his first year at Jordan L. Mott, despite having had no support whatsoever in his classes, but he was at the end of his rope, too. He was totally burnt out, and Charisse was on his ass to get the hell out. He was seriously contemplating bolting, too.

On the last day of school that year, Chris met with the parent-coordinator. They had a deep conversation and it turned out he shared the same concerns as Chris about the state of their female students. Since he'd been working at the school for years, Chris asked him if he had any ideas about how he could help those young ladies. He said the boys' baseball and basketball teams had just won the city championships that year, which seemed to slightly unify the male population of the school.

"That's what these girls need, Astacio. A sport that would unify these girls and give them something to be proud of," he said, then added, "Whatever you choose to coach, I know you can take them to the championship!"

Chris felt that little fire in his belly again. The good kind, not the cancer kind.

He was always up for a new challenge. So he stayed.

Part Two

PRACTICE

Chapter Nine

WHERE'S THE BEEF?

"Sorry, it's not gonna happen."

Mott had hired a new principal—a youngish, hipster Asian dude who had as many lofty ambitions for 22 as he did colorful tattoos. But none of those ambitions included a girls' softball team. The school was failing again, badly, and this guy needed new programs that would instantly raise test scores. The budget had been stripped to bare bones, and every dollar was to be allocated for that one specific goal. Get the school a passing grade and pull 22 out of the gutter. That's what he was hired to do. A girls' softball team wouldn't help achieve that goal. A girls' softball team had nothing to do with raising test scores. At that moment in time, there was absolutely no reason for, or money for, a frivolous endeavor like a girls' softball team. The new principal liked Chris's passion project just fine but he did not have time to care about or fund a girls' softball team. To put it bluntly, he didn't give a shit.

Chris's heart sank. He'd spent the whole summer researching softball, coming up with a budget and figuring out a way he could reel in the most troubled girls. "I didn't want a repeat of the previous year," Chris says. "I barely survived that first year and I was like, 'There's no way I'm going through that again. I have to do something.'" He was desperate to give his female students an outlet for their rage and pain, because he understood the healing power of sports and its correlation with mental health. During his troubled teens, playing baseball and working out had saved Chris from the abyss countless times. The girls at 22 had almost no extracurricular athletic options, besides the basketball team. Even cheerleading had been eliminated from the budget. Chris thought about coaching volleyball for a hot minute, but he knew next to nothing about the sport. He knew the basic fundamentals to teach it in PE but coaching it was a different story. Plus, he only had one pole that looked like it was from the 1970s. Volleyball was not an option. He knew how to play baseball, so how different could softball be? Softball seemed realistic and doable. He headed into the new school year bright-eyed and bushy-tailed with a specific, well-thought-out plan to unveil a softball team. "It's going to happen!" he'd convinced himself.

And now the new principal was telling him nope, definitely not. "Listen," he said, sensing Chris's crushing disappointment, "you can do this if you want. But I can't give you any money."

Bottom line: If Chris were to create a girls' softball program, he got the "green light," but he'd be doing it "on his own." It couldn't officially be organized through LEAP (Learning Enrichment After-School Program), which meant no money for uniforms or equipment. You know, the very things needed to make it feel like a real team. Given that the majority of the girls in the school didn't have any interest in sports, he also had to somehow persuade them to join a team without the very tools needed to make it function. And to make his idea even more appealing, he wouldn't be compensated for his time.

This was going to take that miracle they'd all been talking about.

That night, Chris weighed the pros and cons with his wife, and it didn't take long to reach a final decision. Ignoring her objections, and much to Charisse's chagrin, he committed 110 percent to starting a softball team. "For me it was all about go, go, go, go, go," he explains. After recovering from stomach cancer, he couldn't sit still anymore. "I knew the feeling of not knowing if I'd have tomorrow." Once he made the call, he prayed to God to help guide him and help keep the faith. To give him strength when he would need it most, because he knew he would be tested.

The test began the second those first dozen girls walked into the gym—loud, disrespectful, and, in the case of Rashell, downright scary. These were not athletes; these were the kids with major discipline problems. The ones who roamed the building, like Nicky and Alcielis, and hung with gangbangers, like Alexa. The day after the initial tryouts, Chris sat in his office next to the gym, feeling as if he should just call the whole thing off and preserve his sanity. He recognized a few of the new recruits from his gym classes last year and it concerned him. He jumped onto his ancient, slower than a snail computer and scrolled through some of their progress reports. He read them aloud to Mr. Toro, who'd been promoted from security to the open PE teacher job, and now shared the office with Chris. He had traded in his suits for tracksuits.

"Achelin: poor attendance, has potential to do better, missing a lot of class has caused Achelin to be behind in the material, which is causing her to struggle."

"Alexa: poor attendance, has the ability to do better, low reading stamina, needs to focus on her work and herself and not that of others."

"Heaven: frequent calling out/disruptive yelling, can be disruptive especially with Aleiri, student has to stop playing around socializing and get serious about her school work, distracted easily, easily influenced."

"Nicky: when she comes to class Hamniky is usually a good student. Needs to come to class, stay in class, complete assignments, participate in activities. Easily influenced to get off task."

"Rashell: needs to take responsibility for disruptive behaviors in class, is constantly on her cellphone, below grade level in areas of reading and writing, needs to correct classroom behavior, often a distraction in the class. Does not stay on task. Would rather talk to friends, is capable of more, cutting classes most of the time, often late disrupting lesson."

"Damn," Chris said, defeated.

"I thought you wanted to transform the school?" Mr. Toro asked. "You should be lucky that these girls signed up. They are the very ones you need in this program. If you change them, you change the school."

Chris knew why he needed the girls—there was no team without players. But he misjudged why they even showed up to begin with. He thought they were just using him and the gym as a hangout spot. Or because some, like Rashell and Alcielis, had boyfriends on the baseball team. And that was partly true. But the other big reason was they needed Chris just as much as Chris needed them. "We were lost girls," Heaven explains. "We didn't know what to do or where to turn."

Heaven, who had a rapid-fire, reckless mouth, joined the team to "let my anger go" about her parents' tug-of-war, but also just to avoid trouble herself. "I lived up the block on One Six Four and Sheridan and it was like a lot of drama, a lot of gang banging, boys hanging in the street, violence. I never wanted to be home because of what was going on. My mom always tried to keep me away from it, so when I joined softball she was really glad."

On the flip side, Rashell's mother was against her joining the team. "No you're not!" she screamed at her daughter. "You crazy, what if you break an ankle. I'm not signing no paper, I'm not buying no cleats." Since her father was gone, they didn't have medical insurance or any money to pay for an injury.

"Give me a chance," Rashell begged.

Nicky's mom was not having it either. She didn't want Nicky and her younger sister Gheynee to be on the team because she'd recently had another baby girl and relied on the sisters to take care of her while she was working. Nicky didn't care. She did what she wanted. She was one of the first to sign up for the team after she saw the bright orange poster and sign-up sheet in the cafeteria. She'd been a cheerleader the year before in seventh grade but that wasn't an option anymore. "I watched the Yankees play but playing myself was something new for me." Besides, there was no way in hell she was going home after school every day. "There was so much stuff going on, I needed something to take my mind off it," Nicky remembers. "I didn't want to be getting screamed at for no reason, so I just decided to go into softball."

At this point, Chris knew so little about these girls other than what he'd learned having them for an hour a day in PE, which was minimal since he had 600 students total and up to a 100 in a single class sometimes when he and Mr. Toro taught at the same time. Besides what he read on their progress reports, he had no backstories and no idea what their lives were like outside of school. All he knew was that they were rude and angry and loud and disruptive—and maybe even dangerous.

Chris was clueless about them, but he'd unknowingly already made an impression on some of them, both positive and negative. "When I heard about the softball team, at first I was like, 'I don't want to do that shit,'" Rashell admits. "I couldn't stand him. But stuff was real bad at home."

Genesis was also having a tough time at home. She hadn't seen her mother in literally years, and, in school, she was riddled with anxiety and isolated herself. She joined the team because it was something to do to keep her mind off her misery.

When Johanna first moved to the Bronx from El Salvador, it took her four months to enroll in school. Like Genesis, she was lonely and also painfully bored. Her very first class at 22 was gym and she never forgot how kind Mr. Astacio was, even though she spoke no English and had no idea what she was doing.

Alexa liked Astacio, too. "I had him for gym and he was inspirational. He shared his life with us so he wasn't one of those robotic teachers. I liked softball, so I was there the first day." She adds proudly, "I brung myself and Achelin."

In the beginning, Chris underestimated the girls' drive, which so many adults had already done to them their entire lives. Grateshka wanted to play, she says, because "I've always liked to be active and keep my body in shape." She saw a flyer in the hallway and asked her parents if she could try out. They were super-strict and overprotective, but they trusted their daughter. A lot of her friends were running around in the streets but not Grateshka. "My parents made an effort to give me a better life, so why would I disappoint them?" She was offered marijuana, pressured to cut school, but she never did. She always got her homework done on time and was in bed at her curfew. If not, she wouldn't be allowed to play *Bratz: Rock Angels* or *Forever Diamondz* on her PlayStation 2. "It was my favorite and, if I was good, my mom would let me play on the weekends."

Grateshka's parents would let her join softball on one condition: that it wouldn't distract from her studies. Plus, they'd been through this before. Her older brother was on a baseball team and they'd all wake up early on Saturday mornings to go watch him play. "He inspired me," Grateshka says.

Likewise, Kimberly was inspired by the uncles on her mother's side who all played baseball. Baseball is a religion to many Dominicans. In fact, the Dominican Republic sends more players to Major League Baseball than any other country in the world. So it was a big part of Kimberly's childhood. "We used to play with plastic balls and bats. I wanted to impress them by joining softball." She, of course, came as a package deal with her younger sister Claudia, since their mother did not trust Kimberly being on her own.

A few of the girls were dumped on the team for babysitting purposes, and a couple were unloaded there by Mr. Toro's old boss Richard Frederick, the AP of school safety. Frederick was a "big believer in social emotional learning and restorative justice," and a fan of the softball team as a concept from the get-go. "I support you," he told Chris, before depositing Robin on the team. She'd been sprung from Horizon Juvie after choking the female security guard and spitting in her mouth. "I thought she'd be in jail for the rest of her life," Chris says. "She was the statistic girl, the one it seemed like there was no hope for." Not surprisingly, she was still getting in trouble so much her grandma Redell was called down to the school almost every day. "Everyone was scared of Robin," Chris says.

Frederick convinced Robin join the team. "He felt it was better to keep me occupied," she recalls. So he called Chris and said, "I got a girl for you."

"Let's go," Chris replied. "I'm not scared."

Chris met with Robin and the first thing he told her was, "I actually care about what you do." He also gave her a list of conditions to be on the team. "This shit about you fighting, that's gotta stop. I don't take that shit." Robin promised to try.

Worried that the softball team would become more *Real Housewives of Atlanta* than *A League of Their Own*, Chris tried to enlist some real athletes to tamp down the drama and balance out the roster. He approached Angie again, even though she'd made it clear as ice during the tryouts that she thought the girls who showed up were clowns. "I was on the girls' basketball team already, and I was really dedicated to it. When Astacio came to me and was like, 'I want to make a girls' softball team,' I was like, 'Okay,' I wanted to do it. But then when I seen all the girls joining, I was like, 'Nah, I'm not gonna join them.' They were more of the cheerleading looking girls. They were always talking about boys. So I told Astacio, 'I don't want to do this if it ain't right. Your team is gonna be ass.'"

Strike two.

Chris moved on to Yoshie. She was young, a sixth-grader, and a quiet loner with few friends. But during PE, he saw her whip a volleyball across the gym at warp speed, and he had to have her and that arm on the team. She was shy and wishy-washy about it, though. When Chris checked out her progress report, Yoshie's teachers hinted that she was a good kid, but maybe an underachiever. "Does the work but should work harder to produce quality work. Attendance is a problem. Needs to read for 45 minutes at home every day. Needs to turn in homework. Very cooperative but needs to focus more in class and participate in class discussion." After pestering her a few more times, Yoshie finally agreed to be on the Lady Tigers with a nonchalant, "Sure, whatever."

Johanna, a seventh-grader, wasn't into softball at first either. She was very athletic, but back in El Salvador, soccer was her true love. Chris pulled her aside one day in gym class and asked her too loudly in English, "Do you want to play softball?" He swung his arms as if hitting a homerun. "Soft-ball."

"No, *me gusta jugar el futbol.*"

He brought another student who spoke Spanish over to Johanna. "Can you translate for me?" Chris's Spanish was limited. His mother stopped teaching him when he was a kid because she thought it would hold him back in life, and he gave up trying. "In the eighties, it wasn't cool to be bilingual, it meant you were stupid," Chris says. "It was a false perception. My own grandmother used to make fun of me for speaking like a white guy."

"Tell her to play softball," he said, pointing at Johanna.

"*Quieres jugar beisbol?*"

"*Podria ententar?*"

"She's saying, 'I could try,'" the translator reported.

"Okay, come with me," Chris said. He brought Johanna and the translator over to the wall. "I want you to try and throw the ball." He threw the ball as an example.

Johanna took the ball and threw it against the wall perfectly.

"Try to pitch it and do this." Chris did a lame underhand softball pitch against the wall. Johanna took the ball and pitched it against the wall, better than he had.

"*Asi? Asi?*"

"Like this? Like this?" repeated the translator.

"*Si! Si!* Just like that! Just like that!" Chris shouted into the rafters. "Oh yeah, we're training her!"

Chris was thrilled he'd found enough girls to field a team but there was no guarantee that they'd keep coming back. They didn't exactly have a stellar track record when it came to attendance. He needed some sort of magical superglue to make it stick. Oddly, in the very beginning, the only thing keeping the team together was Rashell. She may have been a bully, but she was also a leader. She just happened to currently use her power for evil. When she talked, the other girls listened. Where she went, the other girls followed. She might have hated Chris, but she hated going home more. So she wanted to play softball. Same with her little eighth-grade clique—Alcielis, Nicky, and Kimberly—they didn't want to go home either. "You could stay at school until 6 o'clock if you were in an activity," Nicky explains.

"The softball team came along and we all went for it," Rashell says. "I told Alcielis and Nicky, and they were like, 'Bro, let's do it! C'mon! Let's go!'" When Chris needed more girls, Rashell helped him recruit. "I was just telling girls, 'Come to softball practice! It's lit!' Mind you, we didn't do anything yet. But I was like, 'Yo, come! In the gym!' 'What time?' 'Come at 4, bro! Go get something to eat and come back!' We literally got girls to go." After the first couple "tryouts," which was basically a half dozen girls sitting on the gym floor listening to Rashell and Alcielis complain about their boyfriends Angel and Wilson, Rashell and her friends managed to convince about twenty-five girls to join the team.

The roster on the first day of practice was pretty impressive:

Achelin

Alcielis

Aleiri

Alexa

Claudia

Genesis

Gheynee

Gianella

Heaven

Jada

Jeelin

Johanna

Kimari

Kimberly

Kyara

Mayoli

Milagro

Natalie

Nayeli

Nicky

Nicolle

Precious

Rashell

Sharlene

Shiadiamond

Tyara

Yoshie

Chris and his ragtag band of players were ready to roll. There was only one problem and it was a big one—they still didn't have any equipment. No bats, balls, or bases. Well, there were faded, painted bases on the concrete field. "We had nothing," Chris says. The principal had told Chris to "search around the school" to find stuff he could use, or ask his fellow teachers. "They play softball, right?" Seriously? He wasn't joking, so Chris rummaged around the campus and found a broken Wiffle ball bat, a bunch of Wiffle balls, and three smelly old gloves. Along with his own personal mitt, those were the only gloves they had for the next couple months.

When the girls gathered on the concrete playground and spotted his weak, plastic baby toys, he could tell they were unimpressed.

"Yo, how we supposed to play, if we can't do nothing?" Gheynee complained.

"Equipment is coming soon," Chris lied. The truth was, he'd already signed up the Lady Tigers on DonorsChoose.org, a website that helps public school teachers get funding for everything from butterfly cocoons to robotics kits. But that could take a minute or a month, or never happen. In the meantime, what was he gonna do with twenty-five impatient, restless girls? In most LEAP programs, students were required to do schoolwork for at least the first fifteen minutes of a club. "We ain't doin' no homework," Rashell warned Chris right off the bat.

Chris agreed. These girls had a lot of energy, like wild horses, and he wanted to harness and rein it in. "I needed to break them and get them winded," he explains.

"Circle up!" Chris bellowed. The team surrounded him.

"Ra-shell, I mean Rach-el, sorry, come join me." He wanted the player with the biggest mouth in the middle with him. "We're gonna stretch out now." They just stood there staring at him. "Do what I do." Chris modeled some moves and they mimicked him.

"Count it out!" he shouted. "I want you to be loud!"

"One, two, three . . ." they shouted back meekly.

"LOUDER!" Chris boomed, as he demonstrated more warm-up stretches. "I want everyone in the whole neighborhood to hear this! Every time we come out here, I want you to be loud! Every time we count! Everything we do is loud!"

"ONE, TWO, THREE, FOUR, FIVE!" Rashell shouted it loud, so the rest chimed in at the top of their lungs, too.

As they did their calisthenics, folks from the neighborhood lined up along the chain-link fence. They'd seen a lot of crazy shit go down on this playground. This was definitely something new that had never happened before. "I want everyone to see that you're here!" Chris roared. "That you're doing something good for yourselves!"

Once they were done with stretching, sit-ups, and push-ups, Chris told them to run around the concrete field twice. They looked at him like he had two heads. "Mister, can we just skip this?"

"No, you're gonna be playing, you're gonna be out in the field and running around the bases . . ."

"What bases?" a smart-ass shouted out.

". . . you can't be tired. What happens if you hit the ball? That's it? You're done?"

The girls trudged up to Chris begrudgingly and unloaded their cellphones into his pockets. There were so many jammed in there, his sweatpants sagged low like a gangbanger. They started off running but couldn't even make it halfway around the field before they stopped and gave up, huffing and puffing like lifelong smokers on oxygen tanks.

Speaking of, Mrs. Holloway, a heavy smoker, walked by the field on her way home, huffing and puffing herself.

"How my babies doing?" she wheezed.

"Hi, Mrs. Holloway!" they all screamed.

"You gotta quit smoking," Chris said. He always saw her struggling to walk up the steps of the school.

"I know, sweetie," then added before walking away, "c'mon, girls, you can do it!"

They couldn't. They were done.

"Are you guys serious?" Chris cried out. "I've seen you run from the deans *and* the cops. I know you can go faster than this!" It seemed like a really light drill to him, then again, it was his first experience working out girls. "I didn't think it was that much, but to them it was like death." The tire obstacle course he'd set up was definitely out.

"Yo! I need two or three of you to run the entire field once before we continue!" Chris ordered.

"You do it."

"No, you do it!"

"I don't want to do it!"

"I ain't doin' it!"

"Can I have some water?"

"My foot hurts."

"I can't breathe."

"Can we have a break?"

"FINE, I'll do it."

Nicky was over it. She took one for the team and completed the lap. Chris wasn't surprised she stepped up. Her sister Gheynee wanted to rip his throat out, but Nicky sort of latched onto Chris last year in her seventh grade PE class. Whenever she was around, she stuck by his side like a loyal poodle. He could tell she liked being his teacher's pet and she, of all the girls, took softball the most seriously. "Don't just do it, be serious about it," she'd bark at the others. "Don't just do it because Juan is doing baseball. Do it because you actually want to do it!"

Nobody else took it seriously. These girls really hated running—and practicing. At first, he scheduled practice three times per week from 4 to 6 P.M. because they had a lot to learn. Chris was starting from scratch and had to teach the most basic 101 fundamentals.

"Okay, show me your athletic stance," he said to blank stares and slack jaws.

"Huh? What's an athletic stamp?" Robin asked.

"'Stance.'"

"What do you want me to do?"

"Just stand there, bend your knees, and squat."

"Squat?"

"Yeah, squat. A little lower. Lower."

"How long I have to stay like this?"

"Well, usually when you play a game it's about two hours."

"I gotta be squatting for two hours?!"

"You want to do this or not?"

Chris had taken certain skills for granted. He assumed they'd thrown a ball a few times in their lives. They hadn't. Most boys grew up throwing a ball or other objects, like frozen eggs, like it was second nature. It was a whole new ballgame for these girls. To teach them, Chris told them to find a spot on the brick wall. He handed them Wiffle or tennis balls, whatever they had on hand that day. Things had a way of disappearing and reappearing. "Try to hit the same spot over and over again," he instructed. "Point your toe at the target." He started them off close, then slowly kept backing them up. Some girls caught on quickly. Yoshie and Gheynee and Alexa had accuracy to match their strong arms. But a lot, like Kimberly and Heaven, really had a problem understanding the follow-through and the flicking of the wrist, and balls sailed haphazardly all over the yard.

"I hate the way I throw," Nicky grumbled.

"Hold up, hold up! Everybody come stand in front of me."

The girls lined up in front of Chris.

Kimberly was first. Standing next to this extremely tall girl, Chris felt extremely small, but regardless of her incredible height, she seemed harmless and appeared as if she couldn't hurt a soul. Along with being totally clueless at times, Kimberly's sister Claudia was the complete opposite and often had a difficult time displaying empathy. Kimberly's teachers had described her as a very bright student who always completed her work but barely spoke in class. She was the epitome of respect, which made Chris question how the other nasty girls in her clique hadn't corrupted her yet.

"I want you to learn how to follow through and flick your wrist. So stand in front of me here, without a ball, and pretend like you're throwing it, but flick your wrist so you slap the top of my head."

"Bald motherfucker!" someone shouted out, probably Gheynee.

"Yo mama so bald," Grateshka joined in, "her cornrows look like stitches!"

Kimberly pretended to throw but barely tapped the top of Chris's head. "I don't want to hit you," she whispered. All the other girls, Chris says, "enjoyed the opportunity to hit me," giggling the whole time.

Smacking Chris's shiny pate was the peak of excitement at the earliest practices. They really wanted to try batting—that looked "dope" to them—but since Chris didn't have any actual bats yet, he could only work on fielding. He unsuccessfully tried to convince them that defense was more important than offense. "We could score a million runs," he explained. "But if the other team scores a million runs in return, it doesn't matter how good we hit if we can't defend ourselves on the field."

Fielding was boring as all hell and they were jonesing to hit stuff. Plus, about two dozen of them had to share four used gloves between them, so drills like picking up grounders or catching fly balls took forever. First, they had to wait their turn, not an easy task for this easily distracted, instantly triggered group. They separated into cliques, mostly based on academy or grade. The nicer, quiet kids, like Yoshie, Grateshka, Claudia, Genesis, and Johanna were all in sixth grade together and clung to each other. Heaven hung with her girl Aleiri. The rough and rowdy clique of Robin, Alexa, and Achelin thought they ruled the team but so did the girlier eighth-graders Rashell, Alcielis,

Kimberly, and Nicky (plus Gheynee because she was her sister and guilty by association). "The older girls were really mean," says Precious, who, by the way, along with her cousin Shiadiamond, had been dubbed "the twin terrors" in Chris's mind.

"Nicky liked to intimidate people," Johanna confirms. "She liked when people feared her. I don't know why." Nobody knew that when Nicky wasn't at softball, her mother was beating the crap out of her.

The biggest problem among the girls was that they "talked behind each other's backs all the time," Precious adds. They also talked smack to each other's faces. So when their turn finally came up in fielding drills, they often had to pass off a glove to somebody they had a beef with. That did not go smoothly.

"Ew, her hands is sweaty!" dainty Alcielis would say. "I'm not touching this!"

Or Kimberly would whine, "This wasn't the glove I used last time!" To make sure it didn't happen again, she wrote her name on Chris's personal glove in baby blue permanent marker. He was not pleased.

The gloves caused a lot of drama. Kimari apparently had a death wish and threw one at the back of Nicky's head. "Kimari was playing with a ball that Astacio didn't want us to play with," Nicky remembers. "I was like, 'Can you please put the ball down?'" See, teacher's pet. "She was not listening to what I was saying. So I said, 'I'm not gonna speak to you for no reason.' I took the ball and started running and she hit me with the glove. So I turned around and punched her and she fell to the ground. We started to fight. Astacio was very mad about that. I explained that she threw the mitt at me. I was trying to help her and she was not listening. I didn't mean to escalate that quickly but she hit me with a glove. In that moment of my life, anything triggered me and got me upset. Like, do not throw stuff at me."

Kimari never came back to practice but her mother did the next day and reamed Chris out. "This is not a safe environment for my daughter!" she complained.

She wasn't wrong.

Local gangs and other hooligans swarmed the practices, bothering the girls and trying to intimidate Chris. "They stared me down," he says. "I'd be like, 'Get your boys out of here!' They didn't back down. I didn't want to get shot, so I'd say, 'Girls, get your stuff, let's go." Sometimes they didn't even have time to grab their gear. Out of nowhere, in broad daylight, "We'd hear gunshots and see boys running around in the street," Yoshie remembers. "We'd just leave our stuff on the playground and take off. It would happen all the time and it would suck. We couldn't practice. Whenever you're around 22, you're not sure what would happen next."

Frederick, the AP of security, wore a bulletproof vest under a hoodie during dismissal. "The outside gangs tried to intimidate me, say 'Yo, mister,' right in my face.' I'd say, 'I don't know who you think you're talking to but I'll get your ass locked up. If you hit me, I'll take you down in one second. Just because I work here doesn't mean I don't know how to play.' If they think you're crazy they don't mess with you. My wife thought I was crazy. She was like, 'You have to get out of there, you're going to get killed.'"

And yet, with that going on, a team of young girls was practicing on the playground with nothing to protect them besides Chris and his wonky walkie-talkies, which rarely worked. "They were like my daughters and I felt like I had to protect them," Chris says. So, after the first few weeks, outdoor practices were temporarily suspended. He moved the girls into the gym, which was even more mind-numbing because there was only so much they could do inside without equipment. Plus, they had to share the space with a bunch of other after-school clubs.

Chris asked the principal for money for a dry-erase whiteboard so he could draw on it while he lectured the team on the rules and fundamentals of softball. He got a "we'll see," which really meant "not in this lifetime." So Chris made his own makeshift whiteboard out of squares of cardboard and taped them up on the gym wall. He drew a diamond on it and let the girls pepper him with questions about the game of softball. The next day, Chris found the whiteboard on the floor ripped to shreds, obviously by the after-school basketball program that came in after them.

"Something new? Fuck you, I'm gonna destroy it," Chris explains. "That's the mentality."

The next time he saw the basketball boys, the same ones who always bent the rims and tore up his beloved whiteboard, Chris walked out of his office with a pair of scissors. When the basketball rolled near him, he picked it up and stabbed it.

"Whoa, what the *fuck*, mister?" they cried.

"You want to play basketball? Go ahead." He threw the deflated ball back to them, and it rolled lopsided down the court due to the scissors sticking out of it. "You mistreat all the other equipment. Why is this so important now?" They all looked at him like he was totally loco. (In future PE classes, as a threat, Chris held that basketball over his head whenever he collected equipment. He wanted his students to know he was capable of taking away their most precious commodity at any time, by any means necessary. To this day, the scissors are still in that basketball.)

Without a field or equipment, and limited time in the gym, Chris had to get creative to teach the basics. "It was a lot of 'pretend' stuff," he says. "*Pretend* you have a glove or a bat, *pretend* this is a real field. If you hit the ball, *pretend* this is how you run to first base. *Pretend* this is how you cover the bases in the field if they get a hit."

It was so pointless and monotonous, the girls stopped caring. Some stopped showing up.

"The first few months we weren't dedicated," Rashell notes. "We would go to practice but we'd just sit on the floor and talk and laugh and take pictures. He couldn't get us to do nothing. He would take us to classrooms to learn and watch softball videos and we would fall asleep. We'd walk in and out like we did in class. We were on our phones or falling asleep. We wanted to practice, not watch no videos. I was like, 'I'm going home.' We didn't really want to do it. We didn't want to go through the process."

Chris was aware that if he didn't act fast, he'd lose the girls. He'd been winging it and he was failing them. He had to step up his game. The team needed a name because there wasn't one single mascot for the school. He thought including them in the selection process might be fun. He regretted asking.

"BAB! Bad-Ass Bitches!"

"Dirty South!"

"Oh Dee!"

"Funky Fresh!"

"Thot Police!"

"Tizzurnt!"

"Chuchifritos!"

"Bronx Flow!"

"Hookie Party!"

"Flippity Floppity Floo!"

"Snacky Smores!"

"FNT! Fear No Team!"

"Southside Barbies!"

"Lady Yankees!"

Hmm, Lady Yankees wasn't bad, since the MLB team was right down the street and most of the girls had grown up in the shadow of the legendary stadium. But Chris wanted them to have their own identity. So he made an executive decision—from now on, they were officially called the mighty "Lady Tigers."

"It's aight," Gheynee grumbled.

The name meant jack if they couldn't play anyway. To be a real team, the Lady Tigers had to get equipment. He went back to donorchoose.org and networked hardcore on the site. He wrote heartfelt campaigns, and posted adorable pictures of his players.

Lady Tigers Swinging for Success!
   Needed:
   • *Heater Softball Pitching Machine & 24' Batting Cage, $872*
   • *16 gloves and catchers gear, $576*
   • *Spring and resistance trainers, big mouth portable net, $917*

Help us become champions! Our very first girls' softball middle-school team who dare to start from the bottom needs a batting cage to take us to the top! My young middle-school students have endured in life what most adults have yet to experience but they still have the courage to continue on.

Battling an environment plagued with poverty, drugs, and gang violence, our school strives to provide these students with hope and inspire them to succeed.

The resources donated to the Lady Tigers will give our girls the opportunity to swing for the fences using a standard softball, which is something we currently can't do due to space limitations. They will have the opportunity to perfect their swing and become fierce competitors, giving them the chance to be true champions!

The obstacle of not having a safe space or a home playing field will no longer exist.

At home, after hours, he'd go online for hours researching charitable companies and email whomever he could find to beg for money. He doesn't remember how, but he finally got connected with a very wealthy philanthropist named Elsa Brule, who helped Chris raise an astounding $5,000. The Lady Tigers were back in the game.

The new equipment really boosted the girls' morale and drive. The first pieces to arrive were a couple of bats and the stationary batting machine. Chris could finally teach them a correct batting stance and how to swing, hopefully at the ball and not each other:

- Feet shoulder-width apart
- Knees slightly bent
- Hands together
- Choke up on the bat
- Elbow up
- Bat perpendicular to the ground

- Keep your eye on the ball
- Step toward the pitcher
- Swing level
- Swing through

The machine was ideal because it was like hitting off a tee but without balls flying all over the place. That seemed too dangerous at this point. Chris was already worried they'd let go of the grip while swinging, and the bat would be become a projectile missile. Nicky refused to put her hands together, so she had an awkward batting stance, but it worked for her. She also had a little Darryl Strawberry-like shimmy that reminded Chris of himself as a kid. Johanna and Grateshka had powerful, hard swings, and Alexa's batting stance was just "scary," Chris recalls. "She had a look in her eye like she was about to kill the ball. She wasn't scared."

Kimberly couldn't swing a bat to save her life, "but I admired her persistence," Chris says. Surprisingly, Yoshie, the natural athlete, was not picking it up at all. She kept swinging and missing. Whiff. Whiff. Whiff. It puzzled Chris, and he vowed to work exclusively with her on hitting.

When the new gloves rolled in, it was a grabby free-for-all. The mean girls claimed the "best" gloves for themselves and refused to share.

"This one is mine," Nicky said. "I'm not giving it up."

"Can I put my name on it?" Heaven asked.

Chris was already peeved that "KIMBERLY" had been permanently tattooed on his mitt. "Don't write your name on the gloves," he demanded. "They're not yours."

Not only did they write their names on the gloves, they hid them in their backpacks. "They wanted to make sure they got to use the same glove at the next practice." So many gloves were taken home, before long, they were short on gloves again. "We didn't have enough. We never had enough. We probably never will."

The resistance bands were a less popular plaything among the girls. Chris attached them to the fence or the wall, put them around the girls' waists, and had them run as fast as they could. "I wanted to increase their speed after hitting the ball and running to first base, because they were very slow." Chris informed them that they needed to get to first base within three seconds. When he did running drills, he'd time them with a stopwatch and sigh loudly as they moseyed down to first base in four, five, six, ten seconds.

"You need to get down there in three seconds or you'll be out!"

"But it's only two seconds off!" Heaven, the hard-headed lawyer, argued.

"But those *two* seconds are *crucial*!" he clapped back, exasperated. Her mouth was not only reckless, Chris thought to himself, her mouth was ridiculous.

At first, the shiny new object was fun, but eventually they remembered to hate it because it meant "exercise." The only girls who really took advantage of it were Nicky and Yoshie. "Yoshi was the fastest by far and Nicky was a little speed demon. They always tried to race each other." After working out on the bungee, both beat the three-second mark down to first base.

Yoshie and Nicky weren't in the same grade, nor were they in the same academy or clique, but they bonded over being two of the best players. "Yoshie wasn't a show-off but she knew she was better than some of the girls," Chris says. "Nicky could play. She was really good. She could catch, she could throw. She got frustrated when people weren't athletic like her. That's why her and Yoshie connected, because they both could play."

Competition pushed them to be better players. They also competed for Chris's attention. Nicky noticed that Coach Astacio gave Yoshie special treatment and she didn't like it. He'd whip out his phone and take videos of Yoshie throwing and batting, so they could watch and dissect her form later.

"Why you recording her?" Nicky complained. "Why can't you record us?"

Yoshie was a gifted athlete and a hard worker, but she was having trouble putting all of her new softball skills together cohesively. Chris saw great potential in her, as a player and a person, and he admits he focused on her a little more than others and didn't even try to hide it. "They were jealous that she had so much talent in such a little body. I was always gassing her up. I used to tell all the girls, 'Why can't you be like Yoshie? You're the oldest you're supposed to be the example. Yoshie is leading by example.'"

Alcielis hated that. "We all know you love her," she whined.

He really did. Yoshie came to practice every day, she did not miss a single one, and she actually wanted more training. "Can I come during lunch for extra help?" she asked. Chris had his eyes on his one prize. Yoshie made him excited to show up every day and be a real coach.

Resentful, Nicky and Rashell tried to intimidate Yoshie. "They'd just stand right in front of me and talk about me," she says. "Nicky was all, 'She's not even that good!' I knew I was good but I was also shy." Still, Yoshie was not threatened by either of them, and if they were trying to get a rise out of her, it wasn't going to work. Not that day, not ever. "I remember this one time I was walking into class and bumped into this girl who was a total drama queen. I ignored her but she kept waiting for me to touch her. I said, 'You're gonna be waiting a long time because I'm not gonna touch you and get in trouble for stupidity.' I just ignored a lot of things. I didn't really have trouble. But if I did, I told the teachers. I would snitch. [Other girls] would get mad but I didn't care."

The girls on the Lady Tigers almost came to blows daily. "It was like a lot of like hate, a lot of animosity," Heaven says. "Everybody had their own crew. Nobody liked each other. We all thought one of us was better than another."

"The team was supposed to keep us calm and humble," Alex adds. "When we were together it was the exact opposite. Nobody put pride aside to practice. Everybody was following each other like monkey-see, monkey-do."

There were a garden variety of "beefs" happening "on the regular," as the kids would say. "There was a lot of girls that was dealing with personal issues at home," Robin explains. "They come to school and take it out on anyone they see."

There were old beefs that had yet to be settled.

"I fought Robin in the yard in seventh grade," Rashell says.

There were beefs between the eighth-graders and the sixth-graders.

The new kids on the block were terrified of older girls. "Rashell was the type of person if you tell her something she's gonna punch you," Johanna claims.

"I felt like I was bullied," Grateshka adds. "I was so small and I remember seeing all these girls like Alcielis and Nicky and being scared." Nicky doesn't dodge it. "I was tiny, too," she says, "but I made up for it with my mouth."

There were beefs between the academies.

Academy beefs were as much about gang mentality as about being smart and dumb. "I don't care what academy you're from! We are one team! I don't care what kind of BS you have in the school, we're not divided!" Chris would shout into the abyss, falling on deaf ears.

There were beefs between the two "popular" groups.

The group led by Robin and Alexa didn't mesh with Rashell and her squad. "Everybody came at me and my clique," Nicky says. "We was always in drama, we was always getting in trouble. It was really crazy."

"I didn't talk to anyone other than Alexa," Robin corroborates. "I spoke when spoken to."

There were beefs between best friends.

This was middle school, after all. "There were arguments every day," Kimberly says. "You'd be friends one second then fighting the next second. If one person stopped talking to you, all of them would stop talking to you."

When Heaven and Aleiri came to the Lady Tigers they were tight, but their friendship fell apart when Heaven started bonding with Nicky and Gheynee. "She talked bad about them and I was uncomfortable. Then when I wasn't there, she talked bad about me to them. I didn't want to associate with someone who talked about me when I wasn't there."

Heaven and Aleiri started arguing so much, Mr. Toro stepped in and tried to fix it. "They were having some sort of disagreement, so I grabbed Aleiri and I'm like, 'Just look at her and smile, and let's see what she does.' Heaven came over and was like, 'Oh, you think it's funny? At least I wasn't kissing my boyfriends in the staircase!' I couldn't believe it. I said, 'Y'all are good friends, you shouldn't have to beef.'"

"A lot of time I didn't want to be on the team because of the tension," Heaven reveals.

There were beefs between sisters.

Kimberly and Claudia were close as kids, but in middle school they barely talked at all. Kimberly was "the brain" and Claudia was "boy crazy." Kimberly stayed out of trouble, but Claudia always had issues with the gang boys. She'd date them and dump them, and when she stopped talking to them, they came for her.

Sisters Gheynee and Nicky were being torn apart by violence at home, and it spilled onto the team. "Our mother made us feel miserable to each other," Gheynee says. "We just hated each other and fought a lot. We physically fought, too."

"They were crazy," Heaven confirms. "They could not be together. They was always arguing against each other."

There were beefs between the good players and the bad players.

There was zero tolerance for the girls who couldn't play well. "It was really corny," Heaven explains. "Girls would throw shade, like, 'That's not how you bat! What are you doing here? You don't even know how to play softball!' Everybody always tryna make others feel bad."

"When I first entered the softball team I felt like I was the worst and it was such a bad feeling," Grateshka says. "I didn't have any skills in softball and they were making fun. I was so scared, I couldn't even catch a ball. Then when I did something wrong, they just laughed. They were not supportive at all."

There were beefs over boys.

Those were the worst and the ones Chris couldn't tolerate. All the girls had their eyes on Wilson, the cutest guy in the whole school. He was dating Alcielis because she was the prettiest girl in school. "A lot of boys liked me but I only had one boyfriend," and "we were the most popular couple," she claims, but Achelin liked him, as well, which caused a lot of corny and petty fights. Back then, some of the girls had their "forever boyfriends," usually a guy on the baseball team, and because it was middle school, they'd be on and off, on and off. Still, that was her "forever boyfriend," so he was off limits. Even when they weren't together, the hard-and-fast rule was, "Don't talk to him, don't even look at him." Well, that didn't happen much.

There were beefs for absolutely no reason at all.

The Lady Tigers may have stunk at softball but they were hall of famers at "grilling," aka rolling their eyes at each other. Getting grilled sounds harmless but in their world, it's very dangerous. It's a sign of major disrespect and could instigate a nasty, claws-out physical fight. "What that bitch lookin' at?" had become the team's unofficial slogan. In the South Bronx, looking at someone "a certain type of way" could get you killed. So it was no joke when a girl on the team got grilled. "You can't just look at somebody, they just feel offended by it," Grateshka says, then notes, "which didn't work for me because eyes were made for looking."

A few team members like Grateshka and Yoshie were able to stay out of the fray. "I used to see them in the hallway and I'd smile because I didn't want to be rude but I'd just walk right past my teammates," Yoshie remembers.

"I got along with everybody, even with drama going on," Achelin brags. Some were clueless, like space cadet Claudia or aspiring singer Mayoli, who was always off in her own world doing runs or listening to music on her headphones. But for the most part, everybody else was mixing it up endlessly, ruthlessly.

"We were a bunch of bad-ass girls who hated each other," Rashell sums it up. "We didn't know what we were there for. All we were doing was fighting each other and not even playing. It was like, 'Fuck you, Astacio. I'm not going to practice.'"

Chris spent an inordinate amount of time at practice screaming himself hoarse. "At the beginning, I tried to talk, but I wasn't getting anywhere. They were not trying to hear it." He found himself repeating everything—drills, rules, and instructions—multiple times because there was rarely a moment when the girls were willing to stand side-by-side as one group. He'd explain something to one clique, then have to walk over and say the exact same thing to the next clique, then to the next clique, and so on. It was like brokering Middle East peace talks, but harder and with less cooperation.

So far, Chris felt like a complete failure as a coach. The Lady Tigers were a disaster. They definitely were not acting like ladies, and they definitely did not resemble anything that looked like a team.

He had to find a way to bring them together.

Chapter Ten

AN ULTIMATUM

"Give a girl the right shoes and she can conquer the world," Marilyn Monroe once said.

Or her own softball jersey.

Chris had been told countless times the school had no money in the budget for the Lady Tigers, but he had an important ally on his side—Richard Frederick. As assistant principal of security, Frederick had some say about the funds that were allocated to the LEAP programs. A few months after Chris started the team, Frederick convinced the powers that be to float him $1,500 for uniforms. He did it for altruistic reasons: he was behind Chris's passion project 1,000 percent, but Frederick himself wanted the team to exist to keep the most troubled girls occupied in a healthier, more productive way. Instead of suspending them, he sent them to Chris. "It became an intervention for me," Frederick says. "Like, 'Hey, do you have any room on the team? I've got this girl, she's a pain in the ass, I think she needs to be on the team.' Astacio would say, 'I really don't have space, but I'll take her.'"

The Lady Tigers basically became an alternative to the SAVE room. The SAVE room (an acronym for Safe Schools Against Violence in Education) at 22 was basically a windowless dungeon in the basement where a terrified teacher babysat the worst behaved students. "At some point, I told Frederick I had enough girls," Chris remembers. "He said he knew I could handle the 'bad' ones. I didn't see them as bad, just misunderstood."

So, because of Frederick, the Lady Tigers got uniforms. Real ones. Wilson brand black jerseys with white piping, orange numbers on the back, orange "Lady Tigers" logo designed by Chis emblazoned across the front, and matching black pants. Of course, the coach had to run the colors and design by style guru Alcielis. "Everything had to be cute for us to wear it," she insisted. Of course, the uniforms showed up a little wonky. They were made of really thick hot heavy polyester, the stirrup socks were mismatched and bizarrely random, several jerseys had the same number, 19, and the pants came in adult sizes. But when the girls saw them, dramatically laid out on the gym floor in a circle, their eyes lit up like it was Christmas morning. It wasn't often that they got gifts like this out of nowhere. It was a rare treat and they didn't even try to play it cool, they were bugging out and squealing with delight.

Naturally, the eighth-graders stepped up and grabbed what they wanted first, calling dibs on the size small pants and the best socks. All the girls tried their new uniforms on over their clothes and paraded around on the basketball court like it was a runway at Fashion Week in Bryant Park. Alcielis wanted to make sure she selected the tightest pants and ran into the bathroom to try them on. When she came out, Chris raised his eyebrows. "That's a little too tight for you, no?"

"I like it like this," she insisted.

"I think you need a medium."

"No, no, no, no, no, this is good!" she said, laughing.

There was a minor skirmish between the number 19s, with each proclaiming, "I'm the real number 19" or "No I'm the real number 19!" But besides that incident, and some players like Yoshie resigned to wear their own pants because the mediums were too big, the Lady Tigers were all about their dope uniforms. They strutted around, took selfies, and posted pics of themselves all over social media.

"Oh my God, I look so good," Alexa said.

"You do, bro," Nicky agreed. "I look so foine, too!"

Nicky and Yoshie picked number 11 and number 12. They liked having numbers right next to each other, and would give each other a knowing look, a "we-know-we-are-the-two-best-players-on-the-team" look, and fist-bump.

The uniforms were a big morale boost, but once the batting cage, bats, and helmets came in, "it all became real for the girls," Chris says. The DonorsChoose.org campaign had pulled through and raised $872 for a 24-foot-long Heater Softball Batting Cage Combo with Pitching Machine. Chris spent a week retrofitting it in the gym, working late into the night. Charisse was annoyed, not only because he was away from his family working extra hours for no pay, but he also spent $200 of their own money on extra materials, like 10-gallon buckets of sand for the stakes, some wood, and a drill. He also bought a saw to create structures to hold the stakes in the buckets and high-tension ropes to secure the nets to the wall.

When Chris unveiled the completed batting cage, the girls were in complete awe. The only problems were that the helmets messed up their hair, and girls claiming bats as their own. There was a lot of "That's my bat!" "We all have to share it!" Everything had been make-believe up to this point. The team had been a joke. The batting cage was proof that the team was not a joke, in fact it was so legit, their coach got them something really fancy and elaborate. He'd invested in them. And Chris refused to let anyone else use it—the batting cage was for the Lady Tigers only. "The boys had everything and the girls had nothing," he explains. "This was theirs."

Even Mrs. Holloway came to check out their new toy. She tried to stop by their practices as much as she could to hype up the girls, but once they moved inside it was hard for her to go up all the stairs to get to the gym. "Everybody knew she wasn't a healthy lady, so when she dropped by it was a big deal to the girls."

Once the cage went up, the team had another new admirer lurking around. Chris had tried so hard to pull Angie into the team but she'd always said, "Hell no!" Now, she was hanging around practice a lot, watching the girls take turns hitting in the cage.

"Yo, this is cool, Astacio," she'd say.

Chris let her loiter because he still wanted her on the softball team. "Why don't you come talk to me about it?" he'd ask her whenever she came by. "Nah," she said. Angie was still on the basketball team but he could feel her contempt for the Lady Tigers slowly melting away.

"I like softball," Angie said one day, as she watched Johanna crush the ball in the cage.

"Y'all should come out," Chris replied nonchalantly, before getting waved off.

The next time she came by, Angie told Chris confidently, "Softball is my sport."

Deep down, she really wanted to play but she wasn't "no quitter." Her basketball coach knew she'd been sniffing around the softball practices and called her a traitor. She didn't like that. Angie put 110 percent into everything she did. Just because she watched the softball team play didn't mean she wasn't dedicated to basketball anymore.

The next time Angie showed up at the batting cage, Chris went in for the kill.

"Hey, I ordered an extra jersey for you," he lied. He had extras, especially number 19s.

Angie quit the basketball team the next day and became a Lady Tiger. "Astacio was really coming for me," she says. "Not many people do that. He made me feel wanted and important. So I was like, 'You know what? I'm gonna join.'"

The uniforms apparently had magical powers. They were so cherished and treasured, some of the girls, including Robin, made it part of their everyday attire. Which was now against the rules. Frederick had recently instituted a wide-ranging swath of new safety measures, including a uniform policy—for girls, that meant khaki pants or skirt, and an orange, white, or black collared shirt. He also banned cellphones during school hours, bandanas, and hoodies, and implemented an ID card system, door alarms, locked bathrooms, and hall sweep teams to make sure every floor, door, and exit were covered. "We stuck to it," Frederick says. "It was about consistency, not the flavor of the month rules."

The Lady Tigers jerseys were black, but they didn't qualify as part of the approved uniform. Gheynee got in trouble a bunch of times for bucking the policy. "I was always in detention for not wearing the uniform." Frederick strictly enforced it. "Why? Because we're a team. Teams wear uniforms," he explains. "If you're on the New York Yankees, you wear a uniform. If Derek Jeter came to a game in jeans and a hoodie, was he allowed to play? No. You want to play? Wear the uniform."

The softball uniforms and the batting cage unified the Lady Tigers, for sure, but in a way Chris hadn't anticipated. They terrorized the school, the other students, and the teachers. "When they all finally became a team, which took months, they were like a gang," he says. "Anyone not part of the team didn't matter. Everyone else was invalid. If anyone stepped to them, look out. They walked the halls like they ruled the school. They thought they were untouchable."

Robin and Rashell brought their girls together in the same way mob dons from different families consolidate power. They were both big girls who had a big presence and even bigger mouths. You could hear them coming from a mile away. Robin's behavior was in your face and impulsive, like the time she opened the SAVE room door and threw in a stink bomb. She also had no filter. If a teacher looked funny, she'd tell her straight up and throw in a "Get the fuck out of my face" or "Fuck you, bitch" for good measure. Rashell's vibe was more subtly scary and manipulative. She liked to brag about how easy it was for her to rattle a teacher. "I'm bored today, let's make her cry," she'd tell her squad.

The Lady Tigers were reckless and running wild, especially Nicky. Chris had to retrieve her from the dean's office almost every day. "It was always Nicky, Nicky, Nicky," he says. "I got tired of seeing her face in the office."

The season had barely begun, and the Lady Tigers already had a rotten reputation. As their coach, Chris was held responsible for their actions. Suddenly, anything they did wrong in school would go straight to Astacio. There was no giving them a chance or even detention. It was, "Your girl did this and this." Every teacher complained about them. He was bombarded with messages about his players cutting class, being disruptive and vulgar, and not doing their work. "The other teachers got on my case a lot. They wanted to see a turnaround in their behavior instantly. I told them, 'You can't expect them to become perfect angels in a few weeks. It's a process.'"

Most teachers weren't patient enough for that process. Everywhere he turned, he heard, "You need to get a handle on your girls, you need to tell them to respect us." The teachers didn't do anything themselves to try to earn respect. If the girls acted out, the teachers immediately called Chris down to their classes to pacify them and defuse the situation. Instead of appreciating his Tiger-whispering skills, they started to resent Chris for being the only one they'd listen to. They seemed weirdly jealous. "I would be in trouble and they'd call him to come calm me down," says Rashell. "This was even me not liking him. He'd say, 'Come on, Ra-shell, speak to me, tell me what's going on. What is it that's wrong with you? I could help you.' I'd say, 'My name is Ra-chel!'

"'Then why does it have an S?'

"I'd say, 'I don't know, ask my mom!' And we laughed."

It wasn't all that funny, though. Chris's reputation was on the line, too. He was staking his career on these girls, what if they cost him his job? He worried the rest of the staff thought he babied the girls too much. So he got a little tougher. He became a helicopter coach, hovering over and around them whenever possible. Every day, Chris did his "rounds." In the morning, he stood at the school entrance waiting for Alexa, who was late every day with an elaborate excuse. "Always a story," Chris sighed, as he walked her to class. He wanted to make sure her "mouth was in control" because she had major attitude with teachers. "My main problem was talking back," Alexa admits.

During his lunch or free periods, Chris wandered around the school looking for the rest of his players, just to make sure they were where they were supposed to be. "Gheynee went to school just to cut class; Heaven was always running from a dean; Nicky and Alcielis were in the stairwells; Robin, Precious, and Shiadiamond were in the basement; and Rashell just liked to leave," he says. "She had a stolen pass in her book bag she used all day long."

When Chris confronted them, they often claimed they'd been kicked out of class. So he'd lead them back and ask their teachers right in front of them, "Did you kick Gheynee out of class?"

"How can I throw them out if they were never here?" was a common answer.

Chris didn't discriminate. He was on top of the good girls, too. Angie was known for wandering the hallways, but she was a smart little girl who always had a pass. "He saw me once," Grateshka adds. "I was on my way to the bathroom with no pass and he literally rushed me into class to prevent me from doing something else."

Chris had no boundaries for his new babysitting job. He'd walk into their classrooms and sit down to embarrass them or just walk by and peer at them through the window. What he saw usually ticked him off. "Everybody was on their phone. Nobody was learning," Kimberly describes. "We controlled the class, the teacher couldn't control us. It was a whole party in the back. My math class had a sub every day. He passed out a worksheet and one kid collected them, ripped them up, and threw them in the garbage. He was like, 'We don't do work when the sub is here.'"

If Chris saw a Lady Tiger acting up or playing around through the door window, he'd knock on the glass, give her a stern look, and point at her to sit down. Then he'd pretend to leave, go back a few seconds later, and see if she was back to her old tricks. If so, he'd go into the classroom and ask the teacher if he could talk to the girl outside in the hallway.

"You think I'm stupid?" he'd ask. "You think I'm not gonna look again?" That usually got a laugh and a promise to go back inside and behave.

Chris rarely felt like he had any leverage for disciplining the out-of-control students at 22. But on the softball team, that was evolving. He was slowly getting to know the girls, and the more he knew, the easier it was to figure out the best way to reach them. Could be a hug, could be taking away time in the cage, could be an old-fashioned threat of telling their parents.

When Heaven sassed teachers, she'd say, "I don't care, you can call my mom!" Chris figured out that she was bluffing. Heaven was petrified of her mother's wrath. She did not want anyone to call her mother. That was the reason she was always running from the dean, she was desperate to avoid a call home. Once, Chris found another player who came from an abusive home hiding outside behind a tree in a park across the street. He snuck up behind her and smacked her playfully on the back of the head. "Want me to call your mom?" he said. "She'll do much worse."

As Chris grew closer to the girls, he got more clues about their lives outside of 22, and in turn, their families. When one of his players got in trouble, he usually dealt with her mom, because almost none of them had a father in the picture, though Robin's grandmother was called down to the school almost every day. "Everyone was scared of Redell, even the adults," Chris recalls. "It was like, 'Robin's grandma is coming in, uh-oh!'"

A parade of parents came through Chris's office, and, just like the other teachers, they expected the softball team to instantly "fix" their children. Alexa was going to practice, but it finished at 6 P.M., and she wasn't getting home until 10 P.M. Sometimes she didn't go home at all and would arrive directly to school the next morning, always late, which was grounds for the school to call ACS. Her mother scheduled an emergency meeting with Chris and a dean. When they asked Alexa where she was in those long windows after practice, she wouldn't budge. "I'm not telling nobody nothing."

"Alexa, please know we are trying to help you," Chris said.

"Why?" she answered, stone-faced. "I just didn't go home."

"Alexa, what are you doing after practice?"

She paused. "I'm just not going home."

After that, Chris made sure his players went straight home after practice. "I had the girls' numbers and asked them to text me when got home. Some did. Some didn't. Some lied."

Like the time Mayoli, the budding singer, told Chris she was auditioning for Kidz Bop, the massively popular children's group that does covers of pop songs. That was a lie. She was smoking weed with the other kids on her block. That wasn't her only lie. After the first few weeks of softball, she stopped showing up to practice. Chris thought she quit because she had no interest in softball. He would see her in school and ask, "Mayoli, when am I gonna see you at practice?" She would always say she was doing something with her mom. A few months later, her mother came to see Chris during parent-teacher conferences. "I have a problem with your team," she told him. "My daughter practices too much and too late."

"Who is your daughter?" Chris asked.

"Mayoli."

"She hasn't been to practice in months," Chris said.

"She's been to practice every day! *Todo dias! Todos dias!*"

"No, she hasn't." Chris showed her the attendance records he was thankfully required to keep.

"But she said she was practicing until 9 o'clock at night!"

"I have not seen her." Mayoli was not at practice. "I found out later she was doing 'very bad things,' which, understanding her past, was smoking weed, drinking, and having sex," Chris says.

She wasn't the only girl using the Lady Tigers as a front for nefarious activities. Natalie was removed from the team after lying for two months that she'd been going to practice. When her mother confronted Chris, he ripped into her. "It's not my fault," he snapped. He'd sent several letters home informing Natalie's parents that she'd been ditching practice and had left messages on her phone, and never received a response. All of a sudden, when she couldn't find her daughter, she wanted to talk. It angered Chris and he got snippy with her, which he rarely did with parents. But he didn't like her tone and retorted, "If you were paying attention, you'd know where your daughter was."

Lying was pervasive among this group. Nayeli showed up to practice one day with her hair shaved completely off. She claimed she had lice. The real story was that her mother cut it off after catching Nayeli stealing. In her defense, if the teachers found out her mom chopped off her hair, they were legally required to report it to ACS.

Chris's relationships with the moms were tricky. He didn't really know the extent of what was happening behind closed doors at any of their homes. At the same time, the girls were totally out of control. He was trying to build trust with his players and didn't want to "rat" on them to their parental figures. He wanted to be fair and diplomatic and neutral, but that wasn't always possible.

Nicky and Gheynee's mom got called down to the school frequently. One time she literally bumped into Nicky running down the hall, grabbed her arm, and yanked it hard. "Don't embarrass me!" she hissed. When she met with Chris, her personality magically transformed. She was charming and saccharine sweet and he bought it. "She put up a front," he remembers. "Nice on the outside until you really know her." If he'd been aware at that time about the beatings, he surely wouldn't have tried to mend the girls' relationship with their mother. "Her mom would come in and I knew how Nicky was back then. I'd tell her, 'To get better you have to meet your mom halfway.' I didn't know the backstory."

That fall, so many of the Lady Tigers were going through intense issues outside of school. "The softball time was the worst time," Nicky confirms. "We been dealing with mad stuff because of my mom. I fell into a depression a lot because that's when it started to happen more. One of the deans had to pull me out of class one day because I was crying nonstop."

Chris could not help getting sucked into their personal lives and problems. It was inevitable. It was unavoidable. And it was necessary. He was a human being with a working, beating heart and he felt it was his duty to help them. Sensing that he actually gave a shit about them, the girls started hanging out in his office, which they loved because it had a private bathroom attached. It was gross, but it was private. They opened up to him about a lot, except for abuse, because they knew that he'd have to report it. But they gabbed about everything else, from serious issues, like not getting along with their parents, to the tragi-comically TMI, like Rashell losing her virginity on her birthday.

"We know what you did this weekend!" Nicky blurted out one Monday afternoon.

Rashell got really upset. "How you gonna say that in front of Astacio? He's like my father!" Then she stormed out. Rashell had professed that she'd remain a virgin until at least high school and took pride that she was not like other promiscuous girls. Even though she was "bad" in terms of behavior, she did not want to be thought of as a "thot."

On the flip side, Alcielis didn't care if she was called a "thot." She liked it and embraced it. She thought she was more grown up than some of the teachers and "she wanted to be a woman," Chris explains. She didn't like being at home and thought it was acceptable to hang out until all hours with her boyfriend, Wilson, even though she was only thirteen. "I felt more mature than my age," Alcielis adds. "I don't know why. I've always been ten steps ahead of myself. I always felt like an old soul."

One day, some of the girls pulled Chris aside in the gym. "Alcielis is not going home after practice," they warned. She was planning on running away and Chris couldn't let that happen. As soon as practice ended, he drove her to her apartment with another teacher in the car and made sure she walked in the front door. The next day, he spoke to her mother on the phone.

"I don't know why Alcielis is like this, she's changed," she cried. "She goes to parties, she stays out late. I need help with her."

Chris had an idea who was to blame. Her mom was the one who bought her provocative clothing. He'd asked Alcielis, "Are those your mom's clothes?" And she'd say, "No, my mom gets me these clothes or she just gives me money. I get it myself."

Alcielis's look was her identity. Her style was influenced by her aunt and her grandma; they were always shopping and were very fashionable.

"I always loved that about them," she remembers. Alcielis bucked the uniform rules. Instead of a frumpy white shirt and khakis, she'd wear a white crop top or a lacey long sleeve shirt and khaki skinny jeans and the hottest sneakers. "It wasn't appropriate, but I didn't care what they said. That's who I was."

Alcielis didn't want to have any kind of rules, so going forward, that's exactly what Chris gave her. He told her that the next time she dressed too provocatively, she was suspended from the team. "If I see that shit, you're not playing." So Alcielis hid from Chris for a whole week. "I didn't see her, I thought she was sick," he laughs. "No one really talked about her. I said, 'Where's Alcielis?' Oh, she's here. She just wanted to wear what she wanted to wear."

Chris knew that Alcielis's mom really cared about her daughter, unlike some other parents he'd dealt with. Many of the girls had no father figure in their lives, like Alexa, Nicky, and Gheynee, or were dealing with daddy issues that were complex, like Heaven and Kimberly. After being on planet earth for thirteen years, Kimberly had just discovered that her birth father owned two cellphone stores right up the block and had three older half sisters and a half brother she'd never met. She wanted to see her father again, so she dropped by to see him. She was nervous. "He shook my hand like I was a customer or something," she remembers, "then gave me money." Kimberly liked getting money, who wouldn't? She didn't feel guilty about it—he had offered and she was "cashing out." But after visiting the store another five times, something didn't feel right and she stopped going. "I don't see him anymore."

Yoshie really struggled with missing her dad, who'd gone MIA after the birth of his son with his mistress/now wife. "I was extremely sad because of him," she says. "I didn't want to be home if he wasn't there." Her connection with her mom was at an all-time low. "She didn't understand the missing my dad thing." And yet her drinking during this time was the worst it had ever been. "She was extremely alcoholic. She was always in the street drinking or up all night drinking." Her mom took her and her little sister to house parties and they didn't get home until

5 A.M., sometimes on school nights. "One time I didn't get home until the next day at noon."

As a sixth-grader, Yoshie was too young to walk home through the South Bronx with her sister. She called her godmother to come get them, but all she got was, "Listen to your mother." In the meantime, her mom was in the next room partying, and often forgot to get the girls dinner. "She would take her time so sometimes we didn't have food. Other people would give me money to run to the bodega or we would have to wait until we got home. I'd be so hungry and tired. I had to watch over my little sister because my mom wasn't paying attention to us."

While the other girls were acting out, Yoshie suffered in silence. Chris noticed that she bottled her feelings up to a point then exploded in anger. "There was only one time I screamed at Yoshie and embarrassed her," Chris says. "She acted like an idiot and I yelled at her. She didn't speak to me for a week." He also noticed cut marks on her arms (as well as Genesis's arms) and tried to talk to her about it, but she was a closed book.

Yoshie had been yearning for a father figure and Chris was it. He taught her about life, he was interested in her life, and, most important, he was always there for her. Even in the middle of the night. One time, she called him four times at 3 A.M. Her mom's ex-boyfriend was banging on the door drunk and Yoshie was "afraid for her life." Chris reported the incident to the school social worker, as he was required to do, who called ACS. Yoshie was mad at him, and her mom was furious at both of them, but Yoshie understood why he did it. "He cared about me."

Now that the girls on the team had his phone number, they called and texted him constantly about their drama in and out of school. "Every day it was something," he remembers. "I couldn't breathe. They were calling me on Saturday nights saying, 'A fight is gonna happen Monday!' I was like, 'It's the weekend. Don't call me!'"

"I remember him being exhausted because he didn't have a plan," Charisse recalls. She also did not like that the girls were calling him at all hours, let alone at all. Charisse expected them to gravitate to Chris as a father figure. "To be honest, I knew that was going to happen because he's just warm that way. He's really patient and he doesn't judge them. He talks to them as a regular person." Still, she was not okay with the constant contact.

"What the hell they have your number for?" she asked incredulously.

"Because I want to make sure they get home or can contact me if something happens! They live tough lives, I want to be there for them."

"You're not their father!"

"I know, but they need someone!"

Now that the girls knew he cared about them, they took advantage of his squishy sensitive heart and begged him for money and food. Nayeli, the girl with the shaved head, was always starving. She said her mom never cooked and she didn't have any lunch money. Chris brought the same lunch to school every day—a honey turkey sandwich on sesame bread, barbecue chips, and a ginger ale. It was the one meal he could count on to not make him nauseous. But lately, he'd been feeling sick to his stomach again, plus he felt awful that a child was going hungry. "Just take mine," he said, then gave her five bucks out of his wallet to boot.

Nayeli's godfather was a teacher at 22 and Chris asked to speak with him about her situation at home. "Yo, you gotta talk to her mother because she doesn't have food at home."

"Whoa, whoa, whoa, she's doing that again?"

"Doing what again? She asked me for money and food."

"She has a history of doing that, pretending that she don't have nothing to eat. Asking for money."

Turns out, Nayeli wasn't hungry. She was a pathological liar.

Yoshie came to school hungry a lot, too, but he was certain her situation was legit. Her mom didn't work and lived off public assistance. So he treated her to a pizza lunch down the block when he could. She kept asking him for more pizza lunches and he had to let her down easy. "Yo, Yoshie, this is costing me too much. I live on a budget and you're breaking my budget right now."

Charisse, again, was livid when she found out how much of their hard-earned cash Chris had been doling out to the Lady Tigers. "He was always putting everything out of pocket and that's just the way he is. Generous. You have to have a limit."

Unfortunately, that year brought out the worst in his wife and Chris knew it was 100 percent his fault. He'd become so fixated on saving the world that he forgot all that they had been through. He was spending money that they really didn't have. Charisse had to remind him that when they got married, they didn't have a dime to their names. They didn't even have rings. And when they saved enough money to get each other rings years down the road, they had to eventually pawn them so they could have money for food. There was a time when they got eviction notices for not paying the rent. Thankfully, their church had something called the "benevolence fund" and paid off three months of back rent. In Chris's heart, he felt that by saving these girls, he was saving his sister, something he could never do. Nothing was going to stop him from doing this. Not even his wife's fury.

Unintentionally, Chris had made his wife feel like she wasn't important anymore, as if their marriage and their family weren't priorities. They had an autistic little girl and a son showing early signs of anxiety, but Chris focused his energy on girls who weren't blood. On girls who were disrespectful and ungrateful at times.

He scheduled practice two to three times per week after school and on Saturdays, so Charisse was basically a single mother. She worked full-time in the billing department of a talent agency in Manhattan, did the cooking and cleaning, and handled everything else in the household. Cristina was still having issues, but Chris continued to come home late and barely interacted with her or Justin.

"I tried to include Cristina with my softball program as much as I could," Chris explains. "I felt that being around girls would help my little girl open up more. They treated her like their little sister and Cristina loved being around them. But since she was still a toddler, I couldn't always take her to practices. I had no one to watch her and Charisse refused to go the practices. I used to spend weekends taking her to the park, but it got to a point that I was so burnt out during the week that I didn't want to take her to the park. My wife would get so upset."

"It was like, 'Hey, we're here, too,'" Charisse recalls. But Chris was either too exhausted or busy writing emails and researching the Internet for donations to help out. "I got the shit end of the stick," she says. "We fought constantly and we got loud. I regret that we did that in front of Cristina."

Blinded by rage, it was hard for Charisse, a person on the outside, to see what Chris was trying to do. "You're not making our family a priority!" she fumed. "You have your softball family, but I'm not a priority! *This* is your first family."

"You're not being supportive of me! This is who I am!"

"You need to get your heart straight!"

"You don't understand what these girls are going through!"

"I do! But you have a little girl at home too! I'm not having it!"

Chris was always exhausted and just wanted to be home. But he wanted to be home and relax, "not hear someone's mouth," he says. As soon as Charisse began complaining and claiming that these girls had replaced his family, he admits he didn't hurry home after every practice. "Sometimes I sat in the car for a few minutes after I parked late at night because I wanted a few moments before the inevitable shouting match."

Charisse had other concerns, other than his physical and emotional absence. His safety. Now that Chris was deep into these girls' personal lives, he was obligated to report abuse to ACS, thereby causing home visits and enraging some of the families. Families, who were, or were connected to, gang members. "What if they try to find you?"

Charisse was torn. She knew 22 needed someone like her husband, someone who was going to step up and try to help. But at what cost? She felt it was totally unfair that she was put in the middle, that she was "the bad guy," and then felt guilty for being mad. Her family was collateral damage for changing these poor girls' lives.

"What kind of person would I be if I was just to stop helping them and end the team?" Chris asked. "This is something that makes these girls get up every morning, something that gives these girls a little bit of hope."

"Who are you talking about—them or you? It's your fault for putting yourself in that position to begin with. Someone is going to get hurt, and it's either those girls or your family."

"Charisse, how can I do that to them?"

After his sister Michelle's death, Chris felt immense guilt that he wasn't there for her. That he didn't help her when he could. Sure, he was young for the majority of her life, but he always felt he could have done more. She'd suffered her whole life and he hadn't cared, since he was focused so much on his own suffering. He promised himself that he wasn't going to be that selfish ever again. When he started softball, he didn't plan on pouring his whole life into the program. When he saw girls that were suffering and in desperate need of help, he felt this was his chance to right so many wrongs. "I couldn't save my sister, but maybe, just maybe, I could save these girls." But he tried to juggle it all: softball, his family, cancer. It just didn't work. Something had to change, but he couldn't just walk away from these girls. It wasn't right or fair to them. It's like reaching to someone who is trapped in a hole and then letting go midway, expecting them to get out themselves. "I know if my sister was alive, she wouldn't give up on them, as she never gave up on me."

Charisse knew all this and felt pressured to be supportive. But she didn't want to be supportive. She wanted a divorce. She gave Chris an ultimatum.

"It's them or me."

Chris refused to be yet another person who just gave up on these girls. The show would go on as long as there was breath in his body, though lately he noticed he'd been getting winded easily and would have to sit down a lot to catch his breath. One time at practice, he got really dizzy and fell. The girls all looked at him weird, but he just said he got up too fast.

The Christmas holidays were approaching, and he needed a break badly. He also felt like he and Charisse could work things out when they had more free time to really sit down and hash it out. "Please, God," he prayed, "just let me make it a few more weeks without any more drama. Amen."

He moved forward. He signed the Lady Tigers up for the Middle School Athletic League, comprised of teams from Manhattan, Brooklyn, and the

Bronx. Actual games against actual opponents were rapidly approaching in April and the girls were nowhere near ready. He had to focus. First, he officially named Rashell captain of the Lady Tigers, but he called her "the leader," so as to not ruffle any feathers. He brought her into his office and announced, "You're my leader." Rashell didn't like or want the title but he insisted. "I want you to take the role." She reluctantly agreed.

Sure enough, there was one angry bird.

"I was very serious about softball, I don't know why I wasn't captain," Nicky still wonders to this day. "I felt very hurt. I was one of the females who always wanted every girl to go to practice and do it right on the field."

Next, Chris amped up the intensity of the practices and made them more structured. At the start of each one, the team had a meeting to talk about the mistakes they'd been making in the batting cage and on the field. Next, leader Rashell went into the middle of a circle, and led the girls in warm-ups and stretching. If they weren't loud enough, Chris made them do it again. After that, they warmed up their arms catching and throwing before getting into the meat of the practice.

Chris assigned the most skilled players to work with the other girls, since he was only one person and couldn't help everyone at the same time. For offensive drills, he had girls alternate between the cage and hitting off the stationary hitting machine. For defensive drills, he split his time between the infield and the outfield, working with one for thirty minutes, then the other for thirty minutes. "Girls would get mad because they all wanted me to help them or watch their progress," he chuckles. After separate drills, he brought the girls together and assigned them either to positions or as runners. He hit the ball to different parts of the field to show them where to throw the ball in specific situations with certain runners on base.

On defense, he taught them to keep their heads down on grounders and use two hands to catch fly balls, "the same way my dad used to teach me." He explained the difference between force-outs and tag outs. How to cover the bases and make double plays—they loved the idea of double plays. You can get two people out at one time? That was dope. Harder to grasp was hitting the cutoff woman, backing up other players, rundowns, and the infield fly rule.

On offense, he showed them where to stand in the batter's box and how to run through first base on a single or round the bases on, God willing, anything more. "Touch 'em all!" he'd scream. The theory of tagging up was not computing. And forget about teaching them how to look to the first-base or third-base coach to wave them around. They did what they wanted. He skipped bunting because the girls had a hard enough time hitting. And he didn't touch sliding, visions of broken bones, bloody raspberries, and angry moms dancing in his head.

They got into a little bit of a groove, especially with the addition of Angie to the roster. She was an excellent player but also a positive influence—she worked hard and set a good example. "I'm dedicated. Even if we're just practicing, I'm giving my all, everything A-1." She stayed out of the beefs and gossiping. "They all fought over boys, they were all chatterboxes, and I was never in that, so they weren't mad at me because I was neutral." But the best part about Angie being on the team was her sense of humor. She was goofy and playful, a vibe sorely missing on the Lady Tigers. Just like at home when her parents fought, she was a peacekeeper. "I guess I was like that light to the team," she boasts. "Don't get it confused. There isn't another Angie in this world."

Angie had a big personality packed into her little body. She made the girls laugh with her one-off comments, random riffs, and off the cuff raps.

"Hamniky? Was your daddy in the hospital eating a ham and cheese sandwich when he named you?" she razzed Nicky.

"I knew a girl who looked like ravioli," she rapped. "I knew another girl who looked like a mouse and had a big butt."

"I'm not an Angelina," she explained to nobody in particular. "I don't even like going by Angie anymore. I go by 'Ange' now. Then it'll be 'An.' Then 'A.' I like 'Ace' better than anything. I be trying to correct it. It don't go nowhere, bro."

Angie made practice fun. At the end, the team came together in a circle again and Chris gave words of encouragement. They put their hands in the middle, or as close as they would allow themselves to get to anyone else, and yelled "LADY TIGERS" on three.

"ONE, TWO, THREE, LADY TIGERS!"

If they weren't loud enough, he screamed, "WHO ARE WE?"

"LADY TIGERS!" they screamed back.

Chris got chills whenever they did that. Months in, he was at last feeling like a real coach. He'd never been one before, so he didn't know what it was supposed to feel like or what he was doing. He didn't try to emulate any coach in particular. He admired Yankees skipper Joe Torre, the epitome of grace under pressure, but the Yankees were excellent and the Lady Tigers were not. If anything, he identified most with Samuel L. Jackson's character in the movie *Coach Carter*, based on the true story of a high school basketball coach who suspended his entire team for failing grades. But Chris didn't like the idea of copying anyone. He wanted to have his own style.

The one area where Chris needed serious help was learning how to throw a fast-pitch. He'd never thrown a fast-pitch before, and certainly didn't know how to teach someone else to do it. It was way more difficult than it looked and much more complicated than an overhand baseball pitch. The underarm windmill is an elegant and smooth motion, but also extremely technical. He had to get down the mechanics because if he taught it incorrectly, or asked a player to do it for too long, it could cause elbow or shoulder injuries. Consistency was key in fast-pitch, but it seemed impossible to master all of the steps—grip, build a load, backswing, rotate the arm, stride, release, wrist snap, hip close, follow through—without overthinking it all and hurling it over the backstop every time.

He watched every Amanda Scarborough and Jenny Finch video he could find and read Finch's book *Throw Like a Girl: How to Dream Big & Believe in Yourself.* Scarborough was an All-American pitcher for Texas A&M, and Finch, also a pitcher, is arguably the most famous women's softball player of all time—an All-American and college world series champ for the Arizona Wildcats, Olympic gold medalist, and pro for the Chicago Bandits. Her influence on the game is epic, from her record fifty-one straight college wins to her signature blond ponytail.

TOP LEFT: At 5 years old, Chris Astacio fell in love with baseball. TOP RIGHT: Chris and his mom Cecilia. BOTTOM: Chris and his father June at the park.

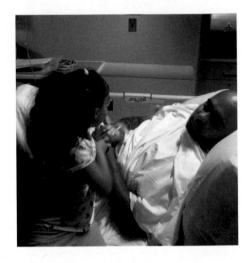

TOP LEFT: Chris and his late sister Michelle at his elementary school graduation. TOP RIGHT: Chris's daughter Cristina nursed him back to health after stomach cancer complications. BOTTOM RIGHT: Chris and wife Charisse on a hot date.

LEFT: Chris and Cristina walked for "Team Cristina" at an Autism Speaks march. BELOW: Cristina and her brother Justin when they were little.

ABOVE: With no funds for a whiteboard, Chris taught the fundamentals on squares of cardboard he taped to the wall. BELOW: Nicky always worked hard, especially in the batting cage Chris built. She loved the game.

ABOVE: Rashell and Yoshie improved their speed to first base working out on the bungee cords.
BELOW: Grateshka built up her monster swing on the stationary batting machine.

ABOVE: Rashell, here leading warm-ups, didn't like being team leader at first but grew into the role. BELOW: The girls were totally out of control on long subway rides to games and Chris was mortified.

ABOVE LEFT: Kimberly wasn't a good player but she'd rather be at softball than at home. ABOVE RIGHT: Yoshie, in ready position at third base, watched Johanna fire up a windmill on the mound. BELOW: Alcielis tried to boost her batting average, with Genesis on deck.

ABOVE: Alcielis and her cute pink glove, of course. BELOW: Chris tried to comfort an upset Angie during a game but she wasn't having it.

ABOVE: As the Lady Tigers got crushed, Chris, Achelin, and Heaven couldn't hide their disappointment. BELOW: The Lady Tigers accepted defeat (again) but, having learned the importance of sportsmanship, lined up to shake hands with their opponents.

LEFT: Robin pretended to be a human softball tee for her best friend Alexa. BELOW: Alexa, Rashell, and Alcielis bonded over the new gear donated through DonorsChoose.org.

TOP LEFT AND TOP RIGHT: Genesis and Alexa were the Lady Tigers' fearless catchers. BELOW: Angie may have been tiny but she was mighty at the plate.

ABOVE: The girls couldn't believe it was another blowout. They wanted to give up. BELOW: Mrs. Holloway, here in her signature sunglasses, was the Lady Tigers' biggest champion and urged them to keep the faith and keep pushing forward.

ABOVE LEFT: Yoshie couldn't buy a hit at first. ABOVE RIGHT: But by the end of the season, Yoshie became co-leader and the team's best hitter. BELOW: Kimberly's sister Claudia, a 6th grader, was protected by Rashell and the other 8th graders.

ABOVE: Refusing to give up, Rashell, Gheynee and her sister Nicky cheered on the Lady Tigers. BELOW: At first, these girls wouldn't even look at each other. Now, they were a team of sisters and a family.

ABOVE: The Lady Tigers took baby steps. A hit one game, a run the next. But a "W" was about more than the score. BELOW: The banquet table, signed by all the girls, and the trophy Chris handed out to each of them.

The Lady Tigers never gave up on themselves and their teammates. And that's why they were winners.

Chris Googled "how to throw a fast-pitch" and soaked up tons of videos on YouTube. "I was learning the game with them," Chris says. He showed the team a slow motion video of Scarborough pitching and they were in awe of her skill and stride. "I can't do that!" they howled. "Astacio, why don't you show us? Show us, Astacio!"

They knew he couldn't do it either. They were making fun of him. They liked to razz him about that and being bald. "Astacio, your head is looking mighty shiny today," Grateshka would tease. Well, *somebody* had to pitch. Chris set up a projector in the gym and put the video on a loop on the gym wall. The girls lined up and gave it a whirl. It was ugly, but two of the girls stuck out. Johanna picked up right where she left off the very first time Chris asked her to join the team. "I just catch on quick," she says. Achelin had some raw talent but would need work. Alcielis really wanted to be a pitcher, because she was pretty like Jenny Finch, but she just couldn't do it.

By now, Chris had figured out who the best players were, who had potential, and who was going to get hidden in right field, the graveyard of softball positions. He started imagining his dream lineup.

Pitcher: Johanna. Skill-wise, education-wise, and following-directions-wise, she was Chris's best player. Achelin could be the backup.

Catcher: Alexa. She was fearless and he needed someone with a good arm who wasn't afraid to crouch down behind the batters and not flinch when they swung the bat.

Shortstop: Possibly Rashell—she was staticky, but a leader plays shortstop. Or Yoshie. She still couldn't put it all together, but the best all-around athlete belongs at shortstop.

First base: Nicky. The best catcher takes first base. Genesis was actually really good at catching the ball, too, but she never said boo. Her self-esteem was so low, he barely noticed she was there.

Second base: Alcielis. She cared more about her acrylic nails than athletics but she was a decent ballplayer. "I wasn't the best, but I wasn't the worst," Alcielis says.

Third base: Angie. The corner has to be ready for hard hit balls. Angie always had her head in the game. Plus, it didn't require the best arm because the distance from third base to first is shorter. Angie, though athletic, had a weaker arm than others and her accuracy was way off. Chris taught her to point her toe at the target, release, and flick her wrist, but she got frustrated and angry and threw her glove down. "Angie, you're just beginning," Chris said. "It's the first time you played softball. Come on. Give yourself a chance."

That left the outfield. Mayoli was perfect out in la-la land because it gave her space to spin around and sing, which is all she did anyway. Gheynee was good but she was hardcore. She only showed one emotion—anger, 100 percent to the fullest. She was still mad at Chris for not getting her name right. "The fuck is wrong with you? How many fuckin' times I gotta tell you?"

"Okay, calm down. I have close to 600 kids. It's hard to remember all the names."

"You should know by now."

She was right. It was very insulting and rude that he didn't make the effort. He promised to make it right.

Grateshka was scared of the ball at first. Heaven "sucked at batting," she admits. Likewise, Kimberly says, "I wasn't good at all. But it was better than being home."

Robin could not play. "At first I didn't know how to do nothing," she says. "I didn't know how to stand. It was rough." She was a tough girl who was better at more physical sports like football or basketball, but that didn't matter to Chris. He wanted to develop her arm and bat to make her more confident, to the point that she liked playing. "I wanted Robin to develop something better than softball skills," he says.

Not just Robin. He wanted all the girls to develop something better than softball skills. Learn how to support other girls, not tear them down. Learn how to be respectful to adults and to each other. Learn how to resolve conflict without violence. All those life skills nobody had ever bothered to teach them before. Resilience. Discipline. Teamwork. Making good choices. Taking responsibility for their own actions.

Like an Amanda Scarborough fast-pitch, the Lady Tigers had already made great strides. But they were still having the same old problems, too, and some girls had been skipping practice lately. It killed Chris when he thought he was making progress but then the girls relapsed into bad behavior. With them, it was always one step forward, two steps back.

One afternoon after practice, close to Christmas break, Chris gathered the girls around. He'd been thinking about his sister Michelle a lot lately—he always did around the holidays because that's when he missed her the most. So, he was already a little on edge and feeling emotional.

"I want to talk to you guys about something. Sit down."

The girls sat down but they were fidgety, hungry, tired. They wanted to go home.

"A lot of you are not showing up to practice. You're cutting school, not doing your homework, being rude to teachers, which means I hear about it."

Nobody was paying attention. They were talking to each other loudly, goofing around, smacking each other, screeching, laughing. Chris got madder and raised his voice.

"You're a reflection of me. I've been letting you girls do these things. I'm not letting you girls do these things anymore."

"You don't know what we go through!" someone shouted out among the racket.

"I don't know what you go through?" Chris asked, then laughed maniacally.

That finally got the girls' attention.

He walked over to a chair, picked it up, and threw it across the room.

"WHAT THE *FUCK*!" he roared, months of frustration loaded into one single curse word.

The girls instantly fell dead silent and stared at Chris in disbelief. They'd never seen him this angry. They'd never even heard him curse. The gym was so quiet, you could hear a pin drop.

"You want to know who I am?" Chris asked, fighting back tears. "I knew a girl way back when. She made bad decision after bad decision, I couldn't do nothing. At thirty-one, she died. My sister is right here now, tattooed on my arm." Chris lifted his shirtsleeve. "Why do I say this? It's not because I think everybody here is gonna end up like this. It's because I see my sister in every one of you. I'll be damned if I'm gonna let you go down the same road that my sister went down. I have girls that say, 'Get off my back, get off my back.' NO. I'm gonna stay on your back. Because I'll be damned if you end up like my sister. I couldn't save her, but I can save you. I love you all. You're my daughters. And I get upset when I see you girls disrespect yourselves."

The girls hung their heads in shame. "We all just looked at each other out of the corners of our eyes, like, 'Oh we messed up big time,'" Nicky says.

"He felt like no one cared," Grateshka says. "He felt worthless."

Chris paced back and forth. At that point, the hurt, angry teen that lost his sister came pouring out of Chris. Who was he kidding, these girls were never gonna change, and his wife was gonna leave him, for what? THIS? He'd been as patient as a saint and now he'd reached his breaking point.

"YOU KNOW WHAT? I DON'T GIVE A SHIT ANYMORE," Chris screamed. "I'LL END THE TEAM!"

"Bro, calm down," Yoshie said. "Relax."

Chris turned toward his favorite "daughter," his eyes turned from fiery to cold and distant. "We're done," he said. "I'll decide over the break if I want to continue the team next year. Give me back my uniforms. I'll give them back to you in January if you change your attitudes. Otherwise, it's over."

The girls couldn't believe what he just said. They didn't want to believe what he just said.

"What if we don't give them back to you?" Robin said. She loved her uniform.

"You're gonna be wearing a jersey for what?" Chris shot back. "I'm not coaching you. Whether you give it back or keep it, there's no team."

Chapter Eleven

A NEW BEGINNING

All of the girls turned in their Lady Tiger uniforms before the Christmas break.

In the South Bronx, the holidays weren't always so holly and jolly. Being home for two weeks straight could be much worse than being at school for a lot of them. There was no escape from the fighting, drunkenness, and physical and verbal abuse, and nowhere to go, especially if it was cold. They were trapped in it.

They also didn't necessarily get lavished with gifts. Yoshie's big presents were a pair of socks and sweatpants. Angie didn't get anything at all, because a babysitter stole all of the cash her mom had hidden in the house. "We didn't really have a Christmas," she says. Rashell was pleasantly surprised that her mom, who was originally opposed to her being on the Lady Tigers fearing she'd break her ankle, got her a $40 used glove and cleats. Even more shocking, Nicky and Gheynee's mom, who often took softball away from them as a punishment, bought them gloves, too. They truly missed softball and played catch outside together, even though it was freezing. "We liked having something to take us away from the house," Gheynee says. "It distracted us."

Chris was having a rough Christmas himself. He was exhausted and burnt out, and the tension was thick in his house, too. He was supposed to work things out with Charisse, but he felt she was gloating about the team disbanding, and it pained him. He struggled with his decision. He'd never been a quitter, and not only had he given up on the Lady Tigers, he had freaked out and thrown a chair. He didn't like or welcome the return of Angry Chris. He felt out of control, like the Incredible Hulk. Plus, he and Charisse were having money problems. Every year, they liked to go all out on Christmas, no matter their financial situation—big tree, lights, decorations, stockings, all of it. They always had presents under the tree, no matter how low their bank account balance. This year they were flat broke and it was partly his fault for spending so much money on the team. They barely had enough money for rent. It was unacceptable to Chris to not have presents at all, but especially not this year, not after his focus had been on his softball family more than his real family. He hadn't exactly been "Dad of the Year." So Chris dipped into his 401(k) and took out a loan from his credit union in order to buy Justin his favorite video games and Cristina a playhouse.

Grateshka was one of the lucky ones who had a fun-filled Christmas with lots of family in from out of state and yummy holiday food, like her favorite fried chicken and Pernil, the classic Puerto Rican pork dish served with *arroz con grandules*. For some of the others, having a lot of family around triggered drama between parents, siblings, and extended family.

In Kimberly's case, the "most wonderful time of year" gave her anxiety and filled her with self-loathing. She wanted to have a good time, but she just dreaded these family gatherings. During the holidays, her half sister's side of the family would be around a lot, including one of Claudia's uncles

Kimberly tried desperately to avoid. Somehow, even with all of her dodging, this man always found a way to isolate her. He'd been doing it since she was seven years old. It was the secret she'd buried deep. That year, on New Year's Eve, he did it again. The uncle found her alone in her room, closed the door, and locked it. When it was over, she told no one.

Over the break, stuck at home, the girls had a collective epiphany—being a member of the Lady Tigers was the best damn thing about their lives. Their homes were totally dysfunctional, their parents ignored, beat, or criticized them, their teachers hated them, they were flunking out, gangs could kill them, other girls wanted to maim them, and grown men abused them.

The Lady Tigers was an island of tranquility in a sea of sewage. If they let it be.

Gheynee and Nicky figured this out while they were playing catch. "Astacio was the only person who cared about this whole team and everybody on it, so we felt like we could trust him," Nicky says. "I don't have a father so I looked at him as my father figure. He'll laugh with me, he'll cry with me. I'll call him at two in the morning and he'll pick up."

"He was like my father figure, too," Angie says. "At home it was a lot of drama. I'll have like rough nights. My dad arguing with my mom, you know, and it will continue in the morning. When I would see Astacio, he was always there to listen or give advice or a shoulder to lean on. Through all my hard times, even outside of the school, I would reach out to Astacio. He was like my second dad in school. As soon as he got there, he warmed my heart. Whenever I was down, he got to know me. He always knew when something was wrong with me and he would say, 'Listen, I'm here for you.'"

"Astacio, he was a father figure, he brung that," Robin says. "He didn't just care about the team, he cared about individuals. We each had our own connection with him."

"He was going to cancel the team and it was a wake-up call," Heaven says. "He wanted us to change our attitude. He wasn't doing it to hurt us, he was doing it to benefit us. He wanted to make us look good. He wanted us to become appreciative of each other. Because one day we could be gone."

"All he wanted to do was help me," Rashell realized. "He wanted to give me a motivation to be a better person."

"Astacio gave great advice," Grateshka adds. "I was always upset or worried that my brother wouldn't come home because of the violence in the streets. I told him I didn't feel safe. And he would sit and listen to me and talk to me the way you're supposed to. He didn't judge. That's why we came back."

When school started up again in January, Chris scheduled a "Come to Jesus" meeting for the Lady Tigers after school one afternoon. He wasn't about to chase anyone down; he didn't have the energy. If they showed up, they showed up. But when the bell rang, almost every single girl on the team walked through the gymnasium doors. "I didn't know back then that I'd have this much love for softball," Nicky says. "I would do anything to play softball again. I didn't care what time of day or how cold it is. I really loved playing softball."

Chris saw Gheynee approaching with a mean look on her face.

"Fuck it," Chris thought. "Let me try again. 'Hey, it's my best friend in the whole world! I missed you!'"

Gheynee walked right up to him.

"Yeah . . . I missed you, too." Then she *smiled*.

Chris made a huge deal out of it. He had everyone stop what they were doing so she could say it again. He wanted to give her a hug but she stopped him and said, "Let's just start with 'I missed you.'"

It was a good omen and a positive first step at changing the narrative of the team. Chris had thought a lot about the problems the Lady Tigers experienced the last semester and he realized he was largely to blame. He'd been too lenient, a doormat even, because he was afraid if he put too many rules in place, the girls would take off and he wouldn't have a team. The bottom line was that the Lady Tigers could not exist or function without rules. So he laid down the law.

"Moving forward, in order to make this team as successful as possible, everyone must follow the rules of the school no matter how much you might disagree with them. If I get a complaint from one teacher, I suspend practice. If I see one girl in the hallway without a pass, I suspend practice. If anyone dares to ignore me, I cancel half the season. And if you continue to act up, the Lady Tigers end. Am I clear? Am I clear! Break any of the following rules, you're off the team. I don't care if there's no team. There will be no exceptions." He then listed the rules:

Rule #1: To be on the team, you must show up to class. Every day. Unless you're dead or dying.

Rule #2: To be on the team, you must be passing most of your classes. You're allowed two exceptions. Since the girls had been failing almost all of their classes, he couldn't expect them to magically jump to passing all of their classes. It was unrealistic.

When the girls moaned about attendance and grades, Heaven, acting as Chris's lawyer, argued his case before the jury of her peers, aka her teammates: "He cannot run a team where everybody is failing and not going to class!" They shrugged their shoulders and nodded in agreement.

Rule #3: Each girl would have a "tracker" conduct sheet that they'd give to their teachers after every single period. The teacher would check off if the player was on time, had done their homework, and was respectful, and add any other comments. Chris would collect them every Friday. "My goal was to always be eligible for the softball team," Grateshka notes.

Rule #4: Behavior that resulted in a trip to the dean's office was grounds for expulsion from the team. Chris was tired of being called down to the dean's office to retrieve them. "Softball became a passion," Achelin says. "I didn't enjoy being a troublemaker anymore. To be on the team I had to go to class. I didn't even mind going anymore."

Rule #5: Practice was mandatory. If you don't show up, you don't play. Mayoli reappeared after the "Come to Jesus" meeting and asked for another chance to be on the team after getting kicked off for lying about where she was every day. "I'm sorry," she said sincerely. "I'm not going to lie anymore." Chris was stern. "If you ever use the team as an excuse again, forget about being on the team." And just like that she was back in the outfield singing and twirling around.

Rule #6: No more fighting or bullying each other. They had to come together as a team. Grateshka was skeptical that was possible but then realized, "The bullies were actually the ones who taught me a lot of stuff about playing." Johanna noticed a change in the older girls, at least toward her. "They all tried to talk to me in English. They were all nice, trying to be my friend."

Chris was kind of blown away by how quickly he saw improvement. "I saw a big change in Nicky right away," Chris remembers. "One day she didn't trust me, then the next day she did. I don't know what happened."

Robin also claimed that she would prove herself to be a better person. She and Chris had a good connection, so he believed she was earnest. She'd been disrespectful to everyone else but "she'd never tried that bullshit with me," he says. She kept her promise for as long she could, keeping her head down and her fists and mouth in check. "She'd come to me every day and say, 'Oh, I didn't have a fight this week, I didn't argue this week!' And I'd say, 'Good job, Robin.'" But then one day, Chris heard through the grapevine she was involved in a fight. He went down the staircase he knew was Robin's favorite hiding spot. He found her with her friends, wearing her Lady Tiger jersey.

"Robin, get over here."

"Why? I'm just hanging with my girls."

"Give me your uniform right now."

Tears welled up in her eyes.

"Do you have a shirt on underneath?"

"Yes."

"Then give me my jersey."

She took it off, reluctantly handed it over, and ran off, like a wounded deer. "She didn't scream at me like other people. She didn't say, 'Fuck you.' She knew better."

"He never got me pissed off or to a point," Robin confirms. "He took my jersey away and I started crying. I was mad at him but I was madder at myself."

In hindsight, Chris felt bad, like he was being too harsh on her. Robin had really been making an effort and she hadn't actually been in the fight, she didn't even throw a single punch. She just had her foot in it. Robin was doing phenomenal and had one setback. Chris found her three hours later and pulled her aside. "Listen, if you pass your math test, you can have your jersey back," he told her. She passed and rejoined the team.

Looking back on the incident, Chris recognized that he bowed to peer pressure. He felt his hand was forced because the staff believed he babied his girls and let them get away with murder. Especially Robin. They'd come up to him about her a lot. That was one of the reasons he'd stripped her jersey. That day, several teachers and a dean had approached him and said, "What are you going to do now about Robin?" He felt like he had to do something to save face because he was looking like a fool.

He'd let the teachers and the dean influence his decisions. "I did not want to operate out of fear like that." Plus, there was no sitting down and working together as a staff to come up with protocols or procedures. It was all trial by error. It was all falling on Chris, which wasn't fair either. He needed more collaboration from everybody but he wasn't going to get it. The teachers threatened to kick girls off the softball team all the time as a weapon. "That baffled my mind," Chris says. "How is that helping you? I would tell a teacher, 'If you take the girl off the team, now we have no leverage. Now I can't help you whatsoever.'"

Once, he saw Yoshie crying in the hallway.

"What's up?" Chris said.

"Mr. Gomez says he's gonna kick me off the team."

"No one kicks you off *my* team, except for me."

Chris found Gomez. "Did you tell Yoshie she's off the team?"

"She's barely paying attention in class. She's barely passing."

Yoshie was quiet but she wasn't a behavior problem. Gomez wanted to make an example out of her but Chris wasn't having it. "Okay, well I understand that. Next time you come to me and I'll deal with it. But you cannot go over my head and take my player off my team. I don't go into your class and say, 'Oh, she's not in your class no more.'"

Those incidents made Chris reevaluate his disciplinary style. He couldn't let the girls get away with murder, but he had to have their backs at all times and be their number one champion. He had a lot of deep discussions with Richard Frederick, the assistant principal of school safety, because they were on the same page when it came to helping the troubled females in the school and had a similar philosophy on what was the most effective and, frankly, humane disciplinary style.

"Listen, every kid in that school is a good kid," Frederick notes. "They have tough lives. If you're loved and you're happy, you come to school to learn. Kids who aren't, come to school to be loved. Kids who are cursing you out are the most fucked-up kids who need love. If you care about them, you got them. It's easy. If they say, 'Mister, why you on me?' 'I care about you and I love you.' If you say, 'Why don't you go to class?' and they say, 'Because I can't read,' then you say, 'Okay so what if I help you?' You had to get to a point where the kids felt safe and loved in that building. That's when things changed."

Frederick also tried to change the mindset of the teachers. If the kids acted out, they expected to be kicked out of class, suspended, or arrested. When students stuffed their book bags with free food provided by Title I federal dollars in the cafeteria, the lunch ladies yelled at them, "You only get one!" Frederick said, "Who cares? Give them more! They're hungry." Robin once started a food fight and one of the deans actually demanded that she pay for his suit jacket dry-cleaning bill. "He was dead serious," she says. "I'm not paying for that!"

Frederick says that's the problem. Piling on students for ticky-tacky transgressions. He'd been bit, kicked, spit on, and worse, but in his opinion, it came with the job. These were things that happened every day. Half the school smelled like weed. It didn't require an arrest. "Flip the script. Do the opposite and you'll blow their minds," Frederick explains.

"Mister, are you gonna call the cops?"

"No."

"Really?"

"Why would I do that? You're high, go get some Visine, get some cologne, and chew some gum. And get to class. Next time I will call the cops."

"Okay, I gotcha."

Now, if a kid brought brass knuckles to school, that was explicitly against the rules and required a suspension. "It's not me against you," he said. "You know you messed up."

For Frederick, it was all about the tone of the conversation, picking his battles, and making allies. "Kids should know one or two people they can go to if they're upset. Need a break, can't handle class? No problem, but don't walk out of class. Have the teacher call me and tell me she's sending you. And I got you."

Like Chris, Frederick was building relationships with the students, and before long, he, too, had kids hanging out with him all the time, including a few Lady Tigers. "He changed so many things," Robin says. "He had a big impact. He was on top of problems. I honestly felt safe." Heaven and Gheynee went from being the most wanted runaways in Frederick's hallway sweeps to permanent fixtures in his office. "I liked Freddy with the nice blue eyes," Gheynee swoons.

"If he told us to stop, we stopped, we didn't even run," Heaven says.

"When I first started there they thought I was a bougie white boy in a suit, probably undercover. After a while they saw I was cool. It was about showing them I'm not just an assistant principal. I'm a person. I talked about my kids, my wife, my life story. How I used to get in trouble. I smoked cigarettes and pot and all these things. When they see you're a person, it changes the whole dynamic."

As the kids got to know Frederick, they started trusting him, too. As they ate fistfuls of licorice, candy, and popcorn he bought by the jugful at Costco, they gave him invaluable intel and became reliable informants. "When Frederick came," Heaven admits, "I didn't cut anymore. He was my best friend. I used to be his eyes!"

Students came to him first thing in the morning to report on the previous night's Facebook war of words, which spiraled into scheduled live fights the next day. "They didn't come to me as snitches, they didn't want bad stuff to happen anymore. They helped me cut it off before it happened."

The kids schooled him on all the lingo, too, and it helped him connect.

"You did me slime."

"It's about to pop off."

"Ratchet."

When he used them, they'd say, "Yo, you're funny, mister!"

On a more serious note, some of the gangbangers liked him enough to warn of real danger in the streets outside of school. "Yo, stay off the corner today," one told him.

"Why?"

"Just stay off the corner."

"They were protecting me from the neighborhood gangs. They knew I was there to help them. Once you broke the shell, which they all have, they're such nice kids."

"I used to take it all personally, like they were rebelling against me," Chris says, "but then I realized they didn't know their own potential. They were wasting it because they'd being knocked down so much by everybody. They thought I was lying when I told them they had potential."

Without encouragement from their parents or teachers or anyone, these girls felt worthless and their self-esteem was a bottomless pit. They had to learn how to boost their confidence on their own, a Herculean task considering all they'd been through. Plus, they didn't have the resources for the intensive counseling most of them needed.

One afternoon, not long after the Lady Tigers had reunited, Chris brought the girls into a classroom. He'd rearranged all the desks into a circle and asked them to take a seat. They naturally sat in their cliques.

"Mister, what are we doin' here?" Alexa asked. "Oh em gee, not another boring video!"

"Forget softball," Chris said. "Today we're not going to touch a softball. We're not going to do anything until we talk to each other." Everybody saw the Lady Tigers as just another sports team, but Chris had discovered that's not what was it was about. "Right now, I see academies. I see Columbia, UConn, and John Jay. I don't want to see those anymore. I want to see a team. We gotta learn to be together. We're going to keep doing this and doing this until I see a team."

Chris called these practices "Circle Sessions." At first, he picked the topics. "Tell me what happened in school today. How do you feel about it?" It was rough in the beginning. Some girls dominated, like Nicky and Rashell. The conversations veered off topic and got a little crazy. "My first initial thing was to listen," Chris says. "I wasn't focused on, 'Oh, is she lying or telling the truth?' Let me just listen. And I listened to everybody. Even if they talked nonsense, I still listened."

Girls were shy at first, but the more they did the Circle Sessions, the more they spoke up. But then it devolved into them talking over each other and the inevitable, "Yo, shut the fuck up, bitch!"

"Yo, we can't have conversations where people are talking over each other!" Chris stressed. "I would get mad, too, if you're talking over me. So you got to give her that right of way." He taught them the etiquette of having a two-way conversation. "If someone's talking, you listen, and when that person finishes, then you can talk or elaborate or ask questions."

The Circle Sessions naturally evolved into therapy sessions, which they desperately needed, but Chris wasn't a real social worker, plus they also competed with each other for the title of Most Fucked-Up Life: "This is what I experienced." "Oh hell, that ain't nothin. This is what *I* experienced." If Grateshka dared speak up, she got an earful. "Shut up! You never been through nothin' rough!" She had a mom and dad that were still together and lived in a good home, so she wasn't taken seriously if she had a problem.

"No one's problem is more important than the other person's," Chris repeated over and over.

Some girls weren't sure if their problems merited complaining, which made them feel stupid and not want to participate. Yoshie, for one, didn't trust her teammates with her secrets. She wasn't about to open up just to get laughed at or worse. She'd seen Kimberly get very emotional and be called out as a "big cry baby." Chris wanted all of the girls to feel safe and contribute, so he made sure that it was a judgment-free space (he also made it clear that he was always available for private conversations). "You're here to talk and listen. Nobody's going to judge you, no matter how many mistakes you've made." To help them feel more comfortable putting themselves out there, he told a lot of his own stories of growing up; about his anxiety and anger, and about his sister Michelle and other females he knew that got in trouble a lot. This angered a few of the girls and made them very defensive.

"Well, I'm not that person!"

"Stop comparing me to this person!"

Chris tried to make a clear distinction—"No, you're not them, but you are on a similar path and could end up like them. Show me you're not that person because right now, you're just like the person I'm talking about."

As trust was earned, the talks got deeper and more painful. Mayoli revealed that her father had been murdered on her birthday and intimated she'd been raped by an uncle. A lot of conversations revolved around not having a dad or how pissed off they were at their fathers or negative experiences with males in general. How their mothers were giving them hell at home. How they felt like they weren't being listened to at home and how they hated going home.

"My mom doesn't even acknowledge I'm there," Yoshie said.

"I stay out until five in the morning and my mom doesn't even know I was gone," Nicky shared.

"My dad only calls me on holidays or birthdays," Gheynee chimed in. She didn't like anyone knowing her business so it was a big deal for her to talk about her feelings. She usually only expressed herself through anger.

"My mom doesn't let me breathe," Alexa confided. "I don't like being at home. I'm not comfortable."

"I can't hang out with my friends. I can't drink, I can't smoke," Alcielis agreed.

"Are you the age to smoke?" Chris asked. "Sometimes we rationalize our behavior even though it's a little bit too grown-up for us." The girls soaked that in and nodded their heads in agreement. He could tell they understood what he was saying and hoped it might help them make better decisions.

Maybe for the first time ever, the girls started analyzing out loud why they might be acting out in such negative ways. Nicky told the group about her birth mother's abuse and that ACS had been called to her and Gheynee's house several times. "The reason I acted the way I acted was because of my mom," Nicky theorized. "Like, I had a bad attitude. I didn't listen to nobody. I didn't care. Don't tell me anything because it'll go in one ear and come out the other ear. I wasn't focused. I was in three fights, always in detention. How I was feeling at home, the only way to release the anger was to fight with people. My mom's a great person, she has a great heart, but she doesn't know how to control her anger. She's got bipolar disorder. Everybody know she has it, I be telling her. She won't get help. She's old school, you don't get diagnosed with a mental disorder 'cause that's weak."

"You gotta understand, I come from a household where I go through stuff," said Robin, who revealed that her mom had died during childbirth and her father had recently gone to jail. She was an orphan living with her grandmother. "We come to school and we take it out on other people because we don't know how to manage our emotions. The reason why us girls are not getting along is we don't know how to communicate and talk and get them to like you. I'm very social. I can start a conversation with a random person and they like me. But it's the way you approach things. Girls thought they was too cute or have to dress a certain way for them to be friends with you. It wasn't right. Me personally I don't care about friends. We all went through something to get where we at right now. Me, Alexa, some of y'all other girls, we still friends to this day. We all been through some hell."

Chris tried to teach them that they needed to accept their fucked-up circumstances or choose to change them, but he couldn't make them do either. "It's up to you. I know it's hard." He understood because of their circumstances they were still "going to do dirt. But the most important thing is you try to fix it and stop making excuses. When you fall you get back up. I'm here to help you but you cannot get mad at me for trying to help you."

Some girls rarely talked at all, like Genesis, who had too much anxiety to reveal that she was being bullied mercilessly in class. "Back then, I couldn't talk to people. I couldn't even blink next to a person," she explains. "I didn't want to go to class because it was tough for me. Some students were just mean. They'd joke about my appearance. For them, a person with large lips was something they'd make fun about. My ass is a little bigger than normal and they'd make fun of that, too. They'd make fun of my weight. They'd make fun of every little thing. Everything I did or said, even my accent." Genesis resorted to cutting. "I had a stupid way of dealing with those types of things to make myself feel better." None of the other players even noticed, because Genesis was so quiet and to herself. Chris noticed marks on her arms, but he couldn't be sure what they were, and he didn't want to accuse her of anything. He wanted Genesis to bring it up on her own when she was ready.

Yoshie wasn't at a point where she felt secure enough to talk about her sexuality, even to Angie who was more open about it. "In sixth grade I was really confused," Yoshie says. "I liked this girl named Jada and I didn't understand why I couldn't stop thinking about her. I was afraid to come out. I didn't really tell anyone. I would question myself, 'Why am I so weird around girls and why do I always wear baggy clothes?'" She dated her first girlfriend, Samantha, that year but didn't know what to do. "We didn't really date for that long because she wanted to do more, and I was like, 'You're my first girlfriend.' I didn't know how to do anything."

She also didn't disclose her sexual abuse but spoke about it confidentially to Mayoli, who'd brought up her similar situation. "When I was crying, she was always there for me. She was the first person I would go to, to vent about my dad or the thing with my cousins."

Sadly, sexual abuse was implied by more than one of the girls, but nobody went too deep into physical abuse, or suicidal thoughts, because they knew

Astacio would have to report it. But due to the Circle Sessions, an amazing thing happened. The girls turned to each other privately.

Claudia got bullied a lot by the gang boys and one posted a photo of her exposed body on the Internet. She wasn't the kind of girl who could stick up for herself. "Everyone in school would laugh at her, especially other girls," Yoshie says. "I said, 'Just stick with me. I'm not gonna laugh at you, I'm not going to judge you.'" Nicky even got involved. "I'm not a big fan of bullies," she says un-ironically. "I was not gonna tolerate that. I approached the girls, mind you, I'm so tiny, and I still approached the girls, there's like three or four of them and I still went up to them. I said, 'Leave the girl alone.' Ever since then, they tried to jump me. I'm not scared of no females. If you jump me there's gonna be a problem. World War III up in this school."

When they couldn't talk about certain things with Astacio, the girls sat in the cafeteria or an office or found an empty classroom (or one that wasn't empty and they would kick everyone out, including teachers) and hold their own Circle Sessions. "We were so down for each other," Nicky says. "Every day we'd come to each other with stories about our boyfriends or what's going on at home. They're all so strong but we always support each other and what we go through. We knew so much about each other that nobody knows. They knew so much about me nobody knows."

Nicky bared all during these private Circle Sessions, including that her mother had been beating her with any object she could get her hands on: sandals, brooms, spatulas. Alcielis had witnessed it many times—Nicky getting things thrown at her and her being thrown against the wall—and bragged how brave and stoic Nicky was. "She never once hit her back, she just put her hands up to protect her face."

It came to a point where Alcielis and Nicky got so close and hung out so much, her mom wasn't even embarrassed to yell at or hit Nicky in front of Alcielis. She even threatened to hit Alcielis sometimes. "I was like a daughter to her, too. She never abused me but if she saw me doing something wrong she would yell at me and threaten to hit me."

Nicky also revealed her deepest darkest secret, that she'd been molested more than once. When she was eight, two cousins "touched me in places that's not tolerated," she told the girls. Another time, she was left alone with a male friend of the family who forced her to "do things that she didn't want to do." Nicky told Mami Gladys and the situation was handled by the police.

Kimberly sat there listening to Nicky, stunned. What she was describing was too familiar and it made her feel nauseous. She had to leave. Kimberly was so young and so inexperienced, she had no clue that the uncle had been doing things that were illegal to her. She knew it felt wrong and shameful, but she had no other frame of reference. She felt tears welling up and thought she might puke. She didn't know what to do. So she stayed silent again.

"I avoided talking about myself and my experiences with anyone," Kimberly remembers. "Instead I would prefer to make a silly show for my friends in class rather than talk about my mom having lupus and my sister Claudia failing every class. When Nicky talked about how her cousin did things to her as a kid and got locked away, I walked away from the conversation. I always wondered where she got the strength to talk about that because little Kimberly was struggling to talk about anything that wasn't math, bachata, or parties. I hung out with the popular girls. They were the pretty girls, the little girls who developed quickly, who had their first boyfriends at the age of seven, and at twelve already dating a high schooler. They were the girls who had been sexually harassed at a young age but were too young to realize what it was. I had nothing in common with them except for the last point."

"I was aware some of the girls were going through their own problems but not aware of the intensity," Heaven says. "Health issues, with parents, dad not in their life, molestation, insecurity, suicidal. Everybody had their own thing. They found the light in softball."

College basketball hall of famer John Calipari, coach of the University of Kentucky Wildcats, once said, "It's not just about working hard, it's about working together. You have to care more about the team than you do yourself."

Coach Astacio's original vision of what the Lady Tigers could be was coming to life. The girls were willing to put their beefs aside to get along for the greater good of the team. They were learning that they had more in common than divided them. They were dissolving their cliques and reaching across the aisle, so to speak. "I though Grateshka was nasty," Heaven admits, "but she can be really nice."

"When people got to know me, they said, 'I thought you was this mean girl," says Nicky. "I'm actually very nice. But I can be very mean, too."

Kimberly, who'd always felt like an outsider in her own home, finally felt like she belonged somewhere: "When we felt comfortable opening up, the girls on the team became a family."

"It felt like family," Achelin agrees. "I loved it. That feeling of being part of a team."

Now that the girls were coming together as one cohesive unit, Chris felt secure enough and brave enough to take them out into the world as a team representing 22. After making a dozen calls to universities in the tristate area, he was able to arrange a practice with a local team, the Monroe College Mustangs, in nearby New Rochelle. The trip had a few purposes:

1. Get coaching from real softball coaches.
2. Learn how to play softball from real softball players.
3. Introduce them to role models, young ladies who looked just like them, who made it out of the 'hood and into college by studying hard and playing harder.
4. Demonstrate what real teamwork looks like.
5. Show them that softball can change their lives.

The girls were excited about the field trip, mostly because they got to wear their shiny black uniforms. The Lady Mustangs could not have been more welcoming to his girls. They held their own Circle Session with the Lady Tigers and brought Rashell in the middle with their captain to lead a discussion about all sorts of topics relating to softball, school, social media, and just life.

"How many of you guys want to keep playing in college after high school?" a Mustang named Paola asked.

All of the Lady Tiger hands shot up.

"This is college and we have to study a certain number of hours. If we don't commit to those hours, we can't play in a game. If you get home and you're tired and don't feel like it, you still have to. It's about time management. You can't just be on Facebook and Instagram all night. Start putting your phone down for two hours to try it. You can get it done. It's hard, but it's worth it for softball."

"This is the time to start making good habits," said another Mustang. "It don't matter what problems you got at home, always stay up. Remind yourself to keep going."

"Softball changes you as a person," another Mustang stressed. "It makes you a better person. You have to work hard at getting better as a person. You guys should really go for it."

After the circle, the Mustangs created a training circuit for the girls, with two to three Mustangs training two Lady Tigers on hitting, fielding, and pitching drills. The joint practice turned out better than Chris could have ever dreamed. Chris summed up the field trip in a glowing mass email he was proud to send to the entire staff of 22:

The girls had the opportunity to talk to and be trained by the Monroe Mustangs. The girls demonstrated immense respect and were in complete awe as the Mustangs explained who they were and how they became softball players. The majority of our girls expressed that they would love the opportunity to play for a college team in the future. The Mustangs conveyed that it took complete dedication in school to become a great student-athlete. During our discussion, the girls sat patiently and posed intelligent questions. It was an awesome thing to witness, the cooperation and determination displayed by our girls.

The highlight of the day was towards the end when one of the Mustangs gave Rashell a hug. Rashell in total shock came running to us and said, "She gave me a hug and I didn't even ask for one. I love this place!" Knowing that she has been struggling in school, we had a talk in which she confided in me that she wanted to become a better student as well as person. I will continue to work with teachers to encourage her success as well as the other girls on the team.

The Head Coach was so impressed with our girls that she has invited us to come back. I am glad that our girls had this experience and hopefully it will increase their focus during school."

Chris could not have been prouder of Rashell. And to think, she'd recently come into his office and asked to be relieved of her leadership duties. "I don't want to be team captain, bro," she said. "I feel like I'm being too bossy, and people be mad that I have to boss them around. I don't want to be team captain no more. You can put somebody else."

"No, you're going to remain team captain," Chris said calmly. "I'm going to tell them that they have to listen to you."

She kept at it and it was paying off.

That night, Chris called Rashell's mother. She'd only ever gotten negative calls about her daughter and it was time for something new.

"Hello?"

"Hi, can I speak to the mother of Rashell?"

"What she do now?" she barked angrily.

"No, she didn't do anything bad. What she did today was great." Chris explained how well-behaved Rashell was on the field trip and how she helped run the drills. "She was a great leader."

"Are you sure you got the right number?"

"Yes, I'm talking about your daughter Rashell. She's making steps in the right direction. I just wanted you to know that."

"Really?" she said quietly, her tone softening. "Oh my God. Thank you."

Chapter Twelve

INNOCENCE LOST

"They killed him. They killed him. They killed him."

Chris was sitting in his office when he heard Alexa wailing in the gym. He ran out and found her shaking and crying, surrounded by the girls on the team.

"I . . . I . . . I . . . was supposed to meet up with him," she cried. She was a mess. She could barely get the words out. Chris brought her into his office and closed the door.

"Alexa, what happened?"

She knew she shouldn't say anything. She didn't even know if she was capable. She was in shock.

"I never even got to meet up with him," Alexa repeated, as tears streamed down her face.

"Alexa, talk to me. It's just you and me."

She couldn't. She couldn't tell Coach Astacio that she witnessed one of her oldest friends from childhood get shot by a gang right in front of her eyes, his blood spattering all over her clothing. They'd made plans to hang out later that night. It never happened. Because he was dead. She'd witnessed a murder the night before, but she couldn't tell her coach. She'd make him an accessory after-the-fact and snitching could put both of their lives in danger.

That was Alexa's big secret. The one thing Chris and her mom and the deans could never get her to talk about no matter how hard they tried. Where was she every night after practice? The answer was, she was in a gang and she'd been hanging out with her gang. It wasn't meant to be a serious gang and she didn't join it for protection. Her crew was small, a group of boys and girls who just wanted to hang out and have fun. "Just 6-7 things," she says, meaning running around the block on 167th Street. They did harmless stuff at first, hopping the gate at the school on Jerome to smoke cigarettes in the park. Or they'd congregate in their regular gathering spot in the tunnel under 167th to drink and smoke weed, even though it was dark and dingy and full of potholes. After a while, they progressed to petty crime, mostly stealing. "It was a lot of theft," Alexa admits. "I was being a tough girl."

Suddenly, one day out of the blue, the shooting happened and "the little gang I was in stopped being kid stuff," Alexa says. "It got real. It got really serious. We didn't expect it. He was humble."

Alexa wouldn't tell Chris, and there was nothing he could do other than be there for her. Even though things were looking up on the team, horrifying incidents like this, completely out of his control, happened every day. Precious had just gotten suspended for thirty days for a fight that started because someone looked at her the wrong way.

"It was always back and forth, back and forth. I couldn't keep up. I was exhausted," Chris says. "It was like you put a Band-Aid on one thing until something else breaks. And the bandage peels off little by little and then you have to go readdress the original wound because you never really fully fixed that problem to begin with."

And it was always never one problem with just one girl. It was fifty problems a day and he tried to catch up and catch up, but he couldn't catch up. He tried to prioritize which girl's issue was more severe immediately, knowing they were all severe. Which one does he address first? This girl's? That girl's? And if he addressed one girl's problem, another girl felt like, "Oh, he don't care about me."

Alexa had witnessed a murder, Precious was gone, and now Nicky and Gheynee were missing practice too much. It wasn't their fault. Their lives were a mess. Between the ACS cases, walking on eggshells in their own home 24/7, and taking care of their baby sister like a full-time job, making softball was impossible sometimes. "Nicky and Gheynee basically raised their little sister," their cousin reveals. "Their mom kept trying to be a mother and it wasn't not working. She tried to stop them from playing softball and make them go to sleep at 9 o clock and miss afterschool programs just because she wanted Nicky and Gheynee to take care of the little girl she gave birth to. They had to be home while she was working all the time. She forced Gheynee not to go to softball practice just to come pick up her baby sister. Gheynee didn't have to but she still did it."

"We had no moments of peace," Nicky says. "I just couldn't focus. Like I just broke down in class. And then my dean, she came in and asked me what was wrong and I just didn't want to tell her anything. And then she had asked me if there was somebody that I was comfortable speaking with and I said, 'Yes, Astacio,' and we went to his office. And we just spoke and I just told him everything that was going on during that year. I was so depressed."

The Circle Sessions had been monumentally and profoundly effective. Most of the girls were expressing themselves in a healthy way and making real, tangible improvements in their behavior, in the classroom and on the field. While everyone else was on a slightly upward trajectory, one girl in particular was spiraling downward fast and it completely baffled Chris.

Kimberly.

Kimberly began to display unusual behaviors that worried him. "I was no longer the silly girl who made everyone laugh, I was now that angry girl who was dangerous to talk to," she says. That desire to excel in softball suddenly disappeared, as she became more frustrated with herself. On one occasion during batting practice, she became so irate she threw her bat clear across the gym and stormed out in tears. When asked, no one had any clue what upset her. Her sister Claudia was no help, she blamed it on Kimberly's "time of the month." After practice that day, Kimberly came back to apologize to Chris. Obviously something was going on and he felt that she was on the cusp of divulging her troubles but he knew she didn't fully trust him yet. "There is no need to apologize for being upset," he said. "We all get frustrated and upset but it helps to talk to someone about it. I'm always here for you whenever you need to talk. I don't care if you want to talk about the weather, I will listen. Just please let me know if you are okay or in any trouble."

Kimberly insisted that she wasn't in any trouble and walked out of the gym with her head down. The next day Chris spoke to Kimberly's teachers to see if they'd noticed any change in her behavior. They said that she'd become more withdrawn during class and stopped completing her work. One teacher reported that Kimberly would often fight back tears but offered no explanation when questioned. "Perhaps she's going through some hormonal imbalance or boy problems," the teacher suggested. As ridiculous as that sounded, Chris held his tongue and told the teacher to keep him posted. Even though Chris was just getting to know Kimberly, he knew something was seriously wrong, but he needed her to open up to him. Chris asked the other girls on the team to keep an eye on Kimberly, to support her and help her find her voice.

Throughout that entire week, Chris continuously checked in with Kimberly to make sure she was okay. On Friday, he received a call from the dean claiming that Kimberly had an outburst during her last period class. Apparently, Kimberly had told her teacher to "suck my dick" and left the classroom in a dramatic fashion. For a second, Chris thought the dean must have gotten her name confused and was talking about someone else. He could not imagine Kimberly cursing at a teacher with such vulgar language or anyone else for that matter. Even Mr. Toro was perplexed when Chris told him what happened. "Are you sure they got the right girl?" Sure enough, the dean had Kimberly in her office hysterically crying. She refused to talk to anyone and had requested her coach.

Chris walked into dean's office to see Kimberly sitting with her head buried into her hands sobbing uncontrollably and shaking like a leaf. The dean looked frustrated, since she couldn't get one word out of her. "If she doesn't calm down and say something, I am going to have to call her mom to come pick her up. I can't send her home upset like this."

"No! No! Don't call my mom!"

For a brief moment, Kimberly resurfaced but only to angrily express her objection. She retreated back into her safe space with her face shoved into her hands. Chris pulled up a chair and sat right in front of her. As he tried to pry her hands away from her face, she resisted and became more hysterical. She began speaking but her hands muffled her voice making her words incoherent.

Finally, Kimberly emerged from her cocoon and repeatedly began to apologize. She tried to explain what happened in the classroom, but her emotions hindered her attempts. Chris grabbed both her hands, like they were praying together, and in the most reassuring voice said, "Kimberly, you are safe. I am not going to yell or get angry. But if you squeeze my hands any harder, we are going to have a problem."

Kimberly mustered strength for a smile and that calmed her down. Eventually, she shared with Chris that she had been depressed the entire week and felt like no one cared. Chis attempted to debunk her claim but she insisted that problems in her life didn't matter. Kimberly admitted that as her teacher circulated the class collecting homework, the teacher had gotten angry that her head had been down throughout the majority of the period. "She could clearly hear that I was crying but all she wanted was her damn work. She kept telling me to get up, where's my work, blah blah blah. Not once did she ask if I was alright. No! Her annoying voice kept irritating my soul. That's when I told her to 'suck my dick' and then I left."

Chris thanked Kimberly for finding the courage to be honest and then asked why she was so anguished. She quickly retracted her hands and cowered back into her chair. "No I can't . . . I can't . . . please leave it alone, it's nothing . . . it's stupid. I'm fine now, can I go home now?"

The dean allowed Kimberly to go home that day but she did call her mother to give her a heads-up. For some reason, Kimberly was afraid to talk to her mom.

Every day for another week, Kimberly cried but wouldn't tell anyone why. Finally, over the weekend, her squad—Nicky, Alcielis, Rashell, and Heaven—had a therapy session at one of their houses. Sex stuff came up and Kimberly realized that she had to talk to someone instead of internalizing her feelings. "Since there was no one at home to talk to, I told my girls," she says. Kimberly revealed that when Nicky shared her stories of sexual abuse it struck a nerve because it had happened to her, too. In fact, it had just happened again on New Year's Eve. And now she knew what happened to her wasn't normal. It had been happening to her since she was eight years old and she was sick of it and she wanted it to stop.

It really frightened the girls because it happened so recently. They were also shocked that Kimberly had *confianca* in them, a Spanish word that roughly translates to giving someone an enormous amount of trust. Kimberly was one of them, she was in the group for sure, but she was different; quiet, shy, and a little awkward. The girls were very affectionate with each other, but Kimberly didn't like to be hugged. She always tightened up when anyone touched her. She'd never really shared much about her personal life. Suddenly, seemingly out of nowhere, she'd trusted the girls with her deepest, darkest secret. "It was like, 'Wow,'" Alcielis says. "It answered a lot of questions about her that we had. For someone to be going through that, it explained a lot about her awkwardness and shyness. So when we found out what happened, it really opened our eyes."

"We have to tell Astacio," Nicky said.

Kimberly didn't want to. She was scared about who she was going to hurt, mostly the people in her family. "I cared too much about others' feelings," she says.

"We're going to Astacio," Nicky ordered.

On Monday, Chris thought he would have lunch for a change before checking on all his Lady Tigers. As he turned a corner in the school, he saw Kimberly clinging to Nicky, struggling to walk up the small flight of steps leading to the gym. She was doubled over and her face was flush with sadness. "She's been like this all morning and she's only getting worse," Nicky said. "We were going to wait until after school to speak to you but this can't wait."

Nicky tried her best to keep Kimberly walking upright, as they walked to Chris's office. It felt like one of the longest walks of his life, because he really didn't know what to expect. "It scared the hell out of me," Chris says.

"What's going on?' he asked.

"She has to tell you something," Nicky said.

Chris encouraged the girls to sit down but they wanted to stay on their feet. Kimberly leaned against Mr. Toro's desk, holding onto it for dear life, while tears fell to the floor. There was an awkward silence as he waited for someone to begin talking. It was obvious that Kimberly wasn't remotely ready to disclose this secret that had been haunting her so Chris suggested that maybe she should take a few minutes to regain her composure before going back to her class. Nicky finally spoke up.

"Well, Kimberly is not the only one who needs to speak to you. I actually have a question for you so I will go first. But before I start, I need you to promise that you will not interrupt me because I might get all emotional and you have to let me finish."

She made Chris pinky swear, cross his heart, and swear on his children, on his life, and on God himself. "You are our coach and in many ways, like our father . . . we all feel like you are the only one who would understand." Nicky explained that during a girls' night at her house over the weekend, the topics of "sex, virginity, and having kids" had come up.

Immediately, Chris threw up his hands and yelled, "Wait!" then asked if anyone was pregnant. The girls erupted in disgust, laying his suspicions to rest.

"Hell, no!" Nicky exclaimed. "We've seen how hard it is to raise a kid. There is no way I am getting pregnant. Besides, what we have to tell you is worse than that. And if you interrupt me again, I am going to leave."

Chris apologized and felt momentarily relieved. But as he leaned back into his chair a wave of dread overcame him. What could be possibly worst than pregnancy?

"Please let me speak and do not try to console me if I get upset. I need you to let me finish because I don't know if I can start up again if you stop me." Nicky began to tremble as the anxiety became a little too much for her to handle. She took a deep breath and told a vague tale that involved the sexual molestation of a very young Nicky. That, many years ago, her mother had been incarcerated, leaving Nicky and her sister Gheynee to live with their aunt Gladys. Sometime during their stay, Nicky was left alone with a male friend of the family who forced her to "do things that she didn't want to do." Fortunately, Nicky did not keep quiet and found the strength to inform her aunt. The individual that had taken advantage of her was "handled," and Nicky received help.

Now, here was Kimberly, who had admitted to her friends something similar had happened a month ago to the day. Nicky started to explain what Kimberly had told them but Chris stopped her.

"Okay, Nicky, hold on, thank you. But now I need to hear it from Kimberly's mouth."

Kimberly revealed what happened and that it had been happening since she was eight years old. That on New Year's Eve, this man locked her in the room and something bad happened.

"Stop, Kimberly. You don't have to tell me no more." He was devastated. As a father, he wanted to embrace her. He wanted to grab her and give her a hug and tell her she'd be okay. But he understood she might not want any male touching her and he knew it wasn't appropriate to ask her for any more details. So he held in his pain and anger, and called the school counselor and the dean. They called the police and they, along with an ACS rep, came to the school to question Kimberly.

"So you waited a whole month to tell your mom," a cop name Omar asked in disbelief, then screamed at Kimberly, "How would you feel if you had a daughter? I'd be mad if I had a daughter who didn't tell *me* for a month!"

Women wait years. Kimberly was only thirteen and didn't even know what sex was.

Next, the school called her mother, who was "sad and disappointed" she didn't know about it, Kimberly says. She met with Chris, the dean, the counselor, and her daughter. After informing her of the molestation, she turned to her daughter and asked only one question, in Spanish. "Are you still not a woman?"

Meaning, did she get penetrated.

"I'm still a virgin," Kimberly answered, humiliated, in front of the entire room.

"Then what's the problem? This is all blown out of proportion. She's fine."

Chris sat there stunned and bewildered. "Are you freaking kidding me?" he thought. But it was all too common in their culture to react to sexual abuse like this.

ACS came to the school three more times to see Kimberly and did one home visit. "I kept repeating my story so many times at school and at my house that it felt like I was singing a catchy song that everyone hates," she remembers. They also interviewed her mom, stepdad, and sister Claudia, but that was the end of it. Nothing happened to the uncle and everyone was furious at her for bringing ACS into their home. Kimberly didn't get punished, but being ignored and exiled was punishment enough. Nobody in her family ever believed her, and they never spoke about it again.

"Dirty laundry gets washed at home," Kimberly says. "But I had too much laundry and not enough soap. I don't know the feeling of coming out but I'm pretty sure it feels close to what I felt in the middle of eighth grade."

The day after Kimberly's harrowing confession, Nicky came to see Chris again. As a result of their talk, she had one more pressing concern. "Like

I said, we were all talking about virginity and stuff and you're a health teacher and I just had one more question: Even though I did those things as a little girl and I know it wasn't my fault, am I still a good girl? Am I still innocent?"

Chris's heart shattered into a million pieces for the millionth time that year.

"No matter what happened to you in the past," he said, "the person you are now defines you. If you feel like you're living an innocent type of life, then that's who you are. It doesn't matter who violated you. That's who you are."

Nicky started crying. "I don't believe that. I'm a horrible person."

"You're not a horrible person, Nicky." He gave her a giant hug. "I'd given out more hugs to these girls then they probably received from any male in their life," Chris notes sadly. "I'd given them more compliments than any male figure. Like Kimberly, she probably hated men, but she had a good reason to hate men. Yoshie did too. I tried to show them another side. Every man is not like that."

That night, Chris took his daughter, Cristina, still a baby, out of her crib and gave her a giant long hug and wept. Charisse asked him what was wrong. "I don't even want to talk about it," was all he could muster.

Chris was traumatized himself and Charisse hated that he was stressed all the time. She was very worried about his health. He was barely eating and lost a noticeable amount of weight recently. He had complained of feeling nauseous all the time. "I remember him throwing up in his office," Yoshie says. "He'd tell us to get the hell out so he could go puke in his bathroom." Chris just told them he ate something bad.

He'd been pretending he was okay until one day he couldn't fake it anymore. Just before Valentine's Day, a stomach bug was going around 22 and Chris caught it, too. He'd been in remission but his immune system was weak, so the virus hit him extra hard. The pain in his stomach became unbearable again and he threw up nonstop for two days straight. When he saw blood in the toilet, he was sure he was relapsing. He had to go back to the doctor ASAP.

At the next Circle Session, Chris knew he finally had to tell the girls the one secret he'd been hiding from *them*—he was a cancer survivor.

When they sat down, Chris said he wanted to go first this time. "You know, I teach you all how to work through pain. Because everyone here is in pain. Because your father's not there, someone died in your family, because you feel like no one cares about you or someone has hurt you so, so badly. I understand that because I have my own pain, but now it's a different kind of pain. It's a physical pain. Four years ago, I got stomach cancer. The doctors had to cut me open and take a third of my stomach out. It was the worst pain I'd ever felt in my life. But I survived, I made it through, and my cancer went in remission . . . but lately I'm not feeling so good again. Some of you probably noticed I'm not myself. So, I gotta go back into the hospital, I'm going to be out for a little while."

The girls collectively gasped.

"We did not know," Heaven says. "He pretended he was okay and we thought he was a happy healthy man. It was heartbreaking."

As soon as it sank in, they all burst into tears.

"Oh my God," Alexa bawled. "Every time something good happens there's always a catch!"

"You can't die!" Nicky cried. "You're the only father I've ever known!"

"I'm not gonna die tomorrow! I just wanted to prepare you!" Chris laughed.

The entire team swarmed Chris and engulfed him in a giant group hug. They all physically touched each other for the first time ever.

Once bitter enemies were now blood sisters.

"Don't give up on me and, more important, don't give up on yourself," he told his Lady Tigers. "Had I given up, I wouldn't be here today."

Part Three

PLAY BALL

Chapter Thirteen

WIN ONE FOR THE MISTER

Dear sisters,

April, we love you, so why are u taking so long to get here? The Lady Tigers are ready to beat those schools. We have no fear and there is nothing impossible. All we have to do is PLAY BALL. Softball is now our life so whatever happens never forget that softball is not just a sport it is our life. Never forget who you are, for surely the world will not either. Make it your strength. Then it can never be your weakness. Armor yourself in it, and it will never be used to hurt you. Strength doesn't come from what you can do. It comes from overcoming the things you once thought you couldn't. I want to give thanks to the team leader, Rashell. You have been there for the whole team and u never betrayed us. You start the day with the best exercise and end the day with a homerun. I also want to give thanks to the

girls that started not great and now getting better every step of the
way. I love you guys! <3
Sincerely,
#11 Yoshie!

Chris always wanted Yoshie to come out of her shell and be a co-captain with Rashell, but she'd been quiet and in the background up to this point, her social anxiety trumping her leadership capabilities. Now that Chris was in the hospital battling a possible cancer relapse, Yoshie stepped up and naturally took on the role, like sending this emotional, rousing letter to all of her teammates.

While Chris lay in a hospital bed hallucinating from a burning fever, his girls actually held practice without him. If he had seen it with his own two eyes, he would have thought he was hallucinating there, too. But it was real. After Chris got deathly sick again, the Lady Tigers were on a mission—work as a team so they could win their games for Coach Astacio. "When we saw he was in a bad place," Grateshka says, "at that moment, we came together and it made the team even stronger. He was strong and it gave us a reason to try and to make him proud."

"The least we could do was make him proud," Alexa adds. "When he got sick, it was an eye-opener."

And a call to action. They held practice at the park on 161st, before and after school, led by their fearless captain Rashell. "When he told us he had cancer, it stressed me out so much," she says. "We all cried. Boy oh boy the tears!"

Just like Coach Astacio, she broke up the girls into groups and gave each one its own leader to run drills. Rashell walked around helping as many girls as she could with the fundamentals, shouting out instructions like, "Fix your feet! Don't forget to twist your back foot!" To her surprise, "They actually listened to me." Well, except for Alexa. She wasn't the type to be bossed around by Rashell.

"She was still nasty but she was the leader," Yoshie says. "If we did something wrong, Rashell would always approach us. She was always saying, 'You have to do this better.' I was scared of her. But once I got to know her, I knew we'd have a connection because we were both leaders."

"Rashell was bossy, but she lead in a way that made you think it's good for you," Johanna notes.

Beefs were put aside, for the most part. "We tried, for him, to get along," Alexa says. "People started to treat me a little bit better."

"Things changed after Astacio got sick," Rashell confirms. "We would be so nice to each other." Nicky transformed into "the sweet one" on the team. She rediscovered the part of her personality she'd buried deep for self-protection when she moved back in with her birth mother. "She always huggin' everyone and we're like get off!" Rashell remembers. "You being *too* nice!"

The girls texted Chris videos and pictures of their practices and it made him smile. As a cancer patient and survivor, he had to go through the whole battery of tests, scans, and blood work again to determine if his disease had returned. Waiting for the results was agonizing beyond belief, but knowing his Lady Tigers were carrying the torch without him helped him get through the scariest moments. That struck him. Being in the hospital was the first time in forever he even had a minute to stop and reflect on the last six months. He thought about all the fights and the drama and the tears and the laughter. He thought about each girl and how far they'd come in such a short amount of time as a player and as a person and felt immense pride.

Then he remembered what Charisse asked him when they were fighting so badly. "Are you doing this for them? Or you?"

The answer, he realized, was "both."

No question being on the Lady Tigers had helped these girls. No question the team helped him, too. Coaching gave him a reason to get out of bed every morning, especially when he was feeling sick. It gave him a purpose higher than himself. He also believed that coaching the team kept his cancer at bay, for as long as possible. Now it might be back again, and he had to prepare himself for the news, whatever it may be.

He turned his head and looked at his wife, sleeping in the uncomfortable chair next to his hospital bed. She'd been there every night for him and he didn't deserve her. On his quest to save the world, Charisse was holding their family together. She kept the house in order. She got Cristina the help she needed for her autism. She soothed Justin when he had anxiety about his papi's cancer coming back. "She was the stability in my chaos," Chris says.

She opened her eyes and caught him staring at her. "What," she said quietly.

"I'm sorry," he said. "I'm going to do better." From now on, he promised, he would manage his time better and make his family the number-one priority. At first, Charisse did not want to compromise. It was softball or the family. Now, she was ready to talk and work out a deal. Chris promised to lessen his practices and not hold them on the weekends. He also had to help out more at home and cook meals on the days he didn't have softball. He had to make sure that he made time for the kids and her. And no more spending their own money on the softball program . . .

His phone buzzed. It was a text from Nicky. She accidentally hit Angie in the head with a bat and they were at the emergency room. "Don't worry, she only got a couple stiches!" she wrote.

Seriously? Chris made a few frantic calls to make sure Angie's head didn't look like a piñata. When he reached her, Angie says she asked him, "Where's my coach? Where's my second dad? You know, it was that love for him." Once he knew she was going to be okay, Chris got in touch with another teacher at the school named Ms. Marte, who played softball in college. She had the background and knowledge of the game. She agreed to monitor the practices while he was laid up in the hospital.

The next texts he received were from the girls complaining about Ms. Marte.

"She's making us run up the steps!"

"So do it!" he texted back.

"I was there the day another coach came," Yoshie says. "She was just there to help. She made the whole team run because we talked back to her. Well, it wasn't me. It was the eighth-graders. She didn't come back the next day. She told Astacio we were bad."

"What she actually said," Chris recalls, was, "Don't ever get sick again. I'm not doing this shit. Fuck those bitches!"

A week after checking into the hospital, Chris was informed that he was cancer-free and released. The next morning, at 6 A.M., Frederick opened the school building and saw Astacio warming up with his girls. "You look terrible, go home!" he said.

"Nah, there's nobody here to do this. They need to practice."

"I've never seen an educator more dedicated," Frederick says. "All he cared about were those kids."

And they cared about him.

Empathy was a new skill some of the girls had never heard of or felt before. When Chris came back, he noticed a completely different team, one that was on its best behavior, brought him cups of water, and, most astounding, actually volunteered to put equipment away. "We helped him out a bit more," Robin verifies. "It lasted like two weeks."

The power dynamic had shifted while he was away, too. Nicky and Yoshie had become an inseparable dynamic duo, having bonded over the absence of their father figure and taking control of the team while Chris was gone. "Nicky made me popular on the team," Yoshie says. "Rashell and Alcielis talked to me now."

No matter how awful Chris felt—he would feel sickly on and off until the end of time after his stomach surgery removed one-third of his stomach—he always showed up to practice, even if he'd just sit and watch his team from the sidelines. "I always tell the girls not to quit," he says. "What kind of example would I be if I quit?"

Nicky was his shadow, always by his side, Rashell his nursemaid. "We got this!" Rashell would tell Chris. "What do you need help with?" Rashell's mom thought she was the devil, now she was an angel. From the moment he made that phone call, he saw a drastic change in Rashell. She almost quit being captain. Now she wanted to be seen as someone who was a role model. He reminded her often that even though he named her leader, the girls really chose her.

The Lady Tigers were rapidly approaching game day. They continued to work their butts off. They worked on fielding grounders and pop flies and line drives. They hit the cage with ferocity and made the necessary adjustments in their stances and swings. Johanna and Achelin perfected their windmills. They watched video without complaining (too much). They even taught themselves some softball cheers so they could intimidate their opponents with their superabundant school spirit:

My name is Gheynee and
You know what I got
(all) What do you got?
I got a team that's hotter than hot!
(all) How hot is hot?
Grand slams and home runs too
(all) Ahuh ahuh
Now, Heaven, do what I do!

11 is her number
Yoshie is her name
And she one of the reasons
We gonna win this game
And if you don't believe us
Try and beat us!

Cheering bonds teammates. It's also a way for a team to rally when they're losing, support players at bat, and rattle pitchers and opponents in dramatic situations, like a 3-2 count or bases loaded. It's a special, unique tradition specific to women's softball. No other women's sport, or any sport for that matter, does it. "How the songs started and why they're only used in softball is a mystery," the *Washington Post* has reported, but speculated it may have "started in softball-crazy California and gradually migrated east."

There are dozens of silly, clever, singsong-y cheers that have been passed around for a couple of generations. There are specific cheers honoring even the most mundane moments in a softball game—like walking or hitting a foul ball. There are cheers that involve back and forth duels between teams, and cheers that include elaborate clapping or stomping. Memorizing them all is a rite of passage. After all, a team's personality is often defined by which ones they choose to chant during games—funny, spirited, or intimidating—how often they do it, and how loudly. Cheering usually only occurs on offense, when the girls are in the dugout at bat. But there are teams that literally sing cheers from the first pitch to the last out. Cheering has become as integral to the game of softball as good pitching.

Now that the Lady Tigers learned some cheers, they were finally ready for the big show. At the end of March, Chris sent a mass email to the staff:

> *Dear 22 Family,*
>
> *The Lady Tigers will embark on their very first season starting the second week of April. If you would like to come out and support our team, please do not hesitate to do so. We are very excited and eager to start playing! I will give our schedule to those who are interested. Have a great and restful weekend.*

On April 9, opening day arrived.

It was time to put all the skills they'd learned to use.

Game on.

Chapter Fourteen

BLOWOUT IN THE BRONX

It was a sight to see. All of the Lady Tigers decked out in their tough black and orange uniforms, marching down College Avenue together like warriors going into battle. Alcielis carried a black and pink glove and a pink bat bag and even donned bright pink cleats. "I didn't care if they even were good cleats or not, I just wanted them to be cute."

It was a twenty-minute walk to the asphalt field on 145th and 3rd Avenue, home of the Lady Eagles, their very first opponents, and the girls were pumped up with adrenaline and nervous energy. Chris lifted them up with pep talks the whole way. "I'm proud of you, Robin, I'm proud of you Claudia, I'm proud of you, Kimberly, I'm proud of you, Alcielis, I'm also proud of you, Nicky, my long-lost daughter, I'm proud of you, Heaven, I'm proud of you, Rashell, and Ms. Yoshie, I will always be proud of you forever. Who are we?"

"Lady Tigers."

"Who are we?"

"LADY TIGERS!"

Middle school girls' softball programs were rare in the Bronx. The Lady Eagles hailed from the Mott Haven section of the South Bronx, which was quite possibly more poverty-stricken than 22's community. MS 223, or the Laboratory School of Finance and Technology, sounded fancy but was far from it. Unlike 22, 223 had made great educational improvements and had recently been named tenth-best middle school in the city by the Department of Education. Like 22, the Lady Eagles' neighborhood was extremely dangerous, and their concrete softball diamond was surrounded by menacing-looking, tall housing projects.

After warming up, the Lady Eagles, decked out in cheerful, bright yellow uniforms, took the field and the umpire announced dramatically, "Play ball!" As the visiting team, the Lady Tigers were up to bat first. Chris ran over to coach third base. They didn't have a first base coach. Nobody else was there. Not even one parent.

The Lady Tigers gave a loud, hearty cheer to get a rally going:

> *She's the l-e-a, d-o-f-f*
> *She the lead off batter*
> *Da da da le, l-e-a l-e-a-d o-f-f*
> *Leadoff batter let's go, Nicky!*

Nicky whiffed three pitches in a row and struck out.

Angie came up next. Whiffed three pitches in a row and struck out.

Yoshie came up next. Whiffed three pitches in a row and struck out.

Three up, three down.

They'd all done so much work in the batting cage but had never faced a live pitcher before. They couldn't practice hitting off Johanna or Achelin outside or inside. Both situations were off limits for different reasons (getting killed, breaking windows). It was a lot different to have a pitch coming from a real person's hand, and not in the exact same spot every time.

"That's okay! We'll get 'em next inning!" Chris said, clapping his hands. "Let's play good defense!"

The Lady Tigers took the field for the first time ever, and Johanna stepped on the mound. What happened next can only be described as "batting practice." The Lady Eagles kept cranking the ball everywhere. Cranking, cranking, cranking. They lit up Johanna like a pinball machine. And it was as if the Lady Tigers had never had one practice. Everything they'd learned went out the window. They apparently didn't know how to catch the ball anymore or where to throw the ball or what the heck to do in any situation. They made error after error, and the Lady Eagles rounded the bases. After five runs, the league's mercy rule kicked in, and it was an automatic three outs.

The Lady Tigers' faces were crestfallen when they came into the dugout.

"Good job out there," Chris said meekly. They shot him daggers. "Let's get some hits now!"

The girls didn't feel much like cheering. But they tried anyway.

Alexa
Let's go
You can do it do it do it do it now
Hit that ball
Just like you should
Right now hit that ball
Hit that ball just like you should

Alexa came up to the batter's box, whiffed three pitches in a row, and struck out.

Rashell came up next. Whiffed three pitches in a row and struck out. Johanna came up next. Whiffed three pitches in a row and struck out. Three up, three down. Again.

All the girls were miserable. They couldn't get a hit.

They walked lazily onto the field, even though Chris had instructed them many times that they should always run to their positions because that's what real pro athletes do. He mixed it up a little in the second inning, to see if that might help their defense. He assigned Genesis a position but she insisted she didn't want to play. "I didn't want to make mistakes and commit any errors. I hated drawing attention to myself. It was my mind playing games with me. I thought, 'You're gonna fail, you're gonna make the team lose.'"

The team didn't need Genesis to lose. They were losing just fine without her.

Achelin was now on the rubber to pitch. She had more velocity than Johanna but was much less accurate. She couldn't find the strike zone to save her life and began walking every single Lady Eagle. Poor Alexa at catcher had to keep running back to the backstop to retrieve wild pitches. With every base on balls, the game slowed to a mind-numbing snail's pace. The girls grumbled obscenities under their breath. Mayoli sat down in the outfield. Achelin started crying. "We was just horrible," Gheynee admits. "Every time we made one mistake, we argued in the middle of the game."

After five more runs, the mercy rule thankfully kicked in again, and they got an automatic three outs. The score was now 10-0.

The next inning was just as disastrous and the softball gods apparently had seen enough. In the middle of the third, with the Lady Tigers in the field, down 12 to zip and counting as the Eagles rounded the bases like a merry-go-round, suddenly, there was a loud *POP POP POP POP POP*.

The unmistakable sound of gunfire.

Apparently a ShotSpotter alerted police, because cop car sirens blared immediately. They all saw lots of smoke and gangbangers running in every direction. *POP POP POP*. "Get behind the fence!" Chris screamed. "Duck! Duck!" All of the players, Lady Tigers and Lady Eagles, ran off the field and dove into their dugouts. They hid there for fifteen minutes waiting out crossfire and police activity. Yoshie remembers crying like a baby. "Me, I was extra scared," she says. "I remember I had a dream the night before that I got shot."

Chris was terrified, too. "It wasn't the first time happening," he explains, "but it was the first time happening in a neighborhood I didn't know. How would I get my girls out of there alive? I couldn't believe this was happening at our first game. I was like, 'Yo, I might have some kids that are going to die today.'"

When it felt safe to come out, Chris ran over to the Lady Eagles coach, who asked, nonplussed, "Want to finish the game?"

What kind of stupid question was that? "Um, no, I do not want to finish the game," Chris replied. "Are we good to go home by ourselves?" He wanted to make sure the Lady Tigers wouldn't be target practice walking around in the wrong neighborhood.

"Yeah, you're fine. Everything's fine."

Everything was not fine. It was obvious to Chris that this guy had seen so many shoot-outs he was numb to it. He knew what that was like. Chris rounded up his girls, who were freaked out about the gang war but more gutted about their humiliating shutout. They packed up their gear in a huff and threw stuff in their bags angrily. "The morale was horrible," Chris remembers.

"Hold up," he said. "Everybody come here." Chris climbed on top of the bench in the dugout so he could see all their faces. He was disappointed, too, because he thought they'd trained really hard. All of that preparation . . . and they still sucked. He'd hyped them up to be the greatest team in the world. The mighty Lady Tigers. He wanted them to have that mentality. In order to be great, he told them, you have to think like you're great. Now he was a liar. They were not great. They figured he only saw them as great because he loved them, like a father-daughter thing.

"This is our first game and we lost. Who cares? We learn. This is what we're here for. You guys are still great. We just have to remember what we did at practice more and utilize it." He tried to build them back up and lift their spirits. After his speech was over, "They were all happy again," he laughs.

"They look like yellow bananas," Nicky said, and they all cracked up.

"They're not very a-peeling!" Grateshka the court jester exclaimed. "After the first game," she notes, "I actually looked at everybody and thought, 'These are not bad people, they're great people.' They're just scared to open up to the world. So I decided from that moment on I'd put my pride aside and just speak to people I didn't normally speak to. That's the way you make friends."

That night Chris sent an email to the 22 staff:

Unfortunately, we lost the game 0–12 and had to end the game early due to gang related activity in the area. But with your support, our girls will move beyond the loss.

It's no problem, Chris thought. If at first you don't succeed, right? There would be more games and plenty more chances to get that first W.

Sadly, one of his players would never get that chance.

Not long after the drubbing, Robin's grandma Redell passed away from complications related to diabetes. The only person who unconditionally loved her, her only guardian left in the world, was gone. Her mother died in childbirth and her father was in jail, now Robin was basically an orphan. Even though she got in trouble all the time, "My grandma was my best friend," she says.

Distraught, she went to school that day anyway. "When I came to school nobody said nothing. No good morning," she remembers. "I was acting sneaky." She hung out in her favorite secret spot in the staircase until lunchtime, then, in a grief-stricken daze, moved into the cafeteria. Cellphone use had been banned by Frederick during school hours, but Robin sat in the lunchroom reading condolence texts from friends and family anyway. A dean saw Robin on her phone and, without warning, snatched it away from her from behind. "I blacked out," she recalls. "I turned around and knocked him out. When he went down I kept hitting him. Multiple times. Security guards didn't do nothing. They just watched me do it. Nobody broke it up."

Robin was arrested but the dean didn't press charges. He knew Robin well and was "mad close" with her grandma since she was always down at the school. He didn't know it was Robin from behind and didn't know her grandma had passed away. He felt bad about grabbing her cellphone, but the bottom line was that she assaulted a dean and had to face the repercussions. Instead of expelling Robin, Frederick arranged for her immediate transfer to the ROADS Charter School II, Bronx regional campus, for troubled students who were overage, homeless, in foster care, or had been in jail. "At ROADS Bronx," the mission statement claimed, "we embrace our students holistically and seek to address all aspects of their wellbeing including healing any past or ongoing emotional traumas, redirecting non-productive behaviors, helping meet basic needs for food and shelter, and, importantly, making up for years of unsuccessful learning experiences."

Robin left PS 22 that very day, and never even got a chance to say goodbye to her teammates. She was no longer a member of the Lady Tigers, but Chris let her keep her beloved uniform jersey. "I was worried about her when she left," he says. "I saw her future in jail. Everybody saw that and said that. I felt like it was my fault. I was too hard on her."

At least Robin got to play in one game. The next game was at home versus another local school, JHS 145 (Academy for Creative Education and the Arts), aka the Arturo Toscanini School, named after the famous Italian composer. All these schools had grandiose names that meant nothing—145 was shut down a few years later due to similar issues at 22, like poor performance and violence. According to an op-ed by former teachers published in the *New York Daily News*, out of 300 students, "20 percent were living in homeless shelters, 18 percent had learning disabilities, and 18 percent had gone extended periods without any education at all." Located just four blocks away in the same Morrisania section of the South Bronx, on 165th and Teller, gang violence was rampant, just like around 22.

Chris was nervous to host a home game, but he felt as prepared as he could be. He had his walkie-talkies and extra security patrolling the playground. The NYPD van was parked in its usual spot on College Avenue, too. If anything went down, they were just a skip away from the back entrance to the school and could all run inside. The girls were also much more prepared than last time. They'd been truly humbled by the shutout. They saw the dumb mistakes they'd made during the first game, and, at practice, talked about those mistakes, took constructive criticism well, and did more drills to correct the mistakes.

When 145 showed up, strutting around the corner all loud and cheering boastfully, Chris's stomach dropped. "Aw shit," he thought on first sight of them. The fronts of their purple and white jerseys were emblazoned with their team name—the Lady Tigers. He didn't know they were also Lady Tigers. He *did* know that would cause a lot of drama.

"They're playing on our field!" Rashell growled. "We have to win now because this is our home and this is our name!"

"Yeah!" all of the original Lady Tigers shouted.

"Who are we?" Rashell screamed.

"LADY TIGERS!" they screamed back.

A for effort, F for execution. The game was a repeat of the last game. No, actually, it was worse. The Other Lady Tigers crushed them like a cheesecake. They had a large African-American pitcher who blew pitches by them as fast as a missile. She intimidated them and they kept whiffing.

"We can't hit off her!" groused Alexa, one of their strongest batters. If she couldn't connect, no way players like Heaven or Kimberly could. They'd still only used the machine in the gym and simply could not adjust to live pitching. In the cage, if they missed the first pitch and the second pitch, at least they knew that the next pitch would be in that same spot. This pitcher was spraying bullets in every corner of the strike zone, high, low, left, right. They could barely see the pitch or get their bats around in time before the umpire called out, "Steeeeeerike!" It was one, two, three, "You're out!" The girls couldn't touch the ball with the bat, so they resorted to the "Statue of Liberty" pose where they just stood there frozen holding up the bat like a sculpture.

Their fielding was a catastrophe, too. Johanna was back on the mound, and she could throw the ball over the plate, but it was such a meatball, so slow-cooked and juicy, the Other Lady Tigers creamed it every time. Once again, Mayoli was so busy singing in the outfield, she had no idea the ball was even heading her direction. On top of that, the girls still had no idea where to throw the ball when it was hit to them. On one play, Alcielis was playing shortstop and when the ball rolled to her, she scooped it up but just stood there. She looked over to Astacio blankly as the runners flew around the bases.

"Throw it!" Chris screamed.

"Throw it!" Nicky and Angie and Yoshie and Rashell screamed.

So she threw it. Randomly in the air. Nowhere near any person covering any base.

"What are you doing?!" Chris shrieked.

Alcielis gave him the finger.

When the inning finally ended by the five-run mercy rule, Chris pulled her to the side.

"If you ever stick your middle finger up at me again . . ."

"Everyone was screaming at me!"

". . . you will never play on this team again. You hear me?"

She nodded sheepishly. Then when Chris turned around, she gave him the finger again.

She wasn't wrong. Throughout the game, after every botched play, the Lady Tigers mocked and ridiculed each other.

"That was your fault!"

"Shut up, that ain't my fault!"

"Why are you even on this team?"

"You suck, bro!"

"No you suck, bro!"

"You have to support each other!" Chris hollered. "You have to communicate!" He looked over at Genesis sitting quietly on the bench observing. "You want to get in there?" Why not, he figured, it couldn't get any worse. Genesis shook her head "no" definitively. She still thought the team would win without her.

"Oh my God, everybody kept getting mad because we were losing," Alexa says. "It was stupid, it was tragic. Girls be flinging the ball and nobody was ready. Or the runner was already safe by a mile and they threw it anyway. They just made the whole team look stupid."

Their opponents were laughing at them—the ultimate sign of disrespect. So was anyone who'd walked by and checked out the game. Home-field advantage was an oxymoron. Nobody really came to see the Lady Tigers play, not their parents, not even Chris's own wife. So their home crowd consisted mostly of loud-mouthed boys from the neighborhood running around recklessly all over the playground. They weren't even cheering on the home team, they were laughing at them and shouting out insults and sexual innuendos. They sat in the girls' "dugout," which was not really a dugout but just outdoor iron park benches. "They came back from the field and didn't have nowhere to sit because all these boys were sitting there," Chris says. He ignored them because they hadn't interrupted the game so far, plus he didn't want to start anything if he didn't have to. "I was new to the neighborhood, they weren't going to listen to me."

One lone teacher, Mrs. Holloway, showed up for the Lady Tigers, wearing her signature sunglasses even though the sun was going down. "Holloway would go to games and support them," Frederick confirms. Adds Grateshka, "She brought a lot of positive energy and vibes." But even Mrs. Holloway's kind encouragement couldn't spur the Lady Tigers to victory. After six painful innings, the torture ended. The final score was 16-0.

As the girls high-fived their opponents and said, "Good game," the mandatory act of sportsmanship after a game win or lose, it took every fiber of their being not to jump the Other Lady Tigers for grilling them. They may have stunk up the joint, but they didn't scratch the other teams' eyes out for making fun of them. So, that was a small but significant step in the right direction.

"Huddle up," Chris said before things could get ugly. Their faces were twisted up in agony and sadness. He tried to look upbeat on the outside, so the girls couldn't tell that on the inside he was totally crushed, too.

"Everybody who's telling you you're not good enough. Stop. Don't let them bring you down. You're strong and even though we lost that doesn't mean nothing. In my heart you won. You know why you won? Because every day you come to school despite what's going on in your life. You feel like the world hates you. Stop. You could have been crying at home but instead you come in, fighting every day. That's better than winning the game."

Mrs. Holloway walked over to the team.

"How'd my babies do?" she asked sweetly and instantly their frowns turned upside down. She just had that way of being able to clear out negative energy.

"We suck, Mrs. Holloway," Heaven said.

"You'll get 'em next time, sweetie."

Chapter Fifteen

SLIDING INTO WORST

The Lady Tigers did not get the next one. Or the one after that. Or the one after that. "Our first home game people showed up to watch, then never came again," Chris says. "A lot of people in the neighborhood gathered around to watch but we sucked so that was it. Who wants to see *us*? It was embarrassing."

The only thing the Lady Tigers excelled at was losing. All over the city. They lost in the Bronx. They lost in Brooklyn. They lost on the Upper West Side. They lost on the Lower East Side. "All Manhattan teams destroyed us," Chris says. The majority of the Manhattan games were played in Chinatown on Cherry Street, next to FDR Drive, in East River Park. The Manhattan teams were comprised mostly of white girls, and the Lady Tigers automatically assumed the white girls were better than them because of the color of their skin, and because they had the best equipment, lots of coaches, and lots of parents, moms *and* dads, cheering on their daughters.

"I told them race has nothing to do with softball, it's about heart," Chris says. But they weren't blind; they saw with their own eyes that they only had one coach, Astacio, no parents at their games, and crappy equipment. Or not enough equipment—it kept getting stolen.

> *Hey 22 family,*
>   *We are missing a bunch of gloves fundraised by DonorsChoose (about 13). The girls did not have enough gloves to play in today's game. Please let me know if you see them.*

The Lady Tigers sometimes had to borrow gloves, helmets, and bats from the opposing teams, who were not always sympathetic to their plight. "Some schools complained about how we weren't ready," Grateshka remembers. "They didn't want to share. One game two of us didn't have mitts in the field." Rashell adds that the Lady Tigers finally learned how to share because they had to. "We still couldn't afford gloves so we'd switch going on and off the field. Bro, I got you, I'll help you."

The Manhattan fields were far from the subway and required long walks. "We were really bad," Heaven admits. "Loud, ratchet kids." Chris remembers walking by an old man sitting on the steps of his brownstone.

"Hey, boy, dat's your team?" the man asked.

"Yeah, that's my team," Chris said wearily.

"God bless you." He didn't mean it spiritually. He said it in a way like there was no way he'd be caught dead with all those girls.

By the time they got to the fields, the Lady Tigers were miserable. It was still windy and chilly in May, especially so close to the water. "We were tired, hungry, and as cold as ever," Heaven adds.

"Can we take a break, mister?" they'd whine.

"No, we're already half hour late!" Chris barked. "Get out there and get your heads in the game!"

Their heads could not be further out of the game and up their you-know-whats. The Lady Tigers could not seem to transfer the skills they'd learned in practice to real game situations. They froze up, literally and figuratively. Against MS 450 (East Side Community School), at Baruch Field in East River Park, they spaced the basic fundamentals they'd gone over a million times. In the field, "if the ball wasn't hit directly at them, they're not moving," Chris laments. "They weren't even covering bases. I used to scream, 'Even if it's hit to her, you have to cover your base! She's running to you!'"

"Oh, I didn't know that."

"But this is what we're doing in practice!"

"Really?"

Mayoli couldn't stop singing and dancing in left field. "Sometimes I pictured myself singing in front of a million people," she says. "It was my dream." That was tolerated, but when she sat down on the ground and took her glove off, the older girls flipped out. "Astacio, look what Mayoli's doing!" Nicky barked. "She gotta pay attention! This is a softball game not a concert!" After that, Mayoli stopped playing and became the team's official photographer, and everyone was happy.

The teams' biggest issue was that the girls watched the game like spectators, instead of playing the game, on defense and offense. As an example, when they hit the ball, they were taught to take off immediately. "But they didn't get that concept of running after you hit the ball. They paused. Like, 'Ooh, I hit the ball!' Instead of, 'I swing the bat, I hear something, I gotta go.' For some of the girls, it was the first time they ever hit the ball in a game so they were like, 'Wow, look where it's going!'"

Then, if they somehow managed to get on base, they still had no idea what to do as a runner, especially tagging up. "How many times did I tell them when the ball is hit, if it's caught in the air, you can't run? Well, they were still running. Or I'd say to them, 'Okay, if it's hit in the air, you stay here until it's caught. Got it?'

"'Got it!'

"Then it's hit in the air and she's gone. And I'm screaming, 'Where are you going?!' They really did not know. Even though I explained it over and over again, it was still a foreign concept. I'm screaming, 'Go back! Go back!'"

"'Go back where?'"

The good news was that, at long last, a few of them had started connecting bat to ball. Racking up some hits was major progress. Yoshie was so frustrated that she kept swinging and missing, she told Chris she wanted to quit. But they kept tweaking her stance until it clicked, and then she clicked. "She started making contact and her making contact gave her more confidence."

Despite their dismal record, the truth was, with each game, the all took tiny steps forward. "People was trying," Alexa says. Chris wanted them to stop and smell the roses, and celebrate the small victories, just not in the middle of the game. Against MS 111, they got their first hit, the next game versus ESMS they earned their first run. The moment the first Lady Tiger crossed home plate, the girls went bananas, even though they were still losing badly, baffling their opponents. "The score was 20-1," Chris laughs, "but we erupted. We finally got one!"

The girls also had individual moments of brilliance, which Chris made sure to praise. "One game, I was so sleepy that day and I was not paying attention," Heaven explains. "I was playing shortstop. Or catcher. Anyway, I was squatting 'cause I was so tired and the ball came to me and I jumped up and caught it. I was like, 'How did I do that?' Then everyone was like, 'Yay!'"

Yoshie started the season unable to hit the ball. With hard work, she'd grown into one of the strongest batters on the team and a star athlete. She'd also quietly become Rashell's de facto co-captain. Both were powerful leaders with different yet effective styles. Yoshie was the strong silent type who shone by example, Rashell the strong outspoken type. They balanced each other out and motivated their teammates in their own ways. "Yoshie would give me the best pep talks before games," Johanna recalls. "She'd say, 'C'mon you got this! It's just you and Gheynee behind the plate.' Gheynee spoke Spanish so she caught for me a lot."

Chris noted the team's micro progressions on the field and off in an email update to the 22 staff after a game that garnered multiple runs but another check in the loss column:

Even though we lost 16–6, I was very proud of our girls for putting up such a great fight to the end. When one of the players on the other team became upset, Rashell encouraged our team to "clap it up" for the player. They demonstrated true sportsmanship.

Sportsmanship was not even in the Lady Tiger's vocabulary a couple of weeks prior. They were finally having fun with each other. They had splits competitions until Gheynee almost split in half. "We were dying. The girls made me laugh and forget about my life," Mayoli says. "The girls were there for me giving me love." They were learning to treat each other as equals and communicate better. "We got used to talking to each other," Yoshie explains. "That was the worst thing before, we were just in our groups. Well, I was by myself half the time, until me and Nicky got closer."

The two had been bonding all season and, in May, their budding friendship blossomed into a young romance, meaning lots of PDA, hand-holding, and hugs (Nicky was a champion hugger). "We got to know each other and she was cute and she told me she liked me," Yoshie says. "So we became girlfriend and girlfriend. We dated and I liked it. Nicky was the person who helped me know who I am. I wasn't open with it. It was Nicky who brought it out and I don't blame her. I thank her for that. If it wasn't for her, I probably would have never opened up that much that year."

"We were an awesome couple that was gonna stay together forever," Nicky confirms. "Just like a little boo thing. She was a good girl, loving and kind."

Everybody on the Lady Tigers was cool with Yoshie and Nicky being boo'd up. Astacio was supportive, too; it was surprisingly socially acceptable for girls at 22 to be fluid about their sexuality. Angie, who was older and had more experience in this arena, gave Yoshie advice. "She was flowing in that same direction, so it was like she looked up to me a lot," she says. "I was always there for her."

Positive stuff was happening but it couldn't cover up the fact that the Lady Tigers hadn't won one single game. "You have to shake hands with the coaches after the games and they all said to me, 'Don't worry, it'll get better.'" It had to get better soon because every loss whittled away at the girls' confidence, which Chris had worked so hard to build up. "Midway through the season we were only losing by three, four, five runs, not a lot. They were like, 'Oh, we lost again.' 'But we scored, that means you're improving!' There was no patience. They needed instant gratification."

He didn't blame them. There was no way to sugarcoat it. Winning obviously felt better, but they'd never known that feeling, on the softball field, at school, at home, anywhere. Sure, a little bit of failure builds character. Everybody knows that old cliché. But losing every single game made these girls feel worthless all over again. "The person who said winning isn't everything never won anything," soccer star Mia Hamm once claimed.

As the losses piled up, the girls' confidence bottomed out, and their behavior got more and more "ratchet," as Heaven would say. The wheels were coming off the train. The team had to take long subway rides together and the girls got increasingly out of control—cursing, yelling, and running around. Chris was so embarrassed he sat as far away from them as possible with his baseball hat pulled low, mortified but fully understanding when the other passengers switched cars to escape their obnoxious, ear-splitting behavior. A couple of the girls, including Angie, did a stripper routine on a pole in one of the cars. "We used to be very reckless on the train," Rashell confirms. "We'd be like, 'Dance, dance!' Clapping and swinging around."

That was all Chris could take. The next day he called a mandatory meeting. "You girls got me in trouble!" he fumed. Chris lied and said the MTA called and was going to ban the Lady Tigers from ever riding the subway again. He even set it up so another teacher busted into the meeting and pretended that he'd gotten a call from the MTA, too. "I got a fuckin' call that you guys want to be acting wild on the train!" Chris raged. "It's a fuckin' embarrassment! How could you do this to me when I present you as the best girls ever? I'm canceling every away game! You'll play in the yard for the rest of the season!"

"Oh snap, he was cursing so we knew it was bad," Rashell says. "What we gonna do? It was hectic." The story was so convincing, Grateshka still believes to this day the MTA called. "Girls was so loud people just complained about it. I guess they saw our jerseys and they wrote down the name and gave a complaint about it. We felt bad."

Chris suspended Angie for two games. He expected that behavior from other girls on the team but not the Angel Kid. It devastated him. He also called her father. "Angie was benched. I didn't even let her go to the games. I was really angry because I expected better from her. It worked because she didn't do it again. They all stopped doing it."

To Chris, there was no question that there was a correlation between the girls losing so many games and losing their focus, their skills, and their minds. It was textbook.

Johanna's arm literally gave out. After being such a reliable pitching machine, slow but steady on the mound, suddenly she tired easily in games and stopped doing the correct windmill motion. "You have to really concentrate on the dynamics or it won't come out naturally, you forget how to actually throw it," Chris says. "When she got tired, she did an underarm pitch. You wouldn't see the windmill anymore."

Once the Lady Tigers started losing and losing and losing and losing, old bad behaviors resurfaced, like Grateshka's clowning. During one game in mid May, she was so busy dancing behind the plate, playing catcher, she let a base runner steal second. Chris thought seriously about hiding the rest of the game schedule from her. "I didn't want her coming to the games anymore because she thought she was a frickin' comedian."

They felt like they were total losers, so they acted like total losers. "Towards the end of the season, they were horrible again," Chris says. They didn't want to do any schoolwork. They stopped showing up to practice. Nicky, Alcielis, and Rashell were running wild around the building again. "If we had our uniforms on, we wouldn't go to class," Rashell says. "We're Lady Tigers! If we had games, I'd cut the whole day, curse at teachers. They'd say, 'I'll get you kicked off the team.' You can't. No teacher could kick me off the team."

It seemed to Chris it wasn't a coincidence that the brattier the girls got, the higher Alcielis's shorts got. "Her butt cheeks were hanging out. If I told her, 'That's too short,' she'd hike them up more. There's no boys around, who you impressing?"

Alcielis's short shorts came out of the closet again, as did Nicky's bullying. "She always had problems with girls on the other team," Yoshie says. "Always drama." The Lady Tigers' thuggish, gang-like behavior reappeared, too. They almost got into a rumble after a game in Chinatown, not with the opposing team but with spectators. A bunch of boys came out of nowhere and started teasing Grateshka. "They were talking at her nonstop," Yoshie describes. "A boy said something, and all the girls reacted. The boys had a weapon and followed us to the subway after the game, so we had to carry bats to the train station."

Old beefs were back. Kimberly and Claudia hadn't hashed out what had happened in their family after the molestation charges, and bad blood was brewing under the surface. During practice one afternoon, they were sitting next to each other on a bench, when Claudia put her hands on Kimberly's lap.

"I don't like anyone touching me," Kimberly said.

"What, are you going to tell on me, too?" Claudia clapped back.

Kimberly bolted up and ran away crying hysterically.

"She's your sister, how can you do that?" Chris said, shaking his head. He didn't know that they'd been ignoring each other since the ACS home visit. They lived in the same apartment and they weren't even talking. Their mother didn't want to hear about any of it, telling Kimberly, "It's not happening anymore so why are you not over that?" But Claudia didn't believe it ever happened to begin with. "She was really mad at me," Kimberly says.

Emotions were running high. When Angie returned from suspension, her behavior was totally out of character. During one game, Chris noticed she was crying while playing first base. Angie rarely cried in public, she always put a happy smile on her face even when she was upset. "I've seen my mom do that so many times. I've seen her go from like tears to just happy. I do it to this day. Go through a problem and just shut down and deal with it on my own. And that causes me more problems. I'm not speaking to nobody getting over my problems, I'm just adding on to my problems. That's the problem with me. I'm too hard on myself. I don't give myself a break."

Now, she was crying out in the field for the world to see but she wouldn't let Chris help her. "Leave me alone, leave me alone, leave me alone," was all she could say to him. "Let me be and let me cry it off, I'll be fine afterwards." He had no idea what she was upset about.

Could have been problems at home, of course. Those hadn't magically disappeared into thin air, for any of the girls. Some got even worse. Like, Nicky's and Yoshie's mothers did not accept their relationship. "I had no type of support at all," Yoshie says. Her cousin sent her mom a picture of Nicky and Yoshie posted on Instagram. Yoshie remembers: "We weren't kissing or nothing like that it was just the caption why she found out. My mom and my aunt and my cousin gave me lots of lectures. Every time we talked about it they said I was confused and made me do girly things. They said it was a sin. 'You can't be doing that, you're young, you're confused.' It was horrible. I was trying to figure out if I wanted to be with girls and they were attacking me."

"Yoshie, it was hard for her to come out," Nicky confirms. "When my mom found out I was dating Yoshie, she was OD upset with me, too. She didn't like the fact that I had turned gay. I kissed girls and liked girls. I was a little ass girl, it was natural. Nobody in my family knew about it, why you gotta know I like girls?"

Nicky's mom confiscated her phone after she saw a racy text from Yoshie saying, "I can't wait to bite your lip." She called up Astacio and blew up on him. "I didn't raise my daughter to be like that!"

Chris was getting creamed from all angles. After losing a staggering sixth game in a row and getting demolished by MS 114 (East Side Middle School), a very white Upper East Side school consistently top-ranked in all of New York state, even Rashell, the pillar of strength and the bad-ass backbone of the Lady Tigers finally broke down. "I'm done!" she wailed. "I'm not losing no more. Enough! They're laughing at us!"

"Why are you doing this?" Nicky questioned her coach. "We travel all over the city and we're always losing. Doesn't that get to you?" Chris didn't confess that he was so frustrated, too, he crumpled up the team's stat sheets and threw them in the garbage after their last crushing defeat.

On the train ride home from the game, Chris stared into space, wondering what the hell he was going to do to turn things around. Genesis, who'd been sitting quietly beside him, tapped him on the shoulder and handed him a letter she'd written, one page, front and back. As he read it, Chris's face turned white.

> . . . *Thank you for all you done for me. You saw something in me no one else could see. I'm sorry for being a huge disappointment to you. I wish I could be that type of person who was a better person that could make you proud. I'm sorry I can't do better in school and in life. I hope you remember me as a good person who always tried my best . . .*

Holy Mother of God. It was a suicide note.

"Her handwriting was very neat, as if she took time to write it. It wasn't something Genesis wrote in five minutes. She made sure it was perfectly written. She put thought into it, then folded it nicely and put it in her pocket. That is what scared me the most."

Genesis was saying goodbye to Coach Astacio. That day, in science class, a group of kids that always sat in the back of the class made fun of her again for the umpteenth time, calling her "fish lips" and other cruel names. "I don't even like saying the words," she says. Genesis didn't want to cry because she didn't want to seem too weak in front of them. Earlier in the year, the teacher was handing back assignments and, in front of everyone, told Genesis she needed to raise her grades or she'd fail the class. "The students heard that and called me stupid and said, 'You're dumb, you're not going nowhere.' At that point I started believing them." Now they were making fun of her looks again and she couldn't take the taunts one second longer. She had to leave. She picked up her stuff and the teacher shouted, "Genesis, where are you going?" Genesis wasn't a rebel, she was going to stop and tell the teacher what happened. But then a student shouted out,

"Yeah, Fish Lips, where are you going?" and everybody started laughing. "What hurt me the most is that the teacher started laughing, too. Right in front of the class. That hurt me so bad."

Genesis walked out and hid in a staircase until it was time for softball. While she sat in the stairs, she wrote the suicide note. She still planned to go to the game, even though she still hadn't played in one, because she figured just being there would be the "last happy moment" she'd have before killing herself. "Apart from the bullying through the years, that day specifically, I tried to reach out for help and that didn't work and I just thought there was only one way out."

At first, during the game, Genesis felt sad, then as it went along, "Honestly I was happy, I forgot all about what happened and stuff." When she got on the train and sat next to Chris, she felt compelled to give him the letter. "The one person I really cared about at that moment was Astacio, so I gave it to him. I don't know why but I felt like I needed to give him that letter at that moment."

Genesis remembers his face transforming from normal to deadly serious as he read it. "I felt so stupid because I didn't want him to be unhappy from my letter." After that, Chris would not leave her side, on the train or the walk home. When her grandfather picked her up, Chris gave him the letter and said, "You need to read this, it's really important. You need to speak to her."

Genesis and her grandfather went home, sat down on the couch and he read the note. "That was the first time I ever saw him cry but he did not want to say anything. Then Mr. Frederick called."

Chris had taken a picture of the letter on his phone and sent it to Frederick, who called Genesis's house at 10 P.M. "How are you feeling?" he asked. He asked Genesis if he could speak to her grandparents but she didn't want him to. He told her she needed them to take her to the hospital. "I don't want to go," Genesis insisted.

The next day, Genesis went to school in a "low mental state" and Chris brought her to his office. A few hours later, her grandmother appeared in the doorway, along with several of Frederick's security officers and an

EMT crew. Genesis tried to run but had nowhere to go. They all blocked her. "You have to go to the hospital," Chris said. Genesis was angry, but he told her, "I'd rather you be mad at me than dead."

The ride to the hospital in the ambulance was terrifying, not because she was scared for herself but because her grandmother was so pissed at her. She was so upset, in fact, her blood pressure shot through the roof. "She turned green," Genesis remembers. "The EMT tried to calm her down." Genesis worried that if something happened to her grandma, it would be her fault. The whole ride in the ambulance, and the whole time at the hospital, they didn't speak. Her grandmother wouldn't even look at her. After waiting for two hours in uncomfortable silence, Genesis's name was called. "A lady asked me a couple of questions like, 'Do you feel like hurting yourself or hurting somebody else? Do you hurt yourself? How do you feel?' I said no to every question because my grandmother was sitting right next to me." The nurse asked to see Genesis's arms and noticed some cuts.

"What is that?"

Genesis made up a lie and they let her go.

"I was afraid of getting help," she says.

All of these girls had been taught somewhere along the way in life that asking for help was a sign of weakness. Lately, all of their behavior seemed like a giant cry for help and Chris couldn't ignore it anymore. They only had three games left in the season but if they lost them all, it wasn't worth shattering their self-esteem, which at this point was as fragile as glass. He didn't start this whole thing to make young girls who were already broken feel even worse about themselves.

Chris scheduled another mandatory meeting and informed the Lady Tigers that the season was canceled until further notice. That they had a lot of work to do on themselves if they ever wanted to win, in life and on the field.

"First of all, I care about you. I don't care if I have to push and push and push, you are not going to give up on yourselves. I know stuff is hard at home I know you feel like you're failing. I don't care if you fail. All I care is that you don't give up. And that you get back up and say, 'I'm gonna try again.' Keep trying. We all fail. I fail every day. Everybody here, you support each other. If she falls, you pick her up! If she falls you pick her up! Do you believe in yourself?"

"Yes."

"DO YOU BELIEVE IN YOURSELF?"

"Yes."

The girls were heartbroken but Chris could sense a little relief, too. The Lady Tigers weren't giving up or quitting, he assured them, they were postponing until they were ready, willing, and able to succeed. They had to discover within themselves what it took to be a winner. It had little to do with a ball, a bat, or the score of a game. Winning was a state of mind and a way of life. He didn't know how long it would take to figure it out. Could be a day, could be a year. It might never happen. The only thing he knew for sure was that they had to help each other through it.

"We're a family first and a team second."

Chris told them he didn't care about winning games anymore. What he cared about was trying to help the girls. But he really didn't like their attitudes, and they needed to fix that before moving forward one step.

"First, let me get one thing straight. I am not your friend, I am not your buddy, we are not cool. I don't call you on the weekend to hang out, we don't chill at your crib. I am your coach. While I might be friendly and ask how you are doing and how your day was, don't get it twisted, I am not your friend. I demand your respect. Now, understanding that, for some reason, girls on this team have the misconception that you can do whatever you want in this school building without feeling the repercussions of your actions. I, your coach, the very person who has sacrificed almost everything to make sure there is even a softball team, that you have uniforms, gloves, equipment, I am blamed for E-V-E-R-Y-T-H-I-N-G."

To show how serious he was, he canceled the next two games, one against IS 276 (Battery Park City School) and one against MS 378 (School for Global Leaders). "At first, I said no practice, let's take a break for two weeks, then we can assess what we're going to do," Chris recalls. But a lot of the players kept showing up in the gym after school anyway. "Fine, you want to call it practice?" he told them. "I'll be here. But we're not going to play, we're going to talk."

For a week, Chris held Circle Sessions. They talked a little bit about softball, but that wasn't the main conversation. "It was more like, what's going on in your life? How can I help?" It opened the floodgate. They bitched about and slagged on everyone and everything under the sun. They blamed their home lives. They blamed their teachers. They said, "They don't care about us" or "They always on my back" or "They always saying they're gonna kick us off the team." The one thing Chris never heard in any of those conversations was any of the girls taking responsibility for themselves or for their own actions. "Because that's how it is in the South Bronx. It's always someone else's fault. If you always have that mentality, you can't fix your life."

Chris had had enough of the victim mentality and laid into them.

"The problem with you girls is all you do is complain and complain and complain. I hear, 'But my class is boring, I don't like the teacher, blah blah blah.' Guess what? TOUGH SHIT. I never said life is fair! If I would've said that, I'd be lying to you. We are people of color living in a poor community, which means we have to work ten times as hard to even prove that we are worthy, to prove we are human beings that deserve an education. We could complain how unfair that is or do something about it! Use your damn mind! Be so damn smart that high schools are lining up waiting to accept you. Be so damn smart that once you graduate high school, colleges are lining up at your door waiting to hand you a scholarship. Be so damn smart that jobs and top CEOs are constantly calling your phone pleading to know when you graduate so that they could hand you your dream career. Be so damn smart that nobody, I mean nobody, will ever doubt you or treat you as less than a human being. I'm yelling at you not because I dislike you personally or I think you are a horrible human being. I am yelling at you because I know your potential and it angers me to watch you destroy yourselves. So the next time a teacher yells at you to do something or gets on your case about anything, I want you to remember, they are pushing you to do your best because they care.

Those who don't care won't push you. Those who don't demand your very best don't believe in you. I believe in you. But you need to start believing in yourselves! I get it, I understand. Most of us lead tough, tough lives and hate going home for whatever reason. You escape your house just to come here. And then us teachers demand your attention, demand you to focus, but you just can't. How can math help my mom to stop drinking? How can science bring back my dad? How can anything in school save me from the hell I am living in at home? I get it. Trust me I do, and I care. But the world does not care. So what you need to do is make them care. Make them see that you are somebody. Get an education, be respectable, do what you need to do to be successful and stop using excuses to hold you back. Many of you already feel like you are in a hole, struggling to get out. What you are doing now—the nonsense and utter stupidity of your actions—is digging your hole deeper and deeper, and before you realize it, you will never be able to escape that hell. Don't be like me. I barely graduated high school and dropped out during my first year of college. I felt too damn proud to reach out for help, so I tried to do everything on my own and it didn't work. The world did not care. When my wife was nine months pregnant, about to give birth, I went to work and informed my boss, 'Hey listen, my wife is due any second now. She might call and I need to leave.' Do you know what he said to me? 'Who is pregnant, you or your wife? Who is giving birth, you or your wife?' I had to take a step back and take a breath because the street in me wanted to punch the shit outta him. He told me that he needed me at my station and I said to him, 'I QUIT.' The world doesn't care about you. So you have to care about yourself. You have to surround yourself with people that lift you up, not tear you down. You have to reach out to people who care, not shut them out. I am reaching out now to all of you. But you need to reach back. I cannot go into the ring of life and take all the hits while you sit in the stands watching. I am willing to fight but you have to fight with me. Fight to become the person, the incredible human being that you are meant to be!"

Chris wasn't sure why he kept urging them not to quit. He'd tried to help the Lady Tigers for months, but he was ready to throw in the towel himself. He felt like a loser, too. He had these lofty goals, he'd worked his butt off to make them happen, and now it looked like it was all for nothing. Plus, his wife still might kick him to the curb. Chris seriously considered disbanding the team, even if it meant he failed. "I don't want to do this next year," he'd mumble to himself. "I'm not doing this next year. This is it. I can't do this again."

Yoshie overheard his mumbling one day, looked at him with saucer eyes, and said, "Oh, you're not going to do this next year?"

"You have to help me a lot more." He couldn't do it on his own.

A couple of days later he got a letter from Yoshie. It was not another suicide note, thankfully.

> *All I wanna say is thank you to the best friend that's always been here for me, to the father I always needed, to the diary that held the deepest secrets, to the coach I'll never forget and will always remember. Thank you Mister Astacio. Since day one you always knew what to say. You are the best and first coach I ever had. You made my dream to play softball in a team. Softball is a thing that takes out my anger and calms me down. Softball is my life. Without a glove ball bat four bases to teams or one winner idk what will I do. #Lady Tigers will always be in my heart no matter what the situation is. We have been through our ups and downs, but look at us now. We are still strong, still as a team. Thank you #Lady Tigers for supporting me thru almost everything. You are the world to me. Yah helped me thru a lot. We have been thru almost everything together. There was no second of the day we wasn't helping and listening to each other. Ya will always be remembered and loved, especially from me. Thank you and I'll always remember ya.*
>
> *Sincerely,*
> *Yoshie #11*

Chris's cold, jaded heart melted into a puddle. There was one more game left in the season. Maybe they should give it one more shot. At the next

Circle Session, he asked the girls if they wanted to play the last game of the season. It was another game against the other Lady Tigers, this time on their home turf around the corner. He reminded his Lady Tigers of the spanking they'd gotten last time. Full disclosure: There was a strong possibility they'd have their asses handed to them again. He wanted to be completely honest about their chances. But he also wanted redemption and revenge.

"We don't have to play, it's up to you," Chris said.

"We want to play, Coach," Alexa said.

"Okay, but if I say yes, we're gonna practice hard," Chris said.

"They're gonna kill us again," Gheynee said.

"No, no, no, no, no," Chris said. "We are going to practice and we are going to find ourselves again."

The girls whooped it up and high-fived each other.

"Who are we?" Rashell shouted.

"LADY TIGERS!"

"THE ONLY LADY TIGERS!"

"THE OG LADY TIGERS!"

For the next week, the team busted their butts in fielding drills and in the cage, in the mornings, during lunch and after school. Nicky, Rashell, Johanna, Alexa, Angie, Alcielis, Gheynee, and Yoshie had a fire in their eyes that Chris hadn't seen before. "I just wanted to hit that ball, hit it out, crush it!" Johanna says. Achelin asked for extra help pitching, and Chris worked with her on her windmill until they perfected it. Genesis was back and seemed in better spirits. They all did. Grateshka the court jester made sure of it. "My main focus at that time was to make my other teammates happy."

"My girls came alive," Chris says. "I never seen such determination in their eyes. We practiced and practiced. Even if it rained, we were outside practicing. They practiced on the weekend without me, in their apartment hallways, and in their sleep. I recall Yoshie telling me that she would throw a ball repeatedly against the wall at night before going to sleep."

Chris wanted to do something extra special for the Lady Tigers to reward them for their hard work, so he organized a field trip to the Turtle

Cove Golf & Baseball Complex. Mrs. Holloway, as school office manager, arranged for a bright yellow bus, which the kids called the Cheese Bus, to take the team to the entertainment complex, which had five batting cages for fast-pitch softball. Chris's cage was fine and all, but here the girls didn't have to wait two hundred turns to practice hitting. They all got plenty of swings, plus free hot dogs, fries, and chicken fingers. Mrs. Holloway came on the excursion, too, and cheered on the girls in the batting cages from the comfort of a lawn chair. It felt like a neighborhood block party. It was a happy, sunny, productive day.

As the rumble in the concrete jungle approached, Lady Tigers v. Lady Tigers, the whole team was killing it, in practice and in school. The girls who weren't very good, like Kimberly and Heaven, were 110 percent dedicated. The girls who hated going to class the most, like Gheynee and Alexa, made sure they showed up and stayed put. Everyone stepped it up so they were eligible to play in the last game of the season.

It was the least they could do. They didn't have any money to buy Coach Astacio a "World's Greatest Coach" mug or an engraved "#1 Coach" whistle. This was the greatest gift they could give him and it was all he ever wanted.

Chapter Sixteen

THE SHOW

There was no way the Lady Tigers were going to make the playoffs. It was the last game of the season and their record was the pits, 0-6 with two forfeits. The general consensus on the team was that they didn't want to embarrass themselves again, but overruling humiliation was the overwhelming urge to exact sweet revenge on the "purple team." They refused to call them the Lady Tigers.

"If this team needs to beat us to advance, I say we make sure they have to take it from us because I will not back down, we will not back down!" Chris proclaimed.

"Yeah, fuck those girls!" Nicky sustained. She was vulgar, but it pumped up her teammates.

Their last matchup with the purple team was a bloodbath, a painful game to play, coach, and watch. That game in particular really broke the spirit of the Lady Tigers, since it was on their turf and they let "the enemy" come in and stomp all over them. Girls were arguing with each other on the field and making careless errors. Alcielis stuck her middle finger up at Chris. They were terrified of the big badass pitcher and couldn't buy a hit. When all was said and done, the Lady Tigers were annihilated 16-0. The purple team left the Lady Tigers' home field laughing at them, saying how "easy" the game was.

Now the Lady Tigers were going to face their tormentors behind enemy lines on *their* home field. It was a death wish, a suicide mission. Some girls laughed hysterically at the thought of it. But Chris juiced them up again and pointed out everything positive that had happened to the Lady Tigers. Toward the end of the season, the scores went from 20-0 to 5-1. Teams had a tougher time scoring on them. They were finally working together and not yelling at each other. "Who cares if they came into our house and stomped all over us? That team doesn't exist anymore. We are different, we are better, we are motivated. And if we play them and happen to lose, then we lose the game but not our dignity or our many successes."

For the last practice before the game, Chris chose not to practice. He told the girls to have some fun. They hung out in the gym, listened to music, and just chilled. He didn't want them all wound up before their big day. He wanted them to enjoy being together as a team. That night Chris was so nervous, he couldn't eat. Charisse kept telling him that they would be fine, to have faith. But he couldn't shake the feeling that if these girls lost again, he'd risk losing them forever. It was a huge gamble and he wasn't sure it was worth it.

The time had finally come. Game day. The girls were as nervous and anxious as Chris. Johanna complained that her arm hurt. She'd pitched almost every game since Achelin had trouble finding a happy medium between burning worms and throwing the ball over the backstop. Johanna had really stepped it up the last few games, striking out at least seven girls per game. But that came with a toll, since she was throwing well over one hundred pitchers per game. The defense wasn't tight, to say the least, and the girls could not get outs easily. So Johanna's arm worked overtime. Chris had her ice it daily, but that day, it was still bothering her. He told her if her arm was really in pain, he wasn't going to put her in.

"NO! I am playing," she insisted.

The last bell of the day rang and it was time to meet the girls in the gymnasium and give them the pep talk of a lifetime. Chris had his speech all planned out; it was going to be epic. On his way down to the gym, he was stopped by Frederick. Chris thought he was going to wish the Lady Tigers luck.

"Astacio, I know you're headed out to play your game, but there's something you need to know. The cops are here and they are about to arrest Achelin for punching a girl and posting a video of the fight on Facebook. The mother of the girl she assaulted pressed charges. I don't want Achelin to be arrested in front of the team, so please just send her to my office. Whatever you do, don't tell her that she is going to be arrested. I'm afraid that she'll run out of the school. I'll wait for you to leave with the team before allowing the arrest. Also, Alexa has been implicated in the fight, as well. She is not going to be arrested, but she can't play either."

Chris was gobsmacked. Achelin was the backup pitcher and Alexa was his best catcher and one of his strongest hitters. Chris had trained them so hard for weeks and now on the day of the game, two of his key players were getting arrested. But that wasn't his main concern. How was he going to tell the team?

Chris waited in the main lobby and directed Lady Tiger after Lady Tiger down to the gym. Girls asked how come he wasn't following them down to the gym and he had to lie. Finally, Achelin came running down the staircase in her uniform, carrying a new softball bag she'd bought, beaming with hope. That killed Chris inside. She stopped in front of him with fire in her eyes and said, "I'm ready, coach."

"Before you head downstairs, Mr. Frederick needs to talk to you for a second."

"Why?"

"I don't know," he said with a pathetic smile. "Maybe he wants to wish you good luck and congratulate you for making such progress. Don't worry, we're not leaving anytime soon."

Chris felt like a punk-ass bitch, setting her up like that. He felt like crying. But he left Achelin there and headed to the gym. "Should I just cancel the game?" he thought. "I have no catcher, the girls are going to lose hope, what should I do? I should cancel. Here we go again. It's an omen. Wait, nope, it's not fair to the rest of the girls. Let's go." He saw Genesis walking slowly down the steps. He remembered her catching once for Johanna during practice a few weeks ago and stated at the time that maybe she should try being a catcher next year. He ran up behind her, beaming with hope once again.

"Remember how you wanted to be a catcher next year? Well it looks like next year is going to be today." Genesis was confused. "I need you. I believe in you."

When Chris walked into the gym, the girls yelled, "Well, it's about time!" They were all ready to kick ass and he still had to deliver the bad news. He got them all together in huddle and let them know they'd be leaving in a few minutes. One of the girls yelled, "Wait, where's Achelin and Alexa?"

Shit, now he was forced to tell them. But what exactly does he say? He hadn't rehearsed this type of speech.

"I have great news!" Chris began. "Genesis is going to be our catcher for today!"

"Genesis?"

"Who the hell is Genesis?"

"What happened to Achelin and Alexa?"

A small little voice in the back of the huddle said shyly, "I'm Genesis." Everyone turned and stared at her as she raised her hand tentatively.

"Ohhhh, I never knew that was your name," Heaven said.

"Achelin and Alexa was involved in an emergency and they might either be late to the game or not make it at all," Chris said.

The girls gasped and wanted to know more. Chris pretended not to know. The Lady Tigers began to unravel. They didn't want to play without their teammates, their friends.

"We should just go home."

"They are going to beat us."

"We cannot play without them."

Their doubts and fears echoed through the gym and it started to make Chris angry. Not angry at them but angry at the world. These girls had worked their asses off and they did not deserve this. Chris erupted:

"Stop, just stop! When life doesn't go our way, do we just quit? You girls have worked so damn hard just to give up now. When they told me I had cancer, yes, I was scared, yes, I wanted to give up, but I said, 'The hell with cancer.' I am not going to quit. I've worked too damn hard. I believe in all of you. And it is damn time that you start believing in yourselves. We are better, stronger, fearless. I say we go over to that damn school and give them hell. And who cares if we win or lose. In my eyes, you are all winners, so it doesn't matter what happens today. But I will not allow you to quit. My sister wouldn't allow you to quit."

It was quiet for a few seconds.

"Let's do this for Michelle!" Nicky shouted.

The fire was back. The Lady Tigers came alive again and chanted Chris's sister's name.

"Mi-chelle! Mi-chelle! Mi-chelle!"

They did one last huddle and all the girls put their hands in. Girls who wanted to speak spoke from the heart.

"We got this!"

"Who are we?"

"LADY TIGERS!"

And they went on their way to what may have been their final demise.

They marched proudly as a team, wearing their tough black and orange uniforms, to the purple team's school six blocks away, through some of the roughest blocks in New York City. And damn if they didn't get smiles from strangers on the street. The twenty-minute walk to the field helped burn some anxiety and ease the tension, and Chris talked game strategy the whole way. Unfortunately, he neglected to take into account the weather. It was unseasonably hot, around 90 degrees, and the humidity made it feel like they were in a sauna. By the time they arrived at MS 145, the girls were soaking wet.

Chris wasn't sure what to expect when they got to the school. He was hoping no one would be there since his girls had very high performance anxiety and they'd buckled under pressure in the past. They reached the front entrance and, oh boy, this school was even worse than theirs. They had even more security than 22 and they were ready for the Lady Tigers. They had to get scanned by metal detectors and have all their equipment and bags rolled through an X-ray machine. For a brief moment, it felt like they were at the airport, and they could just fly away and forget the whole thing. The girls collected their belongings and, to their relief, the school sounded pretty empty. They walked through the school, down some stairs, and out a double door to the field.

As the oppressive heat smacked them in the face, they saw a massive crowd gathered on the concrete field to see their beloved team crush the Lady Tigers once again. The Lady Tigers didn't have anyone there to watch them. Rashell begged her mom to come to her last eighth grade game ever. "Please, please go," she asked.

"Imma go," her mom promised. But she had just started a new job and was nowhere to be found.

Rashell kept blowing up her phone, but got no response.

"Where is she?" she said sadly to no one in particular. "I can't believe she told me she was coming."

Of course, the purple team had a large crowd. They needed this win to make it into the playoffs. Spotting the giant peanut gallery, the Lady Tigers were already grumbling:

"There's more people than last time."

"Fuuuucccckk we are screwed."

"This is too much, I can't do this."

In the distance, outside the center-field fence, their school band marched out, banging drums and chanting for their team. They thought this was gonna be a guaranteed win, and they wanted to show off and rub it in.

"You got to be fucking kidding me."

Rashell turned around and stopped everyone in their tracks. "Stop the shit, this is our day, our time!"

"They can bang their drums and scream out their lungs for all we care," Chris shouted, "but we will shut them up!"

"Yeah!"

And with that, the girls began walking to their dugout with a certain swagger, beaming with confidence. They took out their gloves and warmed up their arms.

Chris met with the other coach on the field to go over the game rules. She looked confident, as if this was going to be a quick game. They shook hands, and the umpire yelled, "Play ball!"

Since it was their home field, the original Lady Tigers batted first. The same pitcher from the last massacre was on the mound, standing with that same annoying intimidating stance. The girls broke out some new cheers to shake her up.

Hey pitcher look at me I'm a monkey in a tree
Aaauuuaaauuaa

Usually, Chris liked to spread the wealth in his batting order, scattering all the strong hitters throughout the lineup. Not today. He decided to put all the strongest hitters first. Yoshie, Johanna, and Grateshka started the team off, to try to crush the other team's expectations. He just hoped it worked, since he only had about four or five strong hitters.

First up, Yoshie.

"Yoshie! Yoshie! Yoshie!" the girls chanted.

Chris grabbed her by her helmet and whispered, "She doesn't know who you have become. Why don't you go show her."

On the very first pitch, Yoshie knocked the cover off the ball, sending it far into left field for a home run. The Lady Tigers were in an uproar, screaming and jumping on Yoshie as soon as she reached home plate.

Chris was completely amazed and so was the other team. But they kept banging their drums and chanting loudly for their team. The coach yelled at her team, "Don't worry about it, it's just one run!"

Next up, Johanna. As he had with Yoshie, Chris grabbed Johanna's helmet and told her in Spanish, *"Mata lo,"* which meant, "Kill the ball," something he had learned from the girls. Their pitcher seemed a little frazzled and kept pitching balls to Johanna.

> *Johanna dame un palito*
> *Eooooo*
> *Que te quien ponchar*
> *Eooo*
> *Manga tu table*
> *Eoo*
> *No te deje tirar*
> *Eooo*
> *Que ta puesto pa ti*
> *Siiiiii*
> *Ta puesto pa ti*
> *Siiii*
> *Quien desaparecerte*
> *Eooo*
> *Sacarte del pais*
> *Siiii*

It didn't help that Johanna's batting stance had become that of a trained assassin. They kept rattling the pitcher on purpose.

> *Watch the pitcher*
> *Watch watch the pitcher*
> *Is she fast*

Is she slow
Is she high
Is she low

When the count was 3-0, Chris told Johanna to take pitches, meaning lay off, until she got the first strike. Did she listen? Of course not. When the first strike came along, Johanna smashed a line-drive home run into left field. She was so fast, she crossed home plate before they even got to the ball.

"Holy shit," Chris thought. "Two home runs in our first two at bats?"

Unfortunately, the next three batters grounded out or struck out. But the Lady Tigers were up 2-0 in the first half of the first inning. Before the girls took the field, he told them, "This is the first time we are in the lead. We are winning, which means we have to work hard to protect ourselves. Drown out the drums, the screaming, the chanting, and shut their offense down!"

The sun was really heating up the asphalt; the blacktop outfield was a cloud of haze and steam. Chris walked with Johanna to the pitcher's mound and handed her the ball.

"Just have fun." She smiled because she knew what he meant.

Johanna hurled strikes one after the other and the other team did not know what the hell was going on. One, two, three outs! It was as simple as that. They had completely shut down their offense in the first inning.

In the second inning, Alexa showed up to the field on her own and walked over to Chris. She'd been questioned by the police about her role in the videotaped fight and released.

"I'm here, I'm ready to play," Alexa said.

"You know I can't," Chris sad sadly. "You can stay and watch."

As much as it pained Chris to do that, rules were rules. Alexa's face completely dropped, and she walked away and went home.

During the second and third innings, the Lady Tiger's offense continued to belt out line drives and grounders that broke through the purple team's defense. But as the game grew longer and the sun shined brighter, Johanna began to tire and the purple team began to answer back. At one point the Lady Tigers were leading 5-0, but then their rivals managed to score three runs. Chris could see frustration seeping into his girls, and he had to constantly remind them that they were in the lead. By the middle of the game, around the fourth inning, Johanna was running out of gas and her arm began to hurt. If that wasn't bad enough, her asthma began acting up. She called time out and Chris ran up to the mound. Johanna was exhausted and literally out of breath. He handed her an inhaler and she took two puffs, wiped the sweat off her forehead, and told him, *"Tengo esto"*—"I got this."

But she really didn't, since she started throwing wild pitches and walking girls. Genesis, in her debut as catcher, was phenomenal. She was making unbelievable saves behind the plate. She was also hitting line drives. "Her athletic ability kind of surprised me," Chris said. "I didn't expect her to be as good as she was. I never trained her to be a catcher and she was scooping up everything. I was like, 'What?'"

Once again, time was called and Chris ran out onto the mound. It was bases loaded and no outs. Chris was ready to take the ball, but Johanna didn't want to quit. All she wanted was a drink from her Gatorade. He reiterated to her that if she didn't start throwing strikes or if she looked like she was going to pass out, he was going to take her out. She said, "I am no quitter, I could do this!" in broken English. Luckily, the next girl hit the ball into the Lady Tigers' very first double play ever. The next batter struck out swinging at a very high pitch. Chris told Johanna she was very lucky to have gotten out of that inning. They might not be that lucky again.

The offensive onslaught continued for the Lady Tigers as they pummeled the defense, increasing their lead to 9-6. Yoshie was crushing the ball each time she went to bat. At one point the pitcher stopped pitching to her and intentionally walked her whenever she came to the plate. The girls were loud as a freight train, rejoicing and cheering for every batter.

Angie is a friend of mine
Rip rip rip
She can rip it any time

Rip rip rip any time any place
Rip rip rip
She can rip it in your face
Rip rip rip

Chris told them all to be quiet. He then asked them, "Can you hear that?" They all responded with a confused, "Hear what? We don't hear anything!"

"Exactly! No banging of the drums, no chanting, no cheering, NOTHING!"

They'd knocked the wind out of the crowd. For the first time in eight months, the Lady Tigers felt like they were a team to be reckoned with, a team that should be feared.

They took the field in the fifth inning with their heads held high. Johanna continued to struggle, but when Chris walked to the mound once again to check on her, she shooed him away with her hand. She was determined to stay in that game even if it killed her. But she continued to walk girls and even pegged a few of them. Girls on the Lady Tigers began to make errors, and the other team inched up the score. Johanna got out of the inning when the other team swung at bad pitches and hit dinky grounders, but some damage had been done. They went into the last inning all tied up 9-9. It was the first time in the game that the Lady Tigers had lost the lead. They had to get some runs because they didn't have last licks or last at bat. The girls answered the call. They got three more runs and with one more last at bat for the purple team, the Lady Tigers led the game 12-9.

Before the girls took the field for the very last time, Chris told them to huddle up and put their hands in.

"No matter the outcome of this game, I'm proud of all of you. You showed a lot of heart and if my sister was alive to see you, she would be more than proud."

"For Michelle!" the girls chanted together, then ran to their positions.

Chris's heart was pounding out of his chest. He kept pacing back and forth after each pitch thrown by Johanna. He tried to look as calm as possible but on the inside he was freaking out. Johanna miraculously struck out the first two batters and all they needed was one more out. But then she utterly collapsed. She was a wreck at this point, grimacing with every pitch. She began throwing ball after ball. Girl after girl walked and the bases loaded up. All they needed was one more out.

"We can't lose like this." Chris agonized over pulling her.

The purple team's best player, their gigantic pitcher, came up to bat. Worst-case scenario, she would hit a homerun to end the game. Chris called time out to take Johanna out the game. He grabbed the ball from her glove.

"No! I am the only pitcher. No one else. I could do this. Please let me do this. I have to do this. You can't take this away from me."

He looked at her with a furrowed brow, not as a concerned coach but as a father protecting his daughter.

"You have nothing to prove," he told her. "I've always believed in you."

She gave him a hug, and he handed the ball back to her. He walked back to the dugout, knowing he should have just taken her out.

Johanna took a deep breath. She wound up her windmill and blew one past the batter for strike one.

The Lady Tigers erupted, "JUST TWO MORE!"

The next pitch was too high . . . but the batter swung at it and missed. "STRIKE TWO!"

The count was 0-2.

"Lay off the high pitches!" the coach of the other team howled. "Make her pitch to you! She is tired!"

Next pitch. BALL.

Next pitch. BALL.

Next pitch. BALL.

The count was 3-2, bases loaded. Runners would be going.

The heavens commanded silence—the ShotSpotters could have heard a pin drop in the South Bronx. Everyone at the ballpark was motionless, holding on for dear life.

Johanna took a deep breath, wound up her windmill, and, with every ounce of power left in her body, let it fly. The batter didn't even swing at it.

"STRIKE THREE!"

The Lady Tigers threw their gloves in the air and rushed Johanna as if they'd just won Game 7 of the World Series. They jumped on top of her and collapsed into a dog pile, whooping at the top of their lungs and crying tears of joy. "I remember Nicky jumping on top of me," Yoshie says. "We were really really happy."

"It was one of the best moments of my life," Nicky confirms.

The girls got up, rushed toward Coach Astacio, and enveloped him in a giant bear hug huddle. They all jumped up and down in unison and chanted as loud as humanly possible:

"WHO ARE WE?"

"LADY TIGERS!"

"WHO ARE WE?"

"LADY TIGERS!"

It was their first "W," but more important, it was their first triumph. Triumph over low self-esteem. Triumph over anger, over rape, over doubt, over everything. The Lady Tigers were winners. They could finally say that now. They'd earned it.

As the girls packed up their gear for the last time that year, they overheard the purple team complaining about them and accusing them of cheating. "It's not fair, those are not the same girls!" one player griped. "That's not the same team!"

"You hear that, girls?" Chris said. "You're not the same team."

Chapter Seventeen

GO FORTH & SET THE WORLD ON FIRE

At the beginning of the year, it seemed highly improbable that all of the oldest Lady Tigers were going to make it out of eighth grade. But here they were in June, and every single one of them had passed their classes, were going to graduate and move on to high school. Chris logged onto his computer and read over his player's updated progress reports.

Achelin: *"Good motivation, great participation."*

Yoshie: *"Great student, completes all class assignments, and is very respectful."*

Alexa: *"Confidence and has great attendance, I am proud of her accomplishments. Completion of classwork. Coming to class prepared."*

Rashell: *"Excellent motivation! Keep up the good work!"*

Heaven: *"Good team skills."*

Nicky: *"Excellent motivation! Keep up the good work!"*

Angie: *"Excellent classwork and class participation, good reading comprehension, is a team player . . . excessive chatter"*

Chris chuckled. Some things will never change.

Chris wouldn't be able to attend the Lady Tigers' first graduation and he was gutted about it. His son, Justin, was graduating from elementary school at the same time on the same day. He wracked his brain to devise a plan that would allow him to attend both events, but Charisse got extremely upset that he even entertained the thought. She didn't explicitly tell him not to go to the girls' graduation, but she did say, in a sarcastic tone of voice, "I know you will make the right decision."

So Chris scheduled an awards banquet instead for another day and ordered snazzy little trophies to give to his team. The Lady Tigers lost every game that season except for the last game, but Chris felt in his heart that his girls were champions who deserved to be recognized. They weren't always champions on the field, but they were champions in life. He'd seen such a drastic transformation in the girls who knew nothing but pain and strife. They battled their inner demons and began to believe in themselves.

Chris invited all of the Lady Tigers (even Achelin, who had been arrested) and all of their parents, and sent an email to the staff at 22 inviting them to a short ceremony in the library after school. He actually got replies back from some teachers who asked why he'd give them "participation trophies," which annoyed Chris. Those trophies represented something more than just playing softball. He'd chosen trophies with flames, since each girl had discovered the fire within that they needed to propel them toward greatness. The flames represented the strength and courage these girls had to change themselves.

All of the girls came to the banquet. Chris wore his jersey proudly. But not one parent showed up, and only one teacher stopped by to show support. It wasn't even Mrs. Holloway. Unfortunately, the principal scheduled a mandatory staff meeting at the last moment and that's where they all were. No matter, the Lady Tigers had gone it alone the whole year. They didn't need anybody else. Chris put together a video montage of their softball journey, which brought some girls to tears. After playing it, he explained why he was giving them trophies:

"There are those of you here that are still hurting. You have endured hell in your lives. Some for many years but you never gave up. How do I know this? Because you are still here. Despite all you have struggled with, you found the courage to believe in yourselves. You found the courage to say that I deserve better, I want to be better, I am better. And no one, I repeat, no one, will ever take away this feeling because I will not allow it. And I know a lot of you feel like you are alone, but understand this, you have each other and you have me. You have become my daughters and I will always be fighting in your corner. I want you to remember this day. Today is the day you will yell out to the world, 'I am and will always be a Lady Tiger and I will never give up.' I am not going to lie, it's going to get very difficult. You are going to feel like you can't take anymore. People are going to disappoint you and you are going to want to give up. And that's okay. Feeling defeated, feeling angry, feeling frustrated, that is okay. What is not okay is convincing yourself that you are not good enough, that you cannot overcome your struggles, that you cannot be that great person that I see every day. Because all of you are great, and no matter what life throws at you, you will remember that you are a Lady Tiger and you will never give up."

Before Chris gave out each trophy, he gave a short speech about each girl and praised her accomplishments.

Angie had strengthened her arm but also her self-care. She learned to stop beating herself up and that she didn't have to please all the people all the time. Her mom was forcing her to wear a white dress and mascara to graduation, so she decided to wear what *she* wanted to prom—a fresh men's suit.

Alcielis was still banned from prom for bad behavior from earlier in the year but the relationships she'd made on the softball team profoundly affected and changed her. "I don't know where my life would be if it wasn't for those girls," she says. "We all have huge personalities, all of us. We were all Spanish and loud and aggressive. We're all fighters but we're all lovers. We can all get so angry and hate you but the next second we love you and are hugging you. We're all like that. Being able to argue and bounce back from it made our relationship so strong. A lot of who I am today is based off of them."

Maybe Heaven was never going to be a star player but she learned to push herself to her maximum potential. "Softball changed me," she says. "My grades were fair, softball made them great. Teachers would push me and push me and say, 'You can do this!' I swore up and down I couldn't. They knew I had a lot of potential but I didn't see it in myself until I started playing softball."

Kimberly was always a stellar student, so she didn't need any help on that front. But being on a team gave her the family she had always craved. And being on the Lady Tigers brought out something just as valuable as her education—her voice. "At home nobody wanted to talk about what happened to me or acknowledge it. Anxiety and depression doesn't exist in our culture. Because of the background we come from it was hard to even recognize it. Being afraid of speaking up can cause inner damage and self-hatred. What this situation taught me was that I have a very powerful voice and if I use it I can dictate my entire life. I realized that it's okay to get help for myself and not wait for someone to advocate for me because it's my life and I'm the only one who can change it.

"We had really bad coping skills that we learned from our families. But softball taught us other ways. I would describe eighth-grade me as traumatized and extremely socially awkward. I barely made eye contact with people and I barely had friends. The softball team changed me because I was introduced to people who had problems and were going through shit a twelve-year-old shouldn't go through. Everyone has a story that makes them who they are today. Lady Tigers allowed us to escape from the world without having to actually run away from our problems. We learned how to cope with things in a helpful way, thanks to Coach Astacio."

Genesis credited Chris with saving her life. She also found her voice on the Lady Tigers and also that she was a pretty damn good softball player. When Chris needed her to be the emergency catcher, she stepped up and killed it. She didn't regret sitting out most of the season because she felt she started playing at the exact right moment. "I loved being there and watching the girls play," she says. "And I loved Astacio. He understood me."

Chris didn't hide the banquet invite from Grateshka. He wanted her there. She couldn't play at all at the beginning and now she'd become a powerhouse. She proved to herself that if she took the important things in life seriously, it paid off. "I noticed going to practice every day and putting your dedication and your effort and your time into it makes you better. It showed me how to dedicate to something and stick to something if you really want to do it. That you should go for it and take a chance. I really love softball now."

Of all the players, softball changed Rashell the most profoundly. "Thank you so much," she told Chris as she accepted her trophy. "I love you, you are the best person." She'd had an edge, to say the least, and the team softened her. Now, Rashell used her immense power and leadership abilities for good instead of evil. "As minorities we all live the same type of lifestyle. I learned that instead of us helping each other, all we do is bring each other down. That isn't what we should do. I owe everything to Astacio. If it wasn't for him I don't know where I'd be right now. I tell my friends, 'Bro, can you imagine us without softball? Who knows when we would've graduated from middle school?' It took a short period of time to make a big change."

As Chris handed out the trophies, making sure to say Gheynee's name right, it became more and more apparent how much he would miss these girls. Especially the girls who'd given him the most trouble. He was scared for them because he knew without continued support, these girls could easily go back to their old ways.

Alexa came up next. Another awesome player, she'd left the gang life behind after the shooting and found solace in her team. "I was humbled," she admits. Softball helped her cope with her anger and the anger of everyone around her. "I was an angry child. The lifestyle I lived, everybody was just angry. Even the teachers were angry at life. When we went to school we didn't see each other as being in the same boat, we saw each other as adversaries. We had enemies at home, too. You expect everyone to be against you. The softball team showed me something different."

Mayoli had become the team photographer, but still loved being included as a real member of the Lady Tigers. "My team was so cool because they treated me like family. Sometimes we got mad at each other, we did make mistakes, but nobody is perfect. It was very special to me. I learned you cannot give up on yourself. No 'I can't do this, I can't do that.' You can do it. You can do better."

Johanna, an immigrant who barely spoke English, also got an instant new American family and mastered pitching the windmill, one of the most difficult skills in this game or any game. "Softball was life changing," she says. "I fell in love with the game and I can't stop playing."

Yoshie made the most drastic improvement as a player. Her talent was raw and untamed in the beginning and she almost quit when she couldn't hit the ball. She was quiet and to herself. But as the season progressed she came out of her shell and the closet. Her May-December romance with Nicky ended up being a short-lived May-June romance. Yoshie got separation anxiety thinking about Nicky leaving for high school and talked to another girl. After a huge argument, they broke up and never talked again. "I was worried about her not being in the same school," Yoshie says. "That ate me up. I was afraid I wouldn't be able to see her. I did the wrong thing talking to another person. She was only my second girlfriend, so I didn't know what to do. I was thirteen. It was heartbreaking because it was like that middle-school love."

Nicky was a great softball player, in particular an excellent first baseman, from day one because she gave it her all. "I used to stand so awkwardly, the way I swung the bat, how far the ball went. I tried to improve everything about myself."

Her growth as a human being was her most remarkable transformation that year. "I wanted to grow up and be better, I didn't want to be the same

Nicky I was in middle school. I feel like I failed so many times in my life. I doubted myself and I was so depressed. I didn't want to be depressed no more. I just wanted to be happy. Depression is not easy to overcome in the nighttime. You're not just gonna wake up and be happy. It's something that takes time. You have to push forward no matter how hard it is. There's always a rainbow at the end that's gonna make it better. I have a better attitude because of Astacio. He's an amazing person. I look at him as a father figure. If something happened to him it would completely ruin me. He's one of the people who shaped me into the person I am today. He just never gave up on me. As much as teachers were sending him messages about me, he knew how great of a student I was and how good of an athlete I was and the person I could become in the future. It's just incredible how a sport can change a person's life."

Chris went through each girl on the team but saved one particular girl for last. He told the team that many people believed that the next girl didn't deserve anything, and that she'd abused all the chances given to her. Out the corner of his eye he could see that Achelin knew he was talking about her because she was already in tears, covering her face with her hands. He praised all of her accomplishments in school and commended her for dedicating herself to be better. "I'm very very proud of this girl. Achelin, come get your trophy."

Achelin was a mess, crying uncontrollably. She hadn't spoken to Chris or the girls about her arrest; she was too embarrassed. Before softball, her fighting was a problem that never stopped. After she joined the team, she changed dramatically. She stopped getting into trouble and became serious about wanting to graduate. She attended her classes, did her work, and was less disrespectful to teachers. Unfortunately, one violent incident came back to haunt her, totally erasing all the good she'd accomplished.

Achelin had never been arrested before in her life and it was a horrifying experience. While the Lady Tigers were kicking butt on the ball field, Achelin was locked up in the local precinct, thrown into a cell with emotionally disturbed career criminals. When she called her mom, she could barely hide her disgust with her daughter, sneering, "I thought you changed." She left for work and left Achelin in jail overnight.

"She left me there because she wanted to," Achelin recalls. "I was so scared and hungry. They took off my shoelaces and I didn't even know why. The people coming in and out, I was not like them. It was a lesson."

Achelin assumed the Lady Tigers and Coach Astacio had written her off. She wouldn't blame them. She'd let the team down in the worst way. As Chris held out a trophy for her, she asked, her chest heaving with sobs, "Are you sure you want to give this to me?"

Chris explained that although he was disappointed when she was arrested, he'd been very proud of her for many months. He made it clear to her that he wasn't rewarding her bad behavior by condoning her actions. Rather, he was acknowledging the fact that for months she had proven to him, the team, and, most importantly, herself, that she had the ability to be great. She put in all the hard work. He was rewarding her for the hard work she'd done. Not for the one mistake she committed. She cried harder and gave Chris a hug.

"I will never disappoint you again," Achelin said.

"Even if you do disappoint me again, I will still love you like a daughter. I love all you girls. You deserve to be happy, you deserve to be successful, and you deserve everything. You're all my daughters."

As soon as he gave out the last trophy, a huge burden lifted from his shoulders. He was done. He wasn't planning on coaching another year—this year had been exhausting and nearly destroyed his family. But then he thought about Yoshie. She still had two years left at 22. She was turning into a phenomenal player. It would be such a shame if she didn't get to keep playing and learning and growing.

As the girls filed out of the library, Achelin asked Chris, "What do I do now?"

"You'll be fine."

"I found someone that believes in me and makes me believe in myself," she said. "How could I possibly go on knowing that you won't be there by my side, telling me what to do or not to do? I will be alone. I can't do this without you."

Chris assured her that she would never be alone and told her to have more faith in herself. She gave him a long hug, as if she didn't want to let go. He knew letting go for her meant she had to face the world on her own. And that was a very scary thought.

But he knew they could make it. In the beginning, he just had a bunch of girls bickering and fighting among each other, mirroring the same violence found outside the walls of their school. Chris had witnessed the girls progress exponentially, not only in their softball skills but also in the way they came together. They were able to overcome their own stupidity and petty differences to bond. Despite their tragic upbringings, despite seemingly insurmountable odds, the girls had learned to love themselves and each other. They'd become a team of sisters and, proudly wearing their black and orange uniforms, a beacon of hope and a symbol of pride in their community.

Chris walked to his car and, as he loaded equipment in the trunk, a woman approached him.

"Where can my daughter get that shirt? Can I buy one?"

"Nope, you gotta be on the team," Chris said. "You gotta be a Lady Tiger."

Epilogue

WINNING CURES ALL

ACHELIN is a senior at Cascades High School and works full-time at a restaurant. "My goal is to be financially free with a happy family and I want a job I won't have to take a vacation from." She's still best friends with Alexa and credits the Lady Tigers for putting her on a better path. "I still got my trophy. I take that with me everywhere."

ALEXA dropped out of high school but recently received her GED. She's currently managing a Domino's Pizza restaurant and saving up to get her own place. In 2019, she started the process to join the army. "The Lady Tigers is good old memories."

ALCIELIS works at Express and attends Westchester Community College, studying fashion merchandising. She hopes to transfer to the Fashion Institute of Technology in Manhattan in order to become an interior designer and decorator. "I've always loved to design and loved the fashion industry so I took everything I'm passionate about and found the perfect career for myself. I work to save money for my future, but my main focus right now is school. I refuse to settle for less, I have big dreams and I will never give up on myself. My philosophy is 'design your future and then do everything possible to make it come to life,' like every good designer. I've been in a relationship with my boyfriend going on two years and he makes me the happiest I've ever been. I've grown so much as an individual and as a woman being with him. We met when I was just sixteen years old, and I'm proud to say that I've matured and changed in all the right ways. I never believed in soul mates before him, but it's an amazing feeling to believe that God placed someone in your life specifically designed for you. I'm still the same girl I was when I was in middle school, just a lot wiser. I am still growing and working on myself. I dream to be the best version of myself, that is working on my selfishness amongst many other things. I will get there one day, but for right now this is only the beginning!"

ANGIE is currently working at Paris Baguette while applying to colleges. She's been with her current girlfriend for more than a year and can't believe how "time flies." She'd still like to either be a psychologist or a rapper. "By the time I'm twenty-five, and that's pushing it, I wanna already live in LA in a nice house, I wanna start a YouTube channel, and I wanna have my music career bumping. But I'll also finish school."

In high school, Angie received life-changing news about her family. Two summers ago, Angie's parents were fighting so badly, she went to live with her grandmother to get "space to breathe. My grandmother always had space for me." While there, her grandmother revealed a huge family secret: The dad Angie grew up with her whole life was not her birth father. Angie was the result of a one-night stand.

When Angie heard the news, it made sense. She'd had hints throughout her life that something was off. Everybody was always telling her she didn't look like her dad, and now she could put the puzzle pieces together. But she felt betrayed and felt like a chump. "Everybody else knew besides me.

I didn't know how to handle it." She's still dealing with the fallout. Angie still has never met her birth father, who lives in Florida, or seen pictures of him. "It was just lies upon lies. My mom said to me, 'I hope you don't hate me.' I'm not mad at anyone, I just want answers. The only father figure I ever knew is not my dad."

She wrote a rap song about it to work out her feelings:

> *"I woke up, me and God had a face off, he said listen to ya momma girl you know it's gon pay off, and you know it's gon pay off, and through all them walking sins there comes a time where you need some, there comes a time where you need some, and through all them walking sins there comes a time where you need some . . . savior*
>
> *(thank you ma) thank you for all them things you did teenage mother couldn't really give me shit, paid checks going to them bills yeah they did straight to them bills oh yeah they did even tho I wanted j's and a iced out fit them new j's and a nice outfit even tho I wanted j's and a iced outfit . . . you couldn't, I seen you struggle just to raise these kids late nights up crying 'cuz my dad ain't shit later to find out that I ain't his kid no! no I ain't his kid but I ain't gon' stress that he played a part in my life no that nigga ain't no step dad but I ain't gon' stress that he played a part in my life no that nigga ain't no step dad. I woke up me and God had a face off, he said listen to ya momma girl you know it's gon' pay off and you know it's gon' pay off and through all them walking sins there comes a time where you need some there comes a time where you need some and through all them walking sins there comes a time where you need some savior."*

GENESIS stopped cutting, and her anxiety and depression eased over time. "I didn't really go to any therapy or anything. I just learned how to express myself a little bit better and actually expressing myself made me feel better and all that weight lifted a little bit." After her mom legally immigrated to the United States, they moved to Allentown, Pennsylvania. Genesis, who plays softball on her high-school team, graduated in 2019 and plans on applying to film school so she can study cinematography. "Whenever anyone asks, I tell them Astacio and softball saved my life."

GHEYNEE played one more year at third base for the Lady Tigers. In high school, she and her sister Nicky moved to Florida to live with Mami Gladys again, but missed New York City and moved back within a couple of months. During her senior year, she moved out of her birth mother's house and in with her boyfriend. "I don't live with my mom and sisters, and our relationship got better since I moved out." Gheynee graduated high school in June 2019 and plans to study acting in college.

GRATESHKA is a senior in high school at the Morris Educational Campus and plays every position on the softball team. She's applying to St. Thomas Aquinas College, where her brother goes, and wants to major in finance. She'd also love to get a scholarship to play on the Spartans' softball team. "It's my dream, I hope I'm able to!" And don't worry, she's still a jokester. "Oh, definitely, I don't change."

HEAVEN graduated high school in 2019 and was accepted to every college she applied to—Binghamton, Stony Brook, Alfred, College of Staten Island, John Jay, Borough of Manhattan Community College, and Bronx Community College. "I can't wait to fulfill my dream and be the best that I know I can be. I'm in a very happy relationship with my boyfriend for a year. My family is good, everybody is progressing and maintaining happiness. At first I wanted to be a teacher but not after what I put my teachers through! Now I want to be a lawyer because I make my points and my points are always right. That is my dream and I shall fulfill it!"

JOHANNA accepted a full scholarship to play softball for the Monroe Express, the same college the Lady Tigers visited, but on the Bronx campus. "I'm really excited because it's a whole new start for me, wearing a different uniform, learning more things, and gaining more experience. I feel like college is going to change the way I think because that's when my transition to adulthood starts. My mom is too happy, she won't stop talking about it with her friends! Sports are good for the soul."

KIMBERLY finally received therapy for her sexual abuse junior year of high school. "As I got older I stopped blaming myself for what happened to me because I was smart enough to see that I didn't do anything wrong. I am strong mentally and emotionally but I still have room for improvement. Of course I'm still affected by it and I still have trouble performing daily tasks. I still have anxiety that something bad is going to happen. I needed to get out of my house and college was the only way to do it." Completely on her own, she discovered and applied for the Educational Opportunity Program at Stony Brook University on Long Island. She was accepted to the program—which provides admission, financial, and academic support services to historically underserved first-generation, low-income, or educationally disadvantaged students—and received a hefty academic scholarship. She's currently a sophomore majoring in engineering science.

MAYOLI dropped out of high school but is still singing like a canary. She costarred in rapper Cashflow Harlem's music video for "Victim," which details her rape by her uncle and the emotional aftermath. The video was retweeted by fellow South Bronx homegirl Cardi B. In March 2019, Mayoli had a baby boy she named Jo'Angel.

NICKY continued to play softball in high school until she was diagnosed with scoliosis. "My body was weak and I just stopped. I miss softball so much." Today, she works at McDonald's while taking online classes at Keiser University. She's thinking about becoming a medical assistant or a physical therapist because "I love to help others." She and Gheynee are very close again and she beams, "She gives me hugs now." She still lives in Harlem with her birth mother, who recently became pregnant with her fifth baby girl.

RASHELL went on an Outward Bound trip freshman year of high school, and, along with softball, it changed her life. "I was in the wilderness for five days, dealing with things I didn't like, like hiking, no food, no showering. That changed me and helped me. My mind is different now." Today, she attends BMCC and works full time at the Bloomingdale's outlet on 5th Avenue. She hopes to become a childhood education teacher or work in criminal justice. "For those who have known me since middle school, they can definitely recognize I'm not the person I was before. I'm no longer the girl who's always loud, arguing, and willing to fight anybody. I'm now the young lady who gets annoyed when it's too loud somewhere or there's drama. I'm all about being with my friends and family and having fun. I enjoy going out. My goal is to be overall happy, as well as become successful and wealthy in life. Not money-wise but successful in opportunities and experiences I can learn from and will help me be the best person I can be. I never thought I'd be a softball player. I never thought I'd be the person I am today."

ROBIN got the help she desperately needed after she knocked out the dean and was placed at the ROADS charter school. "I met this counselor named Izzy. I told her my whole life story and she cried. She helped me a lot. I didn't know how to talk at the time. Now I know how to talk. Izzy got me comfortable to express my feelings without my fists. I started writing poetry, like love poetry. Not too lovey-dovey. A little gangsta." Robin never got into another physical fight again, not once in four years of high school. Today, she's currently working as a medical intern and living with her fiancé Brian in the Bronx. Her goal is to become a pediatric nurse one day, just like her late mother. She'd also like to write a book. "It's rare you catch me home. I'm always at an event or an art show. I'm a totally changed person."

YOSHIE was named captain of the Lady Tigers in both seventh and eighth grade and became the starting pitcher. Once she left 22, she was the star of her high school and club teams. "She's a beast and a monster," Chris says. Unfortunately, junior year, Yoshie spiraled, after a knee injury and a suspension for fighting knocked her off her softball teams. She logged fifty-four absences and started smoking weed. In March 2019, she was rushed to the hospital after threatening to kill herself at school. She's currently getting counseling for depression and is back playing softball on club teams, but she's struggling. "It's not an escape anymore. I just don't know what to do or where to go. I feel so trapped in my head. Everything is blank."

RICHARD FREDERICK spent four years at Jordan L. Mott Middle School but left to take a job twenty minutes from home in Brooklyn after the birth of his first child. He made astounding progress during his tenure at 22. The year the Lady Tigers started, there was a 70.9 percent reduction of incidents in the building. By the time he left, the school was down from 278 suspensions to only 30 suspensions per year. He'll never forget his time at 22 or Astacio and the Lady Tigers. "They absolutely improved the school and community. They wore the clothes with such pride. If you were a Lady Tiger you felt like you ruled the school. Like, 'Yo, I'm on the team. Astacio is my boy, my dad, don't mess with me.' Girls wanted to be on that team."

MRS. HOLLOWAY suffered a stroke and tragically passed away the summer after the first season of the Lady Tigers. In her honor, in future seasons, Chris named the end of season banquet the Holloway Awards. "It was very emotional because, besides Astacio, she was the most supportive teacher we ever had," Grateshka says. "She was a great lady."

CRISTINA ASTACIO still struggles with dyslexia and social norms, and loud sounds and bright lights still bother her. But she loves life and herself. "Cristina doesn't shut up and wants to know everything," Chris beams. "She has lots of energy. Sometimes it's hard to keep up with her!" She goes to public school in an ICT (Integrated Co-Teaching) classroom, where two teachers oversee both general education and special-ed children. "I love when people first meet Cristina," Chris adds. "I always get, 'Well she doesn't look autistic,' and I really don't know how to respond. There is no 'look' for autism. Cristina is highly functioning, and if she continues to get the help that she needs, she will be able to thrive on her own as an adult. I recently heard about a woman who has autism and became a lawyer. So I am hopeful for Cristina because she is so eager to learn."

CHARISSE admits there's still some lingering bitterness over the inaugural season of the Lady Tigers. "It really put a bump in our marriage." After she and Chris hashed out a compromise about how much time he should spend with the softball team and how much time he needed to be home helping out with their kids, Justin and Cristina, "I'm on board now and we're in a good place," she says. Still, she's never been to a game. "I think eventually I will go. I *am* proud of him."

THE LADY TIGERS did not dissolve after the first season. "The main reason why I did it again was Yoshie," Chris says. "She was really good and I felt responsible if I didn't help mature that skill she had." The Lady Tigers lost every game but one the first year, but the next year, the team went undefeated and made it to the Bronx playoffs, only to be eliminated in the first round. The following year, the Lady Tigers once again made the playoffs and, in the most exciting and controversial game ever, won the Bronx Middle School Championship.

Only four girls showed up to the very first Lady Tigers tryout. Four years after it began, 100 girls tried out for the team. Over those years, the Lady Tigers raised more than $100,000 on DonorsChoose.org for equipment and uniforms, mentoring field trips to colleges and universities, and tournaments in Florida and Chicago. In the spring of 2016, the Lady Tigers were invited to Yankee Stadium, right down the street. Brian Smith, a rep from the team, saw a story about the Lady Tigers in the newspaper and visited the school. He invited the whole team to watch a game and promised them a tour of the stadium. They did not know that they were actually going to run onto the field with the Yankee players right before the game started. Girls were in tears as they stepped foot onto the grass. Yoshie turned to Chris with tears in her eyes and said, "We finally made it, Dad."

In 2017, Ellen DeGeneres was also moved by the team's journey. She invited Coach Astacio and several of the players on her show and presented them with a check for $20,000 from Walmart. "I love this story," she said.

CHRIS ASTACIO spent six years at 22 and coached five seasons of Lady Tigers' softball. His final record was 18-16. In 2017–18, the season was canceled after two games due to gang violence. Chris has won numerous awards. Mayor Bloomberg honored him as one of ten "Dads of the Year" in all of New York City, the New York Yankees honored him with "Coach of the Year" at their Hispanic Heritage Month Community Achievement Awards, and he was among thirty teachers honored by ESPN and the College Football Playoff Foundation's Extra Yard for Teachers program in September 2017. Chris never set out to make money or win any awards starting the Lady Tigers. All he wanted to do was help these neglected, abused, and marginalized girls have a shot at a decent life. In return, he believes they helped him get out of bed every morning. His stomach cancer remains in remission.

In 2018, Chris accepted a new job as PE teacher at MS 95 (the Sheila Mencher Van Cortlandt School) in the Kingsbridge section of the Bronx, just two blocks away from his house. He can now pick up his daughter from school and be on time for dinner, no doubt pleasing his wife. Of course, he immediately launched the school's first softball team, the 95 Storm. Even though Chris moved on to a new school, he'll always have a special place in his heart for the original Lady Tigers, and he will be forever grateful to them for never giving up. If they had quit at any point, none of this would ever have happened. "In the beginning, I just wanted to have a team of girls be unstoppable," Chris says. "Even better, I got a family. I'll take that over winning any day."

ACKNOWLEDGMENTS

This book could not have happened without the generosity, love, and support (financial and otherwise) of my parents. My dad, John R.F. Baer, played on softball teams from the day I was born until the day he died and was the greatest third baseman in Chicagoland. He taught me everything I know about the game—he was my best coach and I'm eternally grateful to him. Miss you, Pop. Wish you were here to read this book, because I know you'd love it and buy a copy for everyone you know. My mom Linda Baer has always been my rock, my biggest champion, and my best friend. I thank her profusely for spending the last year in the den so I could write. I thank her for *Jeopardy!* breaks and suffering through Pasta Night for me. Love you so much.

Special thanks to my beautiful English lass Sam Horn for infinite patience, love, and understanding during my "writing process." I'm so lucky.

A big thanks to the following people:

Aaron Rasmussen for the couch, car, showers, food hall runs, and *Love It or List It* marathons. That's right.

Regina Dominican softball coach and superstar shortstop Julie Venn for introducing me to Coach Astacio and the Lady Tigers. Huge shout out to Deerfield Youth Baseball Association (DYBA) and my former softball teammates, the most athletic women on the planet: Jennie Hughes Janda, Jennifer Casey Drevline, MJ Cimbalo Forbes, and Lesley Bernstein Ravenscraft. *"The Deers are blue but the real ones are brown . . ."*

Brett Baer, Cathy Shambley Baer, Gina Bacchiocchi, EJ Boeke, Mary Pender-Coplan, Daniella Wells, Ever Mainard, Jaime Harkin, Tia Brown, Ann Shoket, Marianne Garvey, Chandra Czape Turner, Khali MacIntyre, Matt Sullivan, Katherine Liner, Tess Rafferty and BR, Marisa Sullivan, Melissa Cronin, Fit in 42, EnerGym, Mary Sterton, and Veronica Burgen for moral support.

Personal role models and heroes Hillary Clinton and the Chicago White Sox.

My agent, JL Stermer of New Leaf Literary, for believing in me and never giving up on this book. But even more for just being an all-around incredible person and straight shooter. Hard to find in this biz. You're the best.

Pouya Shahbazian for loving this project and the girls, and tryna make it happen.

Pegasus founder and publisher, and my fabulous editor, Jessica Case, for believing in this project from day one and having the guts to take a chance on a book that's never been done before. You are an absolute joy to work with.

Alexandra Maruri from Bronx Historical Tours (bronxhistoricaltours .com) for all of the incredibly helpful information she generously provided and the great chats, Danny you-know-who-you-are, Shavonda DeRoche, Richard Frederick, and Rafael Toro—Renaissance man, gentleman, and top chef.

The Astacio family—Charisse, Justin, and Cristina. Charisse, you are an awesome woman. I always tell Chris how lucky he is to have you.

The beautiful and brave Lady Tigers—Achelin, Alexa, Alcielis, Angie, Genesis, Gheynee, Grateshka, Heaven, Johanna, Kimberly, Mayoli,

Nicky, Precious, Rashell, Robin, and Yoshie, who gave me their time and their trust. I'm so honored you let me tell your inspiring stories, and stayed so dedicated throughout the process, even though it was emotional and a giant pain in the ass. But you knew you were going to help so many other young girls and gave your all. You're all heroes.

And last but not least, my ride-or-die, Christopher Astacio. Barriers cannot be broken if everyone lives cushy, comfortable lives. Chris is that person who gets uncomfortable and makes huge sacrifices to make change, even when it's hard or seems hopeless. He's truly one of the hardest working guys I've ever known, also the most kind and compassionate. We need more men like him in the world right now. Chris, thank you for always putting 200 percent into this book, through the ups, downs, and obstacles. I'm so proud to call you my friend. I love you. We did it.